RENEWALS 458-4574

they fought the law

Rock Music
Goes to Court

WITHDRAWN
UTSA Libraries

they fought the law

Rock Music Goes to Court

Stan Soocher

Schirmer Books

An Imprint of Simon & Schuster Macmillan

New York

Prentice Hall International

London Mexico City New Delhi Singapore Sydney Toronto

WITHDRAWN
UTSA Libraries

(c) 1999 by Stan Soocher

All rights reserved. No part of this book may be reproduced or transmitted in any form or by any means, electronic or mechanical, including photocopying, recording, or by any information storage and retrieval system without permission in writing from the Publisher.

Schirmer Books
An Imprint of Simon & Schuster Macmillan
1633 Broadway
New York, NY 10019

Library of Congress Catalog Number: 98-15108

Printed in the United States of America
Printing number
1   2   3   4   5   6   7   8   9   10

Library of Congress Cataloging-in-Publication Data
Soocher, Stan.
    They fought the law : Rock music goes to court /
Stan Soocher.
        p.   cm.
    Includes index.
    ISBN 0-02-864731-9
    1. Music—Law and legislation—United States.
2. Rock music—History and criticism.   I. Title
    ML3534.S615 1999
    781.66—dc21   98-15108
                                            CIP
                                            MN
This paper meets the requirements of
ANSI/NISO Z39.48-1992 (Permanence of Paper).

Library
University of Texas
at San Antonio

It's affidavit swearing time

—George Harrison, "Sue Me, Sue You Blues"

Contents

Preface

The portrait of Elvis Presley that has emerged over the years is that of a business bumpkin who deferred to a Svengali-like manager—Colonel Tom Parker—on critical career decisions. Just how much of the blame for Elvis's ruinous finances ultimately fell on Presley's or Parker's shoulders is a question that likely will be debated as long as there is an entertainment business.

Elvis wasn't always acquiescing and unquestioning. He rarely wrote letters, but in February 1959—while he was stationed in the U.S. Army in Germany—Elvis wrote Hollywood producer Hal Wallis, who oversaw nine Presley movies: "I have my records pretty much in a mess concerning my dealings with your studio, please send me my financial records with the studio so that I may straighten out my books." Wallis sent a copy of the letter to Colonel Parker with this note: "Our records are in pretty much of a mess so at this point I don't know what to tell Elvis. Perhaps he can send me his financial records and it might help get ours in shape."

What makes Elvis's letter so startling is that he *had* to know Wallis's loyalties were with Parker. In his autobiography, *Starmaker*, Wallis wrote that he didn't mix socially with Elvis and that the two never visited each other's homes. By contrast, Wallis received correspondence playfully signed "Private Parker" by Presley's manager, who would become Wallis's Palm Springs neighbor. The Colonel also made Wallis a member of his "Snowmen's League of America" and presented the film producer with an honorary Snowmen's banner. ("High Potentate" Parker's Snowmen's League stationery was dotted with expressions like "Snow Jobs for All Occasions," "Free Advice at Reasonable Rates," "Choice Mosquito Manure," and "Don't Put It In Writing . . . Put It In Invisible Ink.")

Was Elvis Presley's letter to Hal Wallis an early attempt to throw off Colonel Parker's chain of command? (All Presley entertainment finances went first through Parker.) Elvis would almost never breach that chain again, though, by the 1970s, Parker would lament he was losing his ability to control his one management client.

The great irony, of course, is that it was only with Elvis's death that his estate was able to gain any real control over his artistic and financial legacy. His estate fought the law and, in some important cases, it won.

That is what this book is about: It is through litigation details that many of the underhanded business practices of the music industry have come to light. The legal issues and lawsuits that artists and their estates become involved in can have as much impact on the music we hear as do the musicians with whom the artists work or even the songs they choose to record. Often, lawsuit begets lawsuit in an ever-deepening pool of claims.

Like Elvis, Billy Joel immersed himself in his music and looked away from the complex business concerns of his career—only to find himself in litigation with his ex-brother-in-law/manager, his former accountants, and his lawyers. George Michael prided himself on his business savvy and hoped to use the law to shake off his teenybopper image for a more mature audience only to have his career wounded by his court fight with Sony Music.

One-time hitmakers B.J. Thomas, Gene Pitney, and the Shirelles got in the detective game to track down long-lost royalties from continuing worldwide record sales. Moe Lytle, the sound recordings owner they chased, had his own collection problems from the widespread piracy of his masters. The Beatles obtained from Capitol-EMI Records the most lucrative settlement ever for recording artists pursuing royalties, but George Harrison soon became entangled in litigation with his long-time manager over the money trail.

The music has often come under legal attack, too. The frequency with which such major artists as Michael Jackson have been hit with song-stealing claims has frightened the music industry, gripped by infringement suit fears, into closing off avenues of access for aspiring songwriters. That groups such as heavy metal rockers Judas Priest and rappers 2 Live Crew could be hauled into suicide liability and obscenity proceedings, respectively, for the lyric content of their songs underscores the connection between music and free expression and both the fragility and strength of the First Amendment.

For the 2 Live Crew, the issue of whether the group's rap parody of Roy Orbison's "Oh, Pretty Woman" was an exercise of its free-speech fair use rights or an illegal encroachment on the "Oh, Pretty Woman" copyright got heated debate in the rarefied chambers of the U.S. Supreme Court. Like many of the cases in this book, the result was the first judicial ruling of its type.

This book begins with Elvis Presley in more ways than one. Elvis was at his early peak when I was in first grade. My grandfather bought me a guitar that I used to work up a routine lip-synching to Elvis records. That got me invited to a first-grade party where I was the only boy. As Presley records spun, I curled my lip, mouthed the lyrics and pretended to play the guitar. The girls began to scream and chased me out the door and around the yard. I quickly saw why Elvis enjoyed what he did.

By August 16, 1977, the day Elvis died, I had long left my Presley passion behind. I had little interest in his 1960s movies or his 1970s jumpsuits and capes. I was on the phone with the Charlie Daniels Band's Nashville area office arranging to write a magazine cover story at Capricorn Studios in Macon, Georgia, when Daniels' representative told me she heard Elvis had died. On impulse, I'd said I'd be in Macon the next day. I also decided to move out of South Florida—where I grew up and had been writing, producing, and drumming on rock demo tapes—to build a music journalist's career in New York. Less than 24 hours after hearing about Elvis, I was in my car, heading north for a new life. For me, Elvis's death became a symbol of dramatic change.

Soon after relocating to New York City, I landed a job as an associate editor at the rock fanzine *Circus* and was lucky to work with a wealth of talented music journalists and critics—many of whom thrive at their craft today. But it wasn't until I entered law school in 1980 that I began to see how the underlying legal issues affect the course that music takes.

The first time I wrote about the intersection of music and law was in a criminal case. It was an article for *The National Law Journal*—for which I also covered the federal appeals courts—on the legal proceedings surrounding John Lennon's murderer, Mark David Chapman.

For a decade after, I wrote a series of occasional articles for *Musician* magazine—beginning with how to find a music lawyer—that I hoped would help musicians learn about their legal rights. In August 1983, the day after I took the New York bar exam, I started a newsletter named *Entertainment Legal News* in my apartment in Queens. In 1985, that publication became *Entertainment Law & Finance*.

Through this, the music has remained the primary thing for me. Rarely a week goes by that I don't listen to my favorite vocal group, the Hollies—particularly their 1960s album output. There is still a sense of discovery, just as there was in researching this book.

At the Nashville federal courthouse, for example, I poured through thousands of pages of documents in a lawsuit between the music publisher Acuff Rose and the estate of Roy Orbison. On the very last page of the very last document box, I found an envelope containing one of the last informal recordings Orbison made, a ten-song demo tape with his writing mate, Bill Dees.

As I sat under a tree on the grounds of Graceland observing the 20th candlelight procession in memory of Elvis, a Presley rendition of the beautiful ballad "I'll Remember You" wafted across the lawn from portable speakers set up at Graceland's gates. I felt reconnected with Elvis's music after more than three decades away from anything but his hits.

This book will have done its job if it provides its readers, too, with a new dimension for the music they love—and with a deeper appreciation of how hard it can be for musicians not only to give birth to their creations but to properly care for them once the music has been born.

—STAN SOOCHER

Acknowledgments

F irst, with love to Susan Barone for her generous and untiring support while I researched and wrote this book.

At Schirmer Books, my editor Richard Carlin, for bringing the book project in-house, and art director Lisa Chovnick, for being there at the right time.

For those whose advice, personalities, and input helped prepare me for this project, I thank: my parents, Barbara and Nat; my sister, Ellen, brother-in-law John, and niece Jenny; my cousins Michael and Aviva; my aunt Marcia (a wonderful mentor for nurturing the creative spirit) and uncle Sumner; Rockerfellas members Craig Ball, Jimmy Muller, and Bob Ronco, as well as vintage guitar expert Andrew Berlin, for helping me keep my concert drumming chops alive; and my decades-long musical comrades Kelly Douthitt and Barry Levine.

All of the sources interviewed for this book were invaluable, including those off the record. In addition, the following individuals and institutions provided support and/or assistance: the Academy of Motion Pictures Arts and Sciences' Margaret Herrick Library; Jeffrey and Todd Brabec; John Bradley; the Broward County Public Library; the Country Music Foundation; Cynthia Cleves; Vincent Cecolini; the Dade County Public Library; Linda Fitchett; Dagmar Hamilton; Marion Hollidge; George Lane; Mark Lee; the Library of Congress; Bob Margolis; the Memphis Room and its curator, Patricia LaPointe, at the Shelby County Public Library; the Middletown, New Jersey,

Public Library; the Nashville and Davidson County Public Library; the National Archives; the New York Public Library; Acelo Pedroso; Kathleen Pellegrino; David Pike; Beverly Pohl; Jeffrey Ressner; James Simon; Miriam Stern; Debbie Thornhill; the University of Memphis Mississippi Valley Collection; the U.S. Supreme Court Press Office; and the staffs at the courthouses where I conducted research.

Special thanks to Leonidas T. Gil de Gibaja III and Ilona Tykotski.

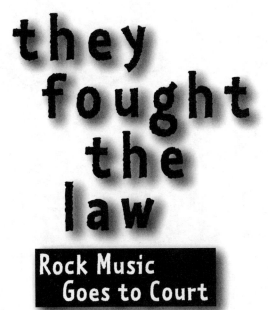

they
fought
the
law

Rock Music
Goes to Court

Elvis Presley: In His Own Image

"It's crazy. It's just crazy."

On the 20th anniversary of Elvis Presley's death, Jack Soden, the chief executive officer of Elvis Presley Enterprises (EPE), walked down the driveway toward the front gates of Graceland. Thirty-thousand fans jammed the boulevard outside that steamy August night waiting for the annual candlelight pilgrimage past the grave of the King of rock 'n' roll. But Soden wasn't talking about the continuing fan dedication to Presley. Soden was referring to an English court ruling earlier that year that Elvis Presley had become so famous EPE could not claim trademarks in his name.

"It's really giving Elvis back to the people, where he belongs," said Sid Shaw, the seller of his own Elvis merchandise who had contested the estate's English trademark effort. Soden claimed the economic impact of Shaw was "practically non-existent. He's one step above a street cart." But a decade after securing precedent-setting judicial approval of its right to Elvis Presley's image, EPE had lost its second case in a year. (Though it was being appealed, a federal district court in Houston ruled that a tavern could continue to call itself "The Velvet Elvis.")

In the age of celebrity, the ability to commercially exploit an entertainer's name and likeness had taken center stage. Through right-of-publicity, trademark and related claims, celebrities were increasingly taking to the courts to protect this fundamental asset.

The right of publicity ironically evolved out of the right of privacy. But it wasn't until 1977, the year Elvis Presley died, that the U.S. Supreme Court ruled the right of publicity was distinct. Since Elvis's death, the entertainer's estate had been on the cutting edge of defining the descendibility of rights of publicity.

Elvis utilized lawyers a lot less during his life than his estate did after he died. Like many performers of his time, Elvis didn't use a general counsel the way entertainers do today. He relied on his manager, Colonel Tom Parker, to handle career contract details for him. Parker, a former carnival worker, explained his negotiating technique in a 1963 interview on the set of the Presley film *Kissin' Cousins*: "You know, the other day a producer told me that Elvis is slipping a little. I said, 'Yeah, I'd heard that,' and the producer said, 'What's your price now?' I said, well, I'd gone up $100,000 [a picture]. He said, 'What? I just told you he was slipping.' I said, 'Yeah, that's why we got to get a little more money. We may need it.' And you know what? He paid it [a half-million dollars, plus 50 percent of the film's profits]."

Frank Glankler, a senior partner in the Memphis firm that has long handled Presley legal issues, recalled what it was like to be a lawyer for Elvis: "In the '50s, we had to drive through the backwoods of Arkansas on 75 cents worth of gasoline to track down a Presley cousin. We needed him to verify the birth date of Elvis's grandmother, Minnie Mae, so she could accompany Elvis on his first trip to Germany. When we finally found the house, there was a goat on the front porch. The cousin didn't want to sign the affidavit because he couldn't read; he was afraid he might be signing away the deed to his house. In the end, he gave us his 'X.'"

Elvis had an accountant and divorce and tax lawyers. Frank Glankler's law partner, Charlie Davis, served as Elvis's legal point man in Memphis; Ed Hookstratten played this role in Los Angeles. "Elvis had access to whatever professional advice he needed," said Memphis attorney Beecher Smith, his estate and tax counsel at the end of Presley's life. "Whether or not he asked for it or listened to it was another story. You had to go see him at odd hours to get him to read papers, if you could get him to read them at all.

"Elvis never allowed anybody to manage his personal business except for [his father] Vernon, who he gave a general power of attorney. Colonel Parker was in charge of making the money. After Elvis got it, Vernon would take care of paying bills and filing the tax returns."

Elvis Presley earned an estimated $79 million in after-tax income during his life. Of course, he gave much of his wealth away to friends and strangers and made few investments. In 1976, Elvis put $520,000 into coal-mine tax shelters that the federal Securities and Exchange Commission later charged had been fraudulently offered by shelter promoters. Elvis had hoped to get a $2.6 million tax deduction from his stake.

"From 1973 on, things were pretty bad," said Memphis attorney Barry Ward, the Presley estate's general counsel for ten years, starting in 1983. "Colonel Parker sold Elvis's royalty rights to RCA for $5.4 million. They made a big to-do of it at the time, it being an unheard of amount of money for an artist. But Elvis got virtually none of it. It went to Parker, to pay Elvis's taxes or to Priscilla Presley for her divorce from Elvis."

Under the infamous March 1, 1973 arrangement—made as both Presley's and Parker's health began to fail—RCA paid Elvis a one-time fee for a waiver of all future royalty rights to his past recordings. Helped by the success of Elvis's *Aloha From Hawaii* TV special in January 1973, Parker claimed he was able to boost RCA's offer from $3 million to $5 million at a time when Elvis's record sales were declining. Elvis also signed a new seven-year recording contract with RCA which, though it contained significant advances, included a starting royalty of just 45 cents per album. This was a mere 5 cent per-album increase from his initial 1956 deal with RCA and less than half of what other superstars were getting in 1973.

"The last few years of Elvis's life were pretty much a vicious cycle. He had a huge retinue of hangers-on and no real money coming in," Barry Ward said. "Graceland was on a revolving mortgage. Elvis would be off tour and the bills would mount up. When the kitty got low, he'd borrow money and hit the road to pay it off." One option Elvis considered was opening Graceland to the public. According to

Jack Soden, Vernon suggested opening the trophy annex that was next door to the residence. "Elvis said, 'Maybe, but then, I don't want people coming through the house while I'm having breakfast.'"

Meanwhile, Elvis was being urged to put his affairs in order, in light of his declining health. "Charlie Davis told Elvis that he needed a will, especially being divorced from Priscilla and having a child," Beecher Smith explained. "I spoke with Vernon and he said, 'Elvis wants to write his will' and he put him on the phone. Elvis told me what he wanted and we spent a good deal of time, about four months, getting the will prepared and executed."

On March 3, 1977, Elvis executed the document in his study upstairs at Graceland. The will provided for his daughter, Lisa Marie—the primary beneficiary—Vernon as executor, and gave financial support to Minnie Mae Presley and Elvis's Aunt Delta. Recalled Smith: "Vernon and my wife [a will witness] were there. I tried to go over it with Elvis in front of [will witnesses] Charlie Hodge [an Elvis confidante and member of his stage show] and Ginger Alden [Elvis's last girlfriend], but Elvis put his hands over the will and said, 'I read it plenty of times. I'm ready to sign.' After he signed it, I held it up and my hands started shaking. Elvis gave me a sheepish smile and said, 'What are you doin'?' I said, 'Tryin' to make sure all the i's are dotted and the t's are crossed.'

"I'd seen Elvis the summer before and he looked heavy, but he looked better in March. It was evening and he was wearing black. He looked like he did in his movies." (There has been talk that Elvis had an alternate will, one that provided generously for his cronies, but Beecher Smith said he never saw it. "Elvis told a lot of people he was going to take care of them in his will, just to keep their loyalty.")

Between March 1977 and August 1977, however, "a lot of things started to unravel," Smith continued. "Elvis's legal problems escalated dramatically. He was going on tour again. His health problems were escalating. He was under a lot of pressure."

Elvis's mounting legal problems included a $6.2 million lawsuit filed against him in Nevada over what Beecher Smith described as members of Elvis's entourage "tap-dancing on some guy's face." After backing out of a guarantee to construct commercial racquetball courts, Elvis also faced litigation by his project partners—Presley road manager, Joe Esposito, and Presley physician, Dr. George Nichopolous. "I explained to Elvis that a guarantor had almost no benefits and all detriment," Smith recalled. "He got livid and said, 'If they sue me, they sue me.'"

In addition, Elvis got caught up in litigation in New Jersey after he sought to terminate a $1.5 million agreement to purchase a jet once owned by fugitive financier and Richard Nixon cohort, Robert Vesco. Elvis wanted out after a South American firm—claiming ownership of the plane—threatened to seize the craft if he bought it. "I'd be damned if I'd let Mr. Presley buy a plane, fly somewhere and have to walk back," David Ravin, Presley's New Jersey attorney, said.

"We were wondering how we'd get Elvis to give a deposition," Beecher Smith said. "He didn't like to do anything like that. He'd say, 'Talk to Daddy.' Elvis'd sign affidavits, but I think the last time he gave a deposition was when he went through his divorce from Priscilla."

There was also talk of Elvis marrying Ginger Alden. Presley insiders told *Nashville Banner* columnist Bill Hance that the 20-year-old Alden was "absolutely running [Elvis] ragged. One time Ginger decided to leave Elvis. She walked out and the only way he could get her back inside the house was to fire a gun in the air."

All of these problems paled when the news came that Elvis had died. Beecher Smith was on vacation when he received the phone call. "I told my office, 'If you tell me he's being sued, I'm not surprised.' They said, 'No, he died.' I said, 'Vernon?' They said, 'Elvis.'"

The true extent of Elvis Presley's financial problems soon became clear. An 82-page inventory of his estate, filed in Memphis probate court by Vernon Presley, listed six bank accounts. The largest, a non-interest-bearing checking account for $1,055,174, was set aside for tax payments. The other five accounts were worth only $24,279, $11,255, $260, $58, and $39—although the Presley estate owned valuable property, including Graceland and nearby acreage. Under joint venture contracts first signed between Elvis Presley and Colonel Parker in 1967—when Elvis's film and recording careers were floundering—Parker became entitled to a one-third to one-half income share from some Presley revenue sources. This included, for example, income from the sale of TV broadcast rights for Elvis movies.

On August 23, 1977, one week after Elvis's death, Vernon Presley agreed to continue the relationship with Parker. After Vernon died in 1979, his will appointed Priscilla Presley, the National Bank of Commerce, and Joe Hanks, Elvis's accountant since 1969, as the estate's executors.

"We weren't aware of the extent of Parker's commissions until Vernon died," Beecher Smith said. "Vernon had been relatively secretive about it. We filed a petition with the probate court to rule on the propriety of the commissions."

Memphis Probate Court Judge Joseph Evans appointed local attorney Blanchard Tual to act as guardian *ad litem* (guardian for a minor) for Lisa Marie Presley. Tual talked to the executors and to entertainment attorneys, executives, and others in the entertainment industry. He also examined whatever Elvis Presley contracts he could find, including those with Parker, RCA, music publishing companies, and for merchandising, concert, and movie deals.

In September 1980, Tual charged in a 300-page report he filed with the probate court that the domineering Parker had kept Elvis "totally isolated" financially. As a result, Tual claimed, Elvis lacked pension plans and other tax-saving vehicles. Tual also criticized the estate's executors. "The most unbelievable thing was that, after Elvis died, the Colonel got $7 million or $8 million and he didn't even have an artist to manage. The big monies came in those first three years. By force of his personality, the Colonel overreached and snookered the estate."

At a raucous December 1980 hearing, Judge Evans gave Tual, who said he had had trouble gathering full financial information on Parker, increased authority to ferret it out. Tual was then able to review copies of Parker's tax returns for the years 1977 through 1980, but he became frustrated by the pace and procedure of document production. Tual blew up at a meeting in Parker's lawyer's office. "Colonel Parker can kiss my ass!!" Tual declared as he stormed out and holed up to write his second report.

It was even more scathing than the first. In it, Tual charged that several sizable side deals Colonel Parker entered into with RCA when Elvis signed the 1973 royalties waiver were in essence a "payoff" to Parker "for keeping Elvis under control." Elvis had approved the side deals, but Tual claimed he had evidence that both Parker and RCA were guilty of conspiracy, fraud, and misrepresentation.

"Elvis signing the '73 contract with RCA was the worst decision ever made in the history of rock 'n' roll," Tual said. "After RCA paid him the $5.4 million and Colonel Parker took his half, Elvis's taxes were 50 percent. So Elvis got only $1.2 million. The more I looked at it, the more incredulous I became. I think the Colonel thought that he better get something while Elvis was alive."

In his defense, Parker told the Memphis *Commercial Appeal* that he "never hid anything" from Elvis. "To suggest that I ever attempted to convince Elvis not to seek legal or tax advice is simply not true," Parker said. Parker told the Memphis *Press-Scimitar* that if Elvis "wanted it, he got it." As for Elvis's state of mind in his last years, "Sometimes it was such a heartache to keep him going," Parker claimed.

For example, when Elvis visited Nashville for a studio session a few months before his death, he instead never left his hotel room. "They say Presley is . . . afraid to record because of recent disappointing record sales," *Nashville Banner* columnist Bill Hance wrote.

"And all this security mumbo-jumbo," a motel staffer said. "[Presley's entourage runs] in doors, out of doors, up and down hallways and elevators trying to hide from people. Who are they hiding from? No fans have come out here. Only you newsmen."

Judge Evans nevertheless ordered the Presley estate to file suit against Parker and RCA. That sparked litigation among the parties in

California, New York, and Tennessee, as well as a partnership suit by Parker in Nevada. The estate was hobbled, however, by diminishing income, a huge tax assessment, and mounting legal costs. "I hope the tax bills and legal fees don't break the estate," Judge Evans worried.

With that to consider, the litigation was settled in 1983. Parker turned Presley audio recordings and concert, film, and TV footage over to the estate in return for a $2 million payment from RCA. RCA also forked $1.1 million over to the estate—over a ten-year period—for unpaid royalties dating back to 1973. Though it footed the settlement bill, "RCA was difficult to deal with," Barry Ward said. "They felt we didn't have a lot to offer because they had already bought Elvis's rights. With the settlement, they felt that they paid twice for the same rights."

"Had I realized that the Colonel [who died in 1997] would live as long as he did, I would never have settled," Blanchard Tual said. "If Elvis had lived and we tried a case against the Colonel, Elvis would have won."

The 1983 settlement agreement severed Parker's ongoing business ties to the estate. But Parker was already trying to re-ingratiate himself with estate representatives. "A couple of weeks after we opened Graceland [in June 1982], someone walked into my office and said that a man is on the phone who says he's Colonel Parker," Jack Soden recalled. "We get a lot of prank calls but I got on the phone and I kinda recognized Colonel Parker's voice from what I'd heard and seen. He said, 'You've got a big challenge ahead. Call me any time. This battle isn't between you and me. You don't have anything to do with it.'

"To him, I was a fresh face. What I saw in the years leading up to his death was frustration and sadness that Blanchard Tual's report had opened up a can of worms about him. I think that Colonel Parker hoped history would treat him kinder. I heard lengthy explanations from him about why he made the decisions he did, but he never said that the deals might have been unfair to Elvis."

"I'm not prepared to paint Parker black," Beecher Smith said. "There were villainous elements but you've got to remember he was like a giant elephant standing on flat ground. He wasn't physically attractive. He smoked cigars and had rough manners. But Parker was instrumental in establishing many of the things the estate benefits from today. His greatest sin was not being savvy about the state of the industry during the last five or ten years of Elvis's life."

In March 1956, Elvis Presley gave Colonel Parker the exclusive right to exploit his name and likeness. Parker claimed that, "at all times, Elvis knew of the uses to which I put his name, image, picture and likeness for commercial purposes on articles of merchandise. Elvis was aware that many individuals were willing to and would commercially exploit his name and likeness improperly for purposes for which he did not approve."

For example, Elvis's talent agent, the William Morris Agency, protested when *Ladies' Home Journal* published a Coppertone suntan lotion ad featuring actress Stella Stevens with the words "Stella co-stars with Elvis Presley in Hal Wallis' 'GIRLS! GIRLS! GIRLS!'"

Still, Parker's carnival background permeated the way in which he busily promoted Elvis's image. Parker wrote film producer Wallis about a 1959 Chicago jukebox convention: "I had my Midget Fanclub there, about 25 midgets with banners reading WELCOME ELVIS PRESLEY MIDGET FANCLUB. We stole the exploitation setups there and left town as soon as everyone had seen the midgets."

In July 1956, Parker signed Elvis to what was the first major merchandising campaign aimed at the burgeoning baby-boomer teen market. The agreement with Hank Saperstein, a successful Beverly Hills children's merchandiser, gave Saperstein's Special Projects Inc. the worldwide, exclusive right to market and exploit 38 categories of Elvis mementos, from anklets and swimming caps to portable typewriters. Presley and Parker received a $35,000 total advance the first year. Special Projects got two one-year renewal options. The licensing fees were split 45 percent each to Saperstein and Presley; the William Morris Agency received a 10 percent commission.

According to Saperstein, "Presley products sold more than $30 million in the first year they were on the market." But, "I know of

nothing like the Saperstein deal going on when Elvis did his movies in
the '60s," Beecher Smith said. (Elvis's merchandising income in 1965,
for example, reportedly decreased to $60,000.)

After Elvis began touring in the 1970s, Colonel Parker set up
Boxcar Enterprises to handle the merchandising, mostly souvenirs
sold at Presley concerts. Elvis paid $3,000 for 75 shares, equal to a 15
percent interest in the company. According to Blanchard Tual's probate court report, in 1974—the year Boxcar was formed—Parker
received $27,650 while Presley got just $2,750.

When Elvis died, Parker gave an exclusive Presley merchandising
license to Factors Etc. Inc. Factors was run by Harry "The Bear"
Geissler, a former steelworker who started in the merchandising business by embroidering customers' names on the backs of bowling
shirts. Geissler ran Factors out of a small factory in the cornfields of
Bear, Delaware. He got into show-business merchandise by selling
bootleg *Peanuts*, *Starsky & Hutch*, and *Sesame Street* items.

"I knew it was illegal. Hell, I ain't gonna kid nobody," Geissler
said. "I knew it as well as the next guy. But I didn't know HOW illegal
it was, you know what I mean?" But after selling 3.5 million authorized heat transfers bearing the image of Farrah Fawcett, Factors was
able to secure the lucrative rights to license *Star Wars* and Sylvester
"Rocky" Stallone merchandise.

Harry Geissler met with Colonel Parker two days after Elvis died
to negotiate a deal that was approved by Vernon Presley. Boxcar got a
$150,000 advance and 5 percent of the net merchandising sales.
Factors received an 18-month initial term with four one-year options,
exercisable upon the payment of just $10,000 at the start of each
option period. "We felt that the Elvis merchandising would go on for
at least a year or so," Harry Geissler's son, Lee, said. "No one really
knew beyond that."

According to Factors' attorney, Greg Kirkelie, Colonel Parker
signed with Harry Geissler "for the purpose of knocking out the boot-
legger. They were out there trying to put up plaques, posters, everything, showing [Elvis] in his coffin . . . it was just outrageous the way

he was being treated. . . . If the bootleggers had not been a problem, I can guarantee you that Factors would not have acquired the rights."

But, "before we could chase the bootleggers, we had to prove that Elvis's right of publicity was descendible," Lee Geissler said. "The law was up for grabs then."

Within weeks of Elvis's death, Factors filed two key lawsuits in Manhattan federal court to protect its exclusive right to license Elvis merchandise. In September 1977, Factors sued the Creative Card Co. over the sale of posters of a jump-suited Elvis. Factors also filed suit against Pro Arts Inc., which was selling an Elvis "In Memory" poster. It was from Pro Arts that Harry Geissler had obtained the Farrah Fawcett merchandising rights. Only five days before Factors filed its complaint, Pro Arts filed suit in Ohio federal court over its business relationship with Factors.

U.S. District Judge Charles Tenney granted injunctions in favor of Factors in both New York cases. The New York right of privacy statute, which provides right of publicity protection, applies to living people. But Judge Tenney ruled that the Presley estate had an independent property right apart from the statute because Elvis exercised his right of publicity during his lifetime. When Pro Arts appealed, the 2d U.S. Circuit Court of Appeals affirmed the ruling in favor of Factors.

After he died on August 16, 1977, the number of Elvis tribute shows ballooned from an estimated 300 to over 3,000 nationwide. Larry Seth had decided to become an Elvis impersonator in 1974, after he hurt his back while working a construction job in southern New Jersey. The six-foot, two-inch-tall Tennessee native donned a sequined jumpsuit and fancy finger rings, coddled pyramid-style sideburns, and launched a new career with "The Big El Show." By 1977, The Big El Show employed 12 musicians and four backup vocalists. It earned about $125,000 in 1976; $300,000 in 1978.

Elvis's estate couldn't help but notice the booming faux Elvis industry. In April 1980, the estate filed suit in Camden, N.J., federal court against The Big El Show's promoter, Rob Russen, to stop use of the Big El name, Elvis's name and image, and the name of Elvis's stage band, TCB.

Russen countercharged the Presley estate with conspiring to engage in price fixing and coercion in violation of federal antitrust law by "restraining and monopolizing interstate commerce with regard to all aspects of Elvis Presley, his name, memory and image."

Russen said that Colonel Parker "was unimpressed by the fact that anyone would bother to do a tribute to anyone. It didn't seem significant to him." Russen claimed that Parker had told him, "As a matter of fact, if you were doing a tribute to Col. Tom Parker, I wouldn't even send you a thank you note."

In 1981, U.S. District Judge Stanley Brotman dismissed Russen's counterclaim and ruled that Elvis's right of publicity was descendible in New Jersey. Brotman issued an injunction on the estate's trademark and unfair competition claims. The injunction barred The Big El Show from selling albums or other merchandise bearing a likeness of Elvis or from using the TCB name or any likenesses of Elvis that could lead consumers into believing the show was sponsored or licensed by the estate. But Judge Brotman allowed the impersonation act—which Larry Seth had by now left—to continue to call itself "The Big El Show" as long as it used a disclaimer stating it wasn't an official Presley estate production.

The ruling didn't trigger a slew of suits against Elvis impersonators, though. Rather, the estate had to pick its fights carefully. "The resources of the estate to litigate weren't as deep as people thought," Barry Ward said. "In fact, they were pretty thin. But the estate wanted people to think it would litigate at the drop of a hat and had the resources of a DuPont to do so."

The Presley estate entered into licenses with some of the bigger-name impersonators, but, according to Jack Soden, "Today we don't really pursue impersonators because there's no question in our minds about the First Amendment. Where they do encroach is when they conduct a substantial part of their promotion by using our trademarks.

"Nobody says I can't wear sideburns, curl my lip, wear high collars and wiggle my hips. Where [a lawsuit] comes into play is when an impersonator advertises 'See Elvis' in big letters, then way down at the bottom of the ad in small letters it says 'as performed by Jack Soden' or whatever."

The Factors and Big El Show rulings were important but indecisive wins for the Presley estate. Not long after Factors sued Pro Arts in New York, it also became involved in litigation with a non-profit organization in Memphis federal court. The Memphis Development Foundation filed suit to prevent Factors from interfering with its use of eight-inch Elvis statuettes to solicit donations to build a large, bronze statue of Elvis in downtown Memphis.

The district court sided with Factors, but in March 1980, the 6th U.S. Circuit Court of Appeals reversed and held that, under Tennessee law, Elvis Presley's right of publicity entered the public domain when he died.

"The impact of the ruling was Godawful," Barry Ward said. "The estate had very little contact with Factors because they'd come through Colonel Parker. The estate hadn't even been involved in the Memphis Development Foundation litigation and its right to license was judicially declared free for anybody to use." Moreover, in New York, the 2d Circuit changed its mind in the Pro Arts case and now ruled against Factors. In June 1981, the appeals court decided that, even though it might disagree with the 6th Circuit, it was bound by that court's decision because Elvis had lived in Tennessee, Boxcar was incorporated there, and that's where the agreement between Boxcar and Factors had been entered into.

This left the Presley estate to enter into whatever licensing deals it could, mostly with mom and pop stores, which could then buy official Elvis merchandise licenses from the estate for as little as $1,000. Fighting the flood of unlicensed merchandise near Graceland after Elvis's death had been "like standing in the middle of a forest fire with a bucket of water," Jack Soden said. The *Memphis Development*

Foundation decision gave new resolve to those vendors. "They were thumbing their noses at us," Barry Ward remarked.

Washington, D.C. area attorney Mack Webner, who worked on the Big El litigation, had filed for the estate's first federal trademark registration in December 1979. When "Glankler Brown [the estate's Memphis law firm] got in touch with me to get a copyright for the epitaph on Elvis's grandmother's tombstone, I told them they ought to think about protecting the Presley name," Webner recalled. "We first got a federal trademark for Elvis's 'TCB' lightning bolt logo [approved in 1983]. Then we got one for Graceland and one for jewelry of a pose of Elvis."

A series of federal and international trademark registrations followed for products ranging from T-shirts to posters, jackets, dolls, key rings, sterling silver spoons, musical instruments, and postcards. "Elvis" was approved for federal registration in 1984, "Elvis Presley" in 1992.

The estate also lobbied the Tennessee legislature for passage of a statute to make the right of publicity descendible. The Personal Rights Protection Act, which took effect in 1984, added Tennessee to a small but growing number of states—like California, Florida, and Texas—to pass right-of-publicity descendibility statutes.

"The Protection Act passed without much difficulty but its effectiveness was hampered because it came so late in the game," Barry Ward said. "What we needed more than a letter from home was to change the 6th Circuit's *Memphis Development Foundation* ruling."

The opportunity arose in the ungainly form of a dispute between two charitable groups out to honor Elvis's memory. On February 24, 1981, two days after the trust created under Elvis's will incorporated Elvis Presley Enterprises, a fan club obtained a state corporate charter for the not-for-profit Elvis Presley International Memorial Foundation (EPIMF). At first, relations between the Presley estate and EPIMF were good. EPIMF helped support the Elvis Presley Trauma Center in Memphis. It also paid for a Tennessee Historical Commission marker placed just outside Graceland's gates. The estate regularly bought tickets for a table at EPIMF's annual Elvis banquet and published items about the charitable organization in its newsletter.

Then in May 1985, the Presley estate incorporated the Elvis Presley Memorial Foundation to solicit funds for a fountain in the Graceland shopping plaza. In July, EPIMF filed an unfair competition suit in Nashville's Davidson County Court to prevent the estate-sponsored foundation from using the Presley name.

The Presley estate argued: "The public is likely to believe that [EPIMF] is somehow associated with or approved by or licensed by the Elvis Presley estate or EPE . . . [The] unauthorized use of the name and likeness of Elvis Presley subjects EPE to injury to the goodwill attached to its marks by [EPIMF's] adoption of a cause or mismanagement of funds or any other error which the higher standard of a not-for-profit organization has imposed upon it. The public is fickle and will overlook acts of commercial enterprises that it will not forgive of charitable groups."

"[N]o one, not even EPE, has raised any objection to our name or logo, until the EPE counterclaim in this action," EPIMF's president, Cheryle Smith replied.

But the court dismissed EPIMF's suit. "I'd never argued before the court in Nashville," Barry Ward recalled, "but when we walked in and the clerk called the case, the chancellor looked up and said sort of in jest, 'The King still lives.'"

In an April 1987 affirmance, the Tennessee Court of Appeals said: "It would be difficult for any court today, especially one sitting in Music City U.S.A. practically in the shadow of the Grand Ole Opry, to be unaware of the manner in which celebrities exploit the public's recognition of their name and image. The stores selling Elvis Presley tee shirts, Hank Williams Jr. bandannas or Barbara Mandrell satin jackets are not selling clothing as much as they are selling the celebrities themselves." The appeals court found Elvis Presley's name and likeness were descendible under Tennessee's common law, but also held that The Personal Rights Protection Act applied to rights of publicity that vested before the act took effect. Ten years after Elvis died, his estate finally had the ruling it needed.

"This was the single most important decision in the whole genre," Barry Ward said. It also breathed life into the estate's efforts against British merchandiser, Sid Shaw.

Londoner Sid Shaw had been selling Elvis Presley merchandise since 1978. He published the *Elvisly Yours* magazine and obtained registered trademarks for the "Elvisly Yours" name. He also ran an Elvis Presley fan club, was involved in bringing English Elvis fans to the Memphis area, and even campaigned for a British Parliament seat on the Elvisly Yours Elvis Presley Party ticket.

"When we opened Graceland, we were just finding our way," Jack Soden said. "Shaw was around and, without really thinking that it could be some kind of precedent, we bought some stuff from him."

"Graceland was the exclusive buyer of Elvisly Yours goods," claimed Shaw, who sold the estate $11,000 worth of his Elvis items for its first gift shop. Shaw also met with Presley estate business manager, Joseph Rascoff, in New York to discuss their merchandising relationship. But Shaw complained Rascoff "demanded a $50,000 licensing fee for each product I sold [approximately 300 items]. I said, 'You're mad.' That would be $15 million, plus payments for the previous four years."

To mark what would have been Elvis Presley's 50th birthday, Sid Shaw convinced post offices in England and in Elvis's birthplace, Tupelo, Mississippi, to issue First Day Cover commemoratives on Elvisly Yours envelopes. This caught the eye of the Presley estate when an advertisement for the British commemorative envelopes appeared in *The New York Times*.

Shaw was called to a meeting at Barry Ward's law office in Memphis. "I thought it would be like, you know, why don't you come over and chat about it. But it was the Spanish Inquisition," Shaw claimed. "I was surrounded by lawyers and had no lawyer of mine own with me. Barry Ward makes a phone call and another guy walks in and serves me with a writ."

"It was fish or cut bait time for Sid Shaw," said Ward. "He had no regard for authority. He's unctuous, like a character out of Dickens."

The estate's federal court complaint charged Shaw with trademark infringement and unfair competition. Shaw had been selling women's underwear emblazoned with Elvis's face and such Presley song titles as "Love Me Tender" and "It's Now or Never."

Colonel Parker claimed that "[n]either [Elvis] nor I would have tolerated" Shaw's panties products. But Shaw argued, "I've got photos of Elvis on stage wiping his brow with a pair of panties. I was at an auction in London where they were offering Presley panties that Colonel Parker licensed in 1956."

In April 1987—three weeks after the Tennessee Court of Appeals issued its ruling in the *Elvis Presley International Memorial Foundation* case—the 6th Circuit ruled in favor of the estate in the Sid Shaw litigation. "Shaw admitted using the same marks on the same goods in the same trade channels to the same consumers as did EPE," the 6th Circuit said about the estate's trademark infringement claim. "From this alone one must infer confusion."

But Shaw wanted a list of the Presley estate's merchandise suppliers and customers, and copies of the estate's licensing agreements and tax returns. He also wanted to depose EPE president, Priscilla Presley. She claimed that Shaw "has no other purpose in mind in taking my deposition than to either annoy or harass me or to gain some other matter about which he may write in his magazine."

Shaw had already written about Priscilla in *Elvisly Yours*, "Many fans would like her to retire, drop the Presley name and get on with her life rearing her child [by boyfriend Marco Garibaldi]."

In October 1990, however, the district court (to which the 6th Circuit remanded the case) issued a permanent injunction barring Shaw from using Elvis Presley's name, likeness, or image for any purpose whatsoever. The 6th Circuit later narrowed the injunction by limiting it to the United States and, in any case, allowing Shaw to write about Elvis or to sell licensed Elvis merchandise.

But Elvis Presley's estate continued to clash with the British merchandiser. When Priscilla Presley was in England, Sid Shaw served her with a lawsuit. "The estate was threatening my customers," Shaw said. "Priscilla was going into a hotel and I walked up and served her a writ inside some flowers." That case was dismissed, but after the estate applied for English trademarks for "Elvis," "Elvis Presley," and an "Elvis A. Presley" signature—to sell perfumes, soaps, shampoos, and cosmetics—Shaw, who had secured his own English trademarks for such Elvis products, filed an objection.

In March 1997, the London High Court ruled in favor of Shaw. "Even if Elvis Presley was still alive, he would not be entitled to stop a fan from naming his son, his dog or goldfish, his car or his house 'Elvis' or 'Elvis Presley,'" Justice Hugh Laddie wrote. "When people buy a toy of a well-known character because it depicts that character, I have no reason to believe that they care one way or the other who made, sold or licensed it."

The ruling, which EPE appealed, applied only to the categories at issue in the case. EPE obtained English trademarks for other goods (though it faced challenges by Shaw in some instances). Still, "My mouth dropped open when I read the case," said Jay Cooper, an attorney with Manatt, Phelps & Phillips, the Los Angeles firm that handled litigation for EPE. "It seems to say the more famous you are, the more you lose your trademark. Elvis Presley Enterprises would have won in the United States."

EPE had recently been told by a U.S. federal judge, however, that it could not stop a Houston tavern from using the name "The Velvet Elvis." The trademark and right of publicity suit was heard just as the estate was about to debut "Elvis Presley's Memphis" in Presley's hometown, the first of a proposed chain of EPE-sponsored restaurants.

Velvet Elvis owner Barry Capece testified during the November 1996 trial that he meant his bar to be a "cheesy, tacky, off-the-wall parody" of American culture. "Elvis Presley has a reputation for having bad taste and not knowing about it and this place plays on that," Capece said. The Velvet Elvis's decor included a velvet portrait of Elvis in a white jumpsuit, a Hawaiian lei around his neck. The bar was furnished with lava lamps, beaded curtains, vinyl furniture, a disco ball, and velvet portraits of Malcolm X, John Lennon, Bruce Lee, and nude women. The menu featured a "Love Me Blenders" drink and a "Hunka-Hunka Happy Hour."

Houston federal Judge Vanessa Gilmore noted that Barry Capece was "All Shook Up" when he received a cease-and-desist letter from Elvis Presley Enterprises. "Stated simply, the Court must determine whether Defendants stepped on Plaintiff's blue suede shoes," Judge Gilmore said.

"Here, the image of Elvis, conjured up by way of velvet paintings, has transcended into an iconoclastic form of art that has specific meaning in our culture which surpasses the identity of the man represented in the painting," Judge Gilmore concluded in favor of the tavern. In addition, except for the velvet portrait, Capece had removed most Presley-related items from his club. Continuing to include a peanut butter and banana sandwich, an Elvis favorite, on the menu or to call "The Velvet Elvis" the "King of Dive Bars" did not violate the estate's publicity rights, Judge Gilmore decided.

She nevertheless enjoined Capece from using Elvis's image or likeness in the bar's promotions or ads, or from using the name "Elvis" in print larger than the word "Velvet." (The estate appealed the rest of the judge's decision.)

Judge Gilmore then ended her decision with a Presleyism: "Thank you. Thank you very much," she wrote. But these weren't the last judicial words in the case. In May 1998, Judge Carolyn King, writing for the 5th U.S. Circuit Court of Appeals, decided that "The Velvet Elvis" *did* infringe on the Presley estate's trademarks. "[T]he defendants have placed the mark in a context that does not alone connote tacky, cheesy art," Judge King concluded.

A few days after the 20th candlelight tribute to Elvis, Jack Soden sat in a conference room at EPE's offices, next door to Graceland. A replica of a young guitar-wielding Elvis stood on a counter near the door. A miniature pink Cadillac sat on a table near the conference room window.

Speaking with a perky mid-Western enthusiasm that draped tough business instincts, Soden confronted the perception that Elvis Presley Enterprises overaggressively sought to protect Elvis's image. "We don't get up in the morning and say, 'Who are we going to sue today?'" the former Kansas City investment banker said. "If Elvis spent 25 years building a tire factory, could you break down the doors and steal the tires after he died? But if we get a guy for stealing Elvis's image, we're this humorless, draconian business. We have to protect and maintain our intellectual property because we run the risk of a claim of having abandoned it."

In the 1990s, EPE pursued, among others, the creator of an unauthorized Elvis CD-ROM and the seller of unauthorized CDs of a Texas radio broadcast of a mid-'50s Elvis concert. It also worried over Elvis materials posted on the Internet, had ongoing tensions with souvenir shops at a strip mall across from Graceland, and, from time to time, sparred in court with its licensees. According to EPE's Memphis litigator, Bill Bradley, EPE sent out about 100 cease-and-desist letters per year, most of them over merchandising issues.

After the successful marketing of the Elvis postal stamp in 1993, Elvis merchandising exploded. Through 1985, estate income from the sale and licensing of official Elvis items was around $2 million; between 1991 and 1996, it was more than $20 million. EPE's licensing agreement revealed a tightly controlled arrangement. "We're not even flexible," Carol Butler, EPE's director of worldwide licensing, insisted. "If licensees fail to follow our guidelines, they don't have the right to sell off the goods they have. We either get them or the goods must be destroyed."

Butler noted that EPE worked with about 100 licensees. The estate's typical deal required a $50,000 minimum payment and a royalty of 10 percent of a licensee's wholesale price, with a two-year licensing term. Butler said she received one to three calls per week requesting Elvis licenses with "a lot of requests for fast foods." Among the more unusual unlicensed Elvis Presley goods brought to her attention: a fly swatter with the saying, "It might have been the King."

Billy Joel: "Honesty Is Such a Lonely Word"

rank Weber was working as marketing manager for a military electronics firm on Long Island when his sister Elizabeth asked him to join her artist management firm, Home Run, which guided the career of Elizabeth's husband, singer/songwriter Billy Joel. "She was sort of secretive about it and invited me and my wife to dinner," Frank recalled. "She said Billy's business had outgrown her ability to handle it, there were so many people—lawyers and accountants—involved."

Frank agreed to oversee operations but claimed his wife "was dead set against it. She said in a facetious way that rock was crazy, full of drug addicts. I love music and play piano, but [the idea of working at Elizabeth's management company] died for a while." Frank nevertheless met with one of Elizabeth's music accountants. "He gave me a graph of how the business worked, the royalties and publishing, and it wasn't all that complicated," Frank said.

Then in the summer of 1978, while he was in a conference at the electronics firm with some government officials, Frank got a call from his brother-in-law, Billy Joel. "I had told my secretary not to disturb me and all of a sudden she busts in. It was Billy and I thought there'd been an accident," remembered Frank. "Billy'd done a concert in Cincinnati and he said, 'We got held up last night. Someone broke into our hotel room with a shotgun and took the concert receipts. You've got to come help us.'"

By the beginning of 1979, Frank was working full-time at Home Run. In 1980, Elizabeth—who would soon separate from and later divorce Billy—stepped down because, according to Frank, "she was bored with the business, tired of hanging out backstage. They had a spat and Billy told me, 'It has nothing to do with your gig.'" Frank, who had never managed an artist on his own before, then signed Billy Joel to a management contract and took financial and creative reins of Joel's career.

Ironically, as Frank Weber told the story in February 1992, he no longer served as Billy Joel's manager. Instead, he sat in the eastern Long Island office of his attorney, Anthony Conforti, in bankruptcy and the target of a $90 million lawsuit Joel had launched against him. The suit charged Weber with, among other things, breach of contract, conversion, and fraud for mismanaging Joel's finances. In the complaint, Joel alleged that Weber had used him as a "personal bank," arranging secret loans for himself and diverting Joel's earnings to fund Weber's gas, oil, horse-breeding, and real estate investments, almost all of which lost money. In addition, the suit named as defendants Joel's former accountants and Weber's wife, sister-in-law, two brothers-in-law, and even attorney Conforti.

"He's sued everybody who's ever had a drink with me," Frank Weber complained that day in Conforti's office.

In fact, Billy Joel had a long history of legal disputes with career advisers but, astonishingly, hadn't discovered the improprieties alleged in the suit against Weber until 1989. That's when, for the first time, Joel had an independent financial audit of Weber's management activities conducted. "I trusted him totally," said Joel, who had made Weber the executor of his will and the godfather of Alexa Ray, Joel's daughter with model Christie Brinkley. "But he seriously damaged my faith in human nature."

Financial insecurity wasn't new to William Martin Joel. Born May 9, 1949, Billy's childhood began in a housing development in Levittown, New York. He started taking classical piano lessons at age four. Then, when Billy was seven, his father, Howard—a General Electric engineer, and himself a classically trained pianist—divorced Billy's mother, Rosalind, and headed back to his native Europe, for Vienna. "He sent a check every month," Billy said, but "we went hungry a lot."

While Billy's mother worked at minimal-paying clerical jobs, his maternal grandfather, Philip Nyman, took the boy to classical music concerts at the Brooklyn Academy of Music. Recalled Billy, "He never had enough money for tickets, so he'd bribe the ushers with a pack of cigarettes."

Inspired by the sounds of James Brown and the Beatles, Billy Joel joined a succession of rock groups with names like the Emerald Lords, the Lost Souls, and the Echoes, earning money as a musician from age 14. He also honed his skills as an amateur welterweight boxer. Rather than concerning himself with graduating from Hicksville High, Billy joined what he described as a gang of junior hoods, "dittyboppers" who would "kick over garbage cans, sniff glue and use phony draft cards to buy beer."

He also hooked up as keyboard player for the Hassles, a band that, in part, emulated the white soul sounds of the Young Rascals and released two albums of its own.

It was around this time that Billy Joel first met Frank Weber, at the funeral of Frank's brother, Harry, who had been the keyboard player in the Hassles before Billy. "I don't remember much about Billy other than that he was at the funeral," Frank said. "Then I bumped into him later on when he was dating my sister Josephine."

Billy went on to form a duo named Attila with the Hassles drummer, Jon Small, whose wife happened to be Elizabeth Weber. Attila released one album—"the loudest thing you ever heard," according to Joel—for CBS Records' Epic label, but the album stiffed. To survive, Billy played clubs and did session work.

At the height of the singer/songwriter phenomenon that swept the early 1970s, Billy turned to writing songs for a solo career. He also began living with Elizabeth Weber, whom he married in 1973.

In 1971, Joel signed a recording deal with producer Artie Ripp and Ripp's Family Productions. In return, Ripp gave Joel an advance and promised to pay Joel's monthly rent. The resulting album, *Cold Spring Harbor*, was not only recorded at too fast a speed but bombed upon release by Paramount Records. When Ripp stopped sending rent checks, a disillusioned Joel left for Los Angeles, found a job as an anonymous bar pianist and renamed himself Bill Martin. The experience gave Billy the lyrics for the title song of his *Piano Man* album, his first release on CBS Records' Columbia label in 1973. To get out from under his obligation to Family Productions, Joel agreed to give Ripp 25 cents from the sale of each copy of any albums Joel recorded.

Frank Weber estimated that, over the years, the financial interest in Joel's albums held by Ripp—"who called every couple of months to exploit the *Cold Spring Harbor* album"—amounted to approximately $20 million. Ripp's financial stranglehold on Joel would continue until Joel's 1986 album, *The Bridge*. In the early 1990s, Billy finally bought out Ripp's interest. "I love this guy from my heart and soul—and pocket," Ripp quipped of Joel.

In 1975, Billy Joel moved back to New York, this time upstate, and worked on his fourth solo album, *Turnstiles*, before being paired with producer Phil Ramone. In 1977, they recorded *The Stranger*, which went on to sell more than nine million copies. By now, Elizabeth had formally taken control of her husband's business affairs, which remained bleak. For example, by 1978 Joel had netted only $7,763 from the *Piano Man* album, which was certified gold by the Recording Industry Association of America in 1975.

As his success on the record charts increased, Billy Joel became a lightning rod for lawsuits, especially copyright infringement claims. "I've got lawsuits up the gazool," said Joel, who claimed he never stole anyone's song. In one notable case, John Powers, a singer/songwriter from Reno, Nevada, alleged that Billy's hit "My Life" was based on a song Powers wrote entitled "We Got To Get It Together." To avoid the high cost of litigation, Joel settled the case on the advice of his lawyers by paying Powers $42,500 but admitting no liability.

The settlement agreement included a confidentiality clause. Powers, however, continued to state publicly that Joel stole his song. Powers even bought newspaper advertisements in which he asked readers to listen to his and Joel's songs and draw their own infringement-claim conclusions. Billy said of Powers in a 1982 *Playboy* interview, "I'm going to kill this guy. I want to break his legs with my own hands." Billy also called Powers a "creep" and "a poor little schlump." Powers filed suit in state court in Reno alleging that Joel had defamed and intentionally inflicted emotional distress on him.

In April 1988, Nevada Judge Charles M. McGee dismissed Powers' suit. Joel had been described in the *Playboy* interview introduction as "a street kid," "a figure of fiery controversy." As a result, McGee wrote: "The reader should be put on notice that many, if not all, of Billy Joel's statements will be nothing more than his opinion. His sought-after opinions as a leading songwriter should not be chilled by litigation, unless he's lying outright." The judge added that Billy's threat to "kill" Powers constituted legally protected "rhetorical hyperbole."

Later, Joel, who once regularly reviewed tapes aspiring songwriters submitted to him, remained wary of copyright infringement claims. "Now I see somebody coming at me with a tape, to me it looks like a subpoena," he said.

When Frank Weber joined the Home Run management firm in 1979, Billy Joel's marriage to Elizabeth was showing the stresses and strains of a couple being both professionally and personally close. According to Billy, "Her function as my manager was to make me a rock star, and I think that's where our paths diverged. I might have become a commodity to an extent, and she might have become the enemy, which is business, capitalism, exploitation."

At first, "I had questions about somebody's brother coming in," Billy said about Frank. However, "because [Elizabeth] had brought Frank in, I thought it would help preserve the marriage by having someone that she brought in, who was her brother, handle the management and the business and for me and her to have, you know, another agreement."

Billy recalled that Elizabeth said, "'If you want this marriage to work and if, as a sign of good faith that you do love me, I want you to sign this agreement which splits our assets 50-50.' And I said, 'That's okay with me. Is it okay if Frank becomes my manager now? Will we be able to live with that?' And she said yes. And that's when I made the decision to go with Frank."

Any misgivings Billy may have had about Frank were allayed when Frank began pointing out "great errors he claimed [Elizabeth] had made in managing me. He expressed great loyalty to me during my separation and divorce from Elizabeth." Frank even accompanied Billy to Haiti to finalize the divorce in 1984. There, artist and manager sat in an airplane in Port-au-Prince, divorce decree in hand, sipping drinks and talking about the meaning of life. "There has always been a sibling clash between us," Frank said about Elizabeth. Before long, Billy Joel relied completely on Frank Weber for all his business decisions. When Billy wanted to buy a new home, Frank found him a real estate lawyer. When Billy married his second wife, Christie Brinkley, Frank advised him on the prenuptial agreement.

Billy didn't bother to independently seek an attorney to represent him on his pre-divorce agreement with Elizabeth. Instead, he chose an attorney that Elizabeth introduced to him. According to Billy, "I met him at a party at our house that Elizabeth had thrown and this guy [Ron Williams] was there. He said he was an attorney and he had some experience in marital agreements. And when Frank asked me to pick an attorney, I said, 'What about this guy from Texas?' and he said, 'You know, go talk to him,' and I did."

Asked several years later about Williams, Joel responded, "I don't know where he is now. . . . I heard he got busted for something."

The divorce decree, like the pre-divorce agreement, provided for a 50-50 split of all of Billy's pre-divorce assets, such as recording and music publishing royalties, including a right for Elizabeth to collect her share from future income earned from those assets. The settlement didn't run smoothly, however. In 1987, Elizabeth filed suit against Billy in New York state court in Manhattan alleging non-payment. Elizabeth claimed that Billy owed her $300,000 in pension-plan funds, $180,000 in music earnings, and $2.6 million that Billy claimed he had used to cover Elizabeth's share of $5 million in tax deficiencies.

Elizabeth and Billy settled the suit, but there was another intra-family squabble to contend with. Frank had sued Elizabeth, alleging that she owed him a portion of his 15-percent share of the income from Billy's pre-1981 music earnings. Frank, who was entitled to the percentage under the terms of Elizabeth's divorce settlement with Billy, claimed he had been forced to file suit against Elizabeth to trigger a promise by Billy to cover any such commission shortfalls.

Elizabeth countered with her own claims against Frank. She asked for $7 million for self-dealing, breach of contract, and breach of fiduciary duty that she claimed Frank had committed in his dealings with her. Based on documents gathered by Elizabeth's lawyers during the suit, Billy Joel for the first time began to believe that Frank Weber might be mismanaging his business affairs. (The sibling suit would lay dormant as Billy pursued his suit against Frank. Frank and Elizabeth would agree in 1993 to discontinue their legal dispute.)

Billy also discovered—as he complained to CBS Records chairman Walter Yetnikoff—that he would have to sell his Manhattan co-op, which he had bought from Frank, in order to have sufficient funds to construct a new home near the fashionable celebrity colony of East Hampton, on the eastern tip of Long Island. The real estate lawyer Frank picked for Billy was Anthony Conforti, who would later defend Frank against Billy's suit.

One of Billy's key friends in the Hamptons was attorney John Eastman, brother-in-law and legal counsel to Paul McCartney. Impressed with Eastman's success in helping the careers of McCartney and other top entertainers, Joel decided in the spring of 1989 to terminate his relationship with his long-time counsel, Grubman, Indursky & Schindler, and to hire Eastman as his lawyer.

Grubman Indursky was widely considered the most powerful music firm on the East Coast and perhaps in the music business. Joel had been the firm's first superstar client; he was also the first major music client to leave the firm.

Eastman immediately appointed the accounting firm of Ernst & Young to conduct a review of Billy Joel's financial records. Manhattan's Berman, Shaffet & Schain, which was hired by Frank Weber, had served as Joel's accountants since 1981.

After completing the audit, Ernst & Young reported to Eastman and Joel that it had discovered a broad pattern of improprieties in the way that Billy's business affairs had been handled by Weber. Ernst & Young concluded that Billy was worth far less than Weber had told him. "I may not be rich at all. I may *owe* money. I may owe a great deal of money," an alarmed Joel said after the audit. Joel claimed that Weber and his associates had used him like "a fire hydrant. They plugged their hose in whenever they needed money and—sploosh."

In July 1989, Eastman notified Weber that Weber's authority to make financial decisions on behalf of Billy had been revoked. In August, Eastman sent Weber a letter of termination, formally ending the management relationship.

Eastman also recruited veteran entertainment litigator Leonard Marks, a senior partner in the New York City firm Gold, Farrell & Marks, to draft a complaint against Weber on behalf of Joel. Marks had already worked on litigation matters for Eastman's other entertainment clients. He also oversaw the complex royalties suit brought by the Beatles against Capitol-EMI Records. In addition, Marks had experience with artist/manager lawsuits and had represented Mike Appel, Bruce Springsteen's former manager, in a protracted dispute with Springsteen in the mid-'70s.

Within two months of the Ernst & Young report, Marks's firm filed suit against Frank Weber in New York Supreme Court in Manhattan. At 7 a.m. on September 25—Weber's birthday—Billy Joel's lawyers had Weber served with an 83-page complaint seeking $30 million in compensatory and $60 million in punitive damages.

"Weber repeatedly has abused his position of trust and confidence to further his own interests, at Joel's expense, and has concealed his abuses from Joel by a systematic practice of non-disclosure and mis-representation," the suit charged.

The complaint further alleged that Weber misused the power of attorney Joel had granted him by obligating Billy, without consent, to millions of dollars in investments in which Weber held a personal interest. These included high-risk gas, horse, oil, and real-estate tax shelters. "Weber concealed his imprudent and improper use of Joel's assets to finance and keep afloat Weber's interlocking network of speculative partnership ventures," the suit alleged. "Weber took more monies from the revenues produced by some of Joel's tours and recordings than Joel himself received." The complaint also asserted that Frank overcharged Billy for music videos made by Weber's pro-duction company and secretly took for himself and his wife, Lucille, hundreds of thousands of dollars in unpaid, interest-free loans. "We found that, in some instances, Weber would sign the loan notes, stick them in his files and take the monies out of Billy's accounts," Marks contended. In addition, at the time Joel's suit was filed, Weber allegedly was about to obligate Joel to a $6 million bank loan.

To make matters worse, the suit charged, Weber improperly pledged all of Joel's song copyrights as collateral for interest-free loans CBS Records gave Joel in lieu of advances. Weber's idea was that the loans were non-taxable income. Weber then took a commission from these loans. (In 1987, Weber and Joel changed their manage-ment agreement to allow Weber to take his 20-percent-of-gross man-ager's commission from any interest-free loans CBS Records made to Joel.) Weber argued that he told Joel about the ongoing business investments. "It's bullshit that he wasn't advised," Weber claimed. Weber also described the interest-free loans from CBS as "a stroke of genius. Some of that money was used to purchase Billy's mansion." As for pledging Joel's song copyrights as loan collateral, Weber insisted, "They were always under Billy's control. All he had to do was hand in an album or pay CBS." Besides, Weber said, CBS knew its liens on

Joel's songs were subordinate to the senior interest Elizabeth held in them under her divorce agreement with Billy.

A burly, apprehensive Weber defended his actions as he sat in the law office of his defense counsel, Anthony Conforti. Sporting a beard peppered with gray and wearing a gray-tweed coat over a blue sports shirt, Weber portrayed himself as a downtrodden ex-confidante out-gunned by Joel's high-powered lawyers.

The state court nevertheless took Billy Joel's charges seriously. In March 1990, Justice Edward H. Lehner—a former state assemblyman who had overseen Elizabeth's suit against Billy and Frank's suit against Elizabeth—awarded Joel $2 million in partial judgment for Weber's unpaid loans, including a $400,000 loan Weber took for himself without Joel's knowledge in 1981 and another $400,000 secret, interest-free loan taken by Weber and his wife in 1986.

Billy managed to collect only $250,000 of the $2 million judgment before Frank filed for bankruptcy. Frank's May 1990 bankruptcy petition in Richmond, Virginia, cited more than 300 unpaid creditors. He listed $652,000 in assets and nearly $24 million in debt, not including what he may owe Billy. In August, the Virginia bankruptcy court ordered Frank's bankruptcy petition transferred to the Eastern District of New York. The bankruptcy court noted, among other things, that Frank had listed several of his corporate and partnership interests in Virginia as being worth only one dollar each.

In New York, Justice Lehner granted Joel's request to attach $675,670 in distributions from real-estate partnerships in which Billy owned an interest. The money had been sent to Weber's management firm and kept by Weber *after* Billy filed suit against him. Justice Lehner also allowed Joel to add attorney Conforti as a defendant based on a claim that Conforti aided and abetted Weber in converting the post-suit earnings. Incredibly, Joel claimed, Weber's management company had dipped into the partnership distributions to help satisfy the $2 million March 1990 judgment Joel won against Weber. "Thus, defendants 'repaid' Joel for their earlier theft of his funds with money that they had later converted from him long after this lawsuit began—using Conforti as the conduit," charged what was now a 133-page complaint, amended by Joel's lawyers for the fifth time.

"I've been paid some money from Weber's companies," Conforti admitted, "but I don't know exactly where the money came from. There's a provision in Weber's management contract with Joel that indicates Weber has a right to post-term monies from work generated during the contract."

(Billy Joel and Frank Weber amended their original 1980 management agreement several times. In 1985, Joel agreed to allow Weber to collect a 10 percent commission after termination of their management relationship, *even if* the termination was due to Weber's "gross negligence, fraud or wilful neglect." Joel also agreed that Weber could be a principal or general partner in business transactions in which Joel had an interest.)

"They've tried to intimidate me and conflict me out of this case to bring Weber to his knees," Conforti insisted. "They're deliberately trying to make this litigation more complicated than it has to be. I get five pounds of paper a week from Billy's lawyers."

With Frank Weber in bankruptcy, Billy Joel's lawyers focused on recovering money from "deep-pocket" defendants. In May 1991, a New York appeals court reinstated previously dismissed fraud claims that Billy filed against the Berman, Shaffet & Schain accounting firm. Billy sought recovery from Berman Shaffet's $10 million malpractice policy. He charged that the accounting-firm had failed to disclose to him that they were also working for partnerships in which Weber had been involved. The complaint also alleged that accounting firm partner Howard Schain invested in one or more thoroughbred horse-breeding partnerships in which Weber was a general partner.

Horse breeding apparently was a favorite Weber investment. It led Frank to use his power of attorney to sign Billy to an investment in a horse named John's Gold, owned by music mogul Morris Levy. Law enforcement officials had long believed that Levy functioned as a key music-industry front man and source of money for organized crime. CBS Records chairman Walter Yetnikoff and Tommy Mottola, who Yetnikoff would bring in to be CBS Records U.S. president, were among Levy's co-horse-breeding investors and closest music industry friends.

In 1988, a federal jury in Camden, New Jersey, convicted Levy of conspiracy to extort in an attempt to seize control of the cutout records business of John LaMonte, a convicted record counterfeiter. Levy, who died before he could serve his ten-year jail term, received treatments for liver cancer at a Manhattan hospital. At one point, in a bed in the room next door lay Billy Joel, contending with kidney stones he had developed shortly after filing suit against Frank Weber.

Frank Weber responded to Billy Joel's legal maneuvers with a legal barrage of his own. When Joel first fired him, Weber filed a $33 million breach-of-contract suit against Joel in Richmond, Virginia, seeking a portion of monies from Joel's upcoming tours and future album sales. In April 1990, the Circuit Court of the City of Richmond dismissed Weber's suit on the ground that any breach had occurred in New York. If Weber were allowed to proceed in Virginia, the court reasoned, then he would unfairly be able to sue Joel in any state in which Billy's records or concert tickets were sold.

That didn't stop Frank from filing a breach-of-contract action against Billy in Georgia. Weber had Joel served with the suit just before Billy got on stage to give a concert in Atlanta. A good reason for pursuing Billy outside New York was that courts in other states were likely to be less sympathetic to New-York-native Joel. Weber agreed to withdraw the Georgia suit, however, and instead file a counterclaim for post-termination commissions in New York.

Frank then turned his sights on Billy's wife, Christie Brinkley. Weber accused Brinkley of maliciously interfering with his relationship with Joel. According to a $12 million suit Weber filed in New York state court, Brinkley "harbored ill feelings and malice" toward him for advising Billy on the artist's 1985 prenuptial agreement with Brinkley. As a result, Weber claimed, Brinkley "did wrongfully, knowingly, intentionally, maliciously and without reasonable justification or excuse, induce, persuade and entice" Joel "to violate, repudiate, and break" the management agreement with Weber.

In March 1992, however, Justice Lehner ruled in Brinkley's favor. He said that, without allegations of such wrongful conduct as fraud or physical threats against Frank, the discussions between Christie and Billy were protected by New York's marital privilege.

One afternoon in June 1991, Arthur Indursky sat in his office on West 57th Street in Manhattan, in a tower next to Carnegie Hall. Coat off, glasses pushed up on his forehead, he puffed on a cigar. Abrupt and even brash at times, Indursky jumped up every few minutes to pick up a telephone near his pipe rack to consider the details of a contract negotiation. Indursky was the managing partner for what was then known as Grubman, Indursky, Schindler, Goldstein & Flax, a law firm with perhaps the most impressive client roster in the music business. Among the firm's many well-known clients were David Geffen, Bruce Springsteen, Madonna, and Sting, as well as top managers, record labels, and record-company executives. Grubman Indursky had recently settled into its new 20,000 square-feet offices. Dark mahogany woods accented the hallways; expensive marble tile lined the reception area.

When Billy Joel, the firm's first superstar client, decided to leave Grubman Indursky in 1989, industry observers bet that other big-time clients would follow. The problem was, these observers noted, Grubman Indursky had served at times as legal counsel to Frank Weber, Billy Joel, and CBS Records.

The law firm had in fact long been subject to conflicts-of-interest criticism and had faced two suits over the issue. In one, Sandy Linzer—a former Allen Grubman client and partner with Tommy Mottola in the artist management firm Champion Entertainment—claimed Grubman favored Mottola, another law client, over him. The case was settled. In the other suit, an independent record label in California charged Grubman with withholding detrimental information about an act the label signed. Grubman's insurance company settled the suit for $1 million, though Grubman later obtained his own settlement from the insurer's law firm, which had triggered a default judgment against Grubman by failing to file a timely answer to the malpractice suit.

Of course, potential conflicts of interest are a common problem in an industry as close-knit as the music business. "In many cases, it exists on paper," Madonna's manager Freddy DeMann admitted. "But as long as everyone is aware of it, it seems to work," he said of Grubman Indursky. So Grubman Indursky remained at the top of the music-business law-firm heap. "We are a league unto ourselves," Indursky boasted.

Brooklyn Law School graduates Grubman, Indursky, and Paul Schindler had worked together since 1974, when the firm was located in an 800-square-foot converted apartment building next to the Friars Club. "We even shared space with clients to keep our overhead down," Indursky recalled. The self-described "relentless and tenacious" Grubman had become a legend for having his shirt ripped to shreds by CBS Records' Walter Yetnikoff in 1981, while "negotiating my *tuchus* off" for Billy Joel. The negotiation resulted in what was then the largest artist deal ever with CBS.

Elizabeth Weber had used New York attorney Ina Meibach to handle Billy Joel's legal matters. Frank Weber hired brash Manhattan lawyer Michael Tannen to represent Joel. But Yetnikoff disliked Tannen and helped push Joel to Grubman Indursky, which had long sought Billy as a client.

By June 1991, Allen Grubman, Arthur Indursky and Paul Schindler had been pulled into the Frank Weber/Billy Joel litigation. The three lawyers were named along with Joel as defendants in a suit filed in a Suffolk County, New York, court by the Union Savings Bank. The bank sought to enforce two $40,000 promissory notes the lawyers had issued in connection with investments in Jericho Breeding Associates, a horse venture in which Frank Weber was general partner. Grubman, Indursky and Schindler claimed that Weber fraudulently procured the notes, then signed them over to the bank to reduce his debt.

Indursky stated in an affidavit, "Weber represented that the Jericho investment was important to Joel, and that it was important to Joel that my partners, Grubman and Schindler, and I also join in the investment. It was clear from Weber's statements that our refusal to invest in Jericho would have a negative impact on the Firm's relationship with Joel."

But Billy hadn't invested in Jericho Breeding. Instead, Frank Weber allegedly used his power of attorney to execute a promissory note in Joel's name, without Joel's knowledge or consent. It was unlikely, though, that Grubman Indursky would have had a chance to ask Billy about this directly because, Grubman complained, Weber had kept them away from Joel. Grubman became angry when he wasn't invited to Billy's marriage to Christie Brinkley in 1986 and concluded that Weber—in order to take credit for the CBS Records deals and to justify his management fees—had told Joel that Grubman and Indursky were merely "scribes."

(By contrast, once free of Weber, Billy Joel mingled freely with his lawyers. For example, Billy attended Leonard Marks's 50th birthday party at the trendy Tribeca Grill—a show business hangout in lower Manhattan in which Grubman Indursky client Robert De Niro held a business interest. Joel mingled comfortably with party guests, while Christie Brinkley engaged in small talk with Alan Friedman, a litigator from Gold, Farrell & Marks heavily involved in the Frank Weber litigation. Joel even broke into an impromptu doo-wop performance with Kenny Vance and the Planotones, an a cappella group performing at the event.)

It turned out that the Jericho Breeding promissory notes weren't the only payments Grubman Indursky made to Weber. The U.S. Attorney's Office for the Southern District of New York—for which Marks had worked early in his career—launched a criminal investigation into Weber's diversion of the $675,670 in real estate partnership distributions made after Joel filed suit against Weber. In addition, the FBI began investigating allegations that Weber planned to have horses killed to collect insurance-policy money. The FBI interviewed Grubman, Indursky and Sony Music president Tommy Mottola about the matter. Mottola had been a close friend and client of Grubman's since the mid-'70s, when he had operated Champion Entertainment.

Grubman acknowledged—when interviewed at his offices in May 1992, by FBI agent Tim Crino—that Mottola told him several years before about Weber's plan to "burn horses." Mottola described Weber as "crazy," Grubman said. But at Weber's request and without Billy Joel allegedly knowing, Grubman and Indursky made an unsecured loan of $250,000 to Weber's Silver W Stables in February 1986. Weber, who said he was "desperate for money," used the funds to purchase a horse that died a few months later. Weber then collected a large insurance policy payment.

In a January 1993 letter to Justice Lehner, Weber admitted that he collected $640,000 in insurance monies after the horse, Vers La Caisse—for which Weber paid $600,000—died following a racetrack injury. But Weber insisted that he lost money after the horse's training and boarding fees were deducted. (Weber also acknowledged that he had collected an additional $250,000 following the death during training of the horse Raisin Taxes.)

Grubman and Indursky claimed that the Silver W transaction was the only time they had loaned money to a client. They had made the loan the same year Weber paid Grubman Indursky $450,000 for helping conclude a renegotiation of Joel's deal with CBS Records.

During the FBI interview, agent Crino questioned Grubman and Indursky about a series of payments—totaling over $180,000—that the lawyers made to Weber between 1982 and 1985. Invoices issued by Weber's companies indicated that Grubman and Indursky had paid Weber for "financial consulting and tax planning." In 1985 alone, the payments amounted to $100,000, though Indursky admitted Weber did "nothing that would take more than 5 minutes." Armed with this information, Billy Joel's lawyers began preparing a malpractice suit against Grubman Indursky. They filed the state court complaint in Manhattan in September 1992. The suit charged Grubman Indursky with fraud, breach of contract, and breach of fiduciary duty. Joel's suit characterized the payments that Grubman and Indursky had made to

Weber as "kickbacks" to retain Joel's business. The suit also claimed: that Grubman Indursky failed to tell Joel that the firm simultaneously represented Joel, CBS/Sony, and CBS/Sony executives; that the defendants received secret investment rebates from Weber, "so they were paying less for their investments in the same deal . . . Joel was investing in"; that Grubman should have had Joel's financial status investigated after Walter Yetnikoff told the lawyer that "something was wrong," following Joel's complaint to Yetnikoff about his finances; and that Grubman should have told Joel about Weber's alleged horse-killing scheme.

Grubman Indursky called the malpractice suit "a contrived and libelous attempt to cause severe injury to a prestigious law firm and to extort a settlement." Arthur Indursky noted that Billy Joel had made it clear that he deferred to Frank Weber's judgment on matters concerning Grubman Indursky's work. For example, Indursky pointed out, when Billy met with firm lawyers to review the terms of the 1981 contract renegotiation with CBS Records, "Joel expressed no interest in reading the contract; upon hearing the material terms of the deal . . . his only words were, in effect, 'Where do I sign?'"

Grubman and Indursky denied that the payments to Weber were kickbacks, insisting instead that they had been "impressed with Weber's understanding of financial and tax planning"—although Weber had had no formal financial training.

One particularly intriguing aspect of Billy Joel's legal battle with Frank Weber and Grubman Indursky was the dynamics between the lawyers involved. Just as there are only so many superstar artists and executives in the record business, there are but a few truly powerful music attorneys. As a result, their orbits intersect on a regular basis. For example, Leonard Marks worked at New York's Paul, Weiss, Rifkind, Wharton & Garrison before co-founding Gold, Farrell & Marks in 1970. For a year in the early 1970s, John Steel, who would become Elizabeth Weber's long-time counsel, worked with Marks as a law partner.

Grubman Indursky hired Paul Weiss to handle the malpractice suit filed against them by Joel. Paul Weiss lawyers Martin London and Gerard Harper then moved to have Marks disqualified as counsel to Joel on the ground that Marks had become a necessary witness by being present during the FBI interview of Grubman and Indursky. Marks in turn moved to have Paul Weiss disqualified because the firm had represented Billy Joel in contract negotiations with Frank Weber in the early 1980s. Both sides agreed not to proceed with their motions.

But that wasn't all. Paul Weiss would hire Marks's firm to file suit against Morris Levy's estate over Levy's failure to pay legal fees for the work Paul Weiss did defending Levy against the federal extortion charges in the cut-out records scam involving John LaMonte. And both Los Angeles entertainment litigator Bert Fields—Grubman Indursky's co-counsel in the Joel malpractice suit—and Leonard Marks regularly handled legal claims on behalf of the Beatles.

Grubman and Indursky attacked Marks in the Joel malpractice litigation. They charged that they had made their personal investment files available to him before the FBI interview took place because Marks had convinced them that their interests were aligned with Billy Joel's against Frank Weber. Marks then used Grubman's and Indursky's files to prepare Joel's malpractice suit, the law partners charged. Marks countered that "not a single one of the documents" attached to the malpractice complaint came from the Grubman Indursky files. "When your defense is weak, it's standard operating procedure to attack the lawyer on the other side," Marks chided.

Claiming they wanted to expedite the legal proceedings, Billy Joel's lawyers asked the New York court to consolidate Joel's suit against Grubman, Indursky and Schindler with his suit against Frank Weber. When Justice Lehner denied the request, a pleased Bert Fields announced that now a jury wouldn't become "confused as to whether Grubman was committing the same alleged bad acts as Weber."

In August 1993, Billy Joel spent the first seven days of the taking of his legal depositions at the offices of Paul Weiss, where, at various times, Frank Weber, Allen Grubman, and Arthur Indursky were present. During one session, Weber tauntingly whistled the refrain from one of Billy's songs, "Honesty is such a lonely word."

By October 1993, Billy's career had reached a new peak. His *River of Dreams* album debuted at number one on the *Billboard* charts and his latest concert tour sold out six nights at Madison Square Garden. Billy had also been able to schedule the remainder of what would be a total of 30 days of depositions to fit between his tour dates.

But Pat Monaghan, a lawyer for Frank Weber and Weber's brother-in-law, Rick London—also a defendant in Joel's suit against Weber—subpoenaed Joel's drummer, lighting man, and sound man. Leonard Marks argued this was "sabotage" because the crew members "knew nothing about [Joel's] financial affairs." Marks claimed that London and his wife, Mary Sue—another of Elizabeth Weber's sisters—hid in bushes outside the crew members' homes, though Monaghan denied it.

Then on October 25, Billy Joel and Grubman Indursky announced their legal dispute was over. Joel's legal advisor, John Eastman, insisted, "It's done. Full-stop. No one is going into any detail. Everyone believes it should remain dead-ass neutral." The terms of the Joel/Grubman Indursky deal were confidential, but Allen Grubman allegedly began telling the press that he had "totally defeated" Joel. Grubman's comments prompted Leonard Marks to reveal in court documents that, to help Grubman Indursky save face, Sony Corp. of America had agreed to "funnel" $3 million to Joel to end the entertainer's suit. "Virtually every settlement agreement was transmitted by counsel for Mr. Joel and the Grubman defendants through the offices of Sony," Marks stated. One early settlement draft would have obligated Grubman Indursky to pay several million dollars directly to Joel.

Sony Music Entertainment chairman Michael Schulhof had met with John Eastman twice in October 1993. Sony had a lot at stake. An unfavorable conflicts-of-interest ruling against Grubman Indursky could have wounded Sony's relationship with other Grubman artists, like Bruce Springsteen and Michael Jackson, who were signed to the record company. Besides, Schulhof liked Grubman. He had purportedly offered Grubman the job as president of Sony Music before it had been given it to Tommy Mottola.

Frank Weber and his bankruptcy trustee, Allan Mendelsohn, reached an agreement as early as 1991 that would allow them to concentrate on fighting Billy Joel, rather than each other. Mendelsohn was to get a percentage of any post-termination commissions Weber might collect from Joel, with a guaranteed minimum of $300,000. The trustee would also drop fraud claims he had brought to void the transfer by Weber of: Weber management company stock to Rick London and Weber's wife, Lucille; and the sale and transfer of Weber's personal real estate to Lucille's sister, Rosemary Haliasz and her husband, Edward.

The bankruptcy court refused to approve the trustee deal, however. According to Gold, Farrell & Marks lawyer Alan Friedman, this represented a "pivotal" point in the Joel/Weber litigation because it denied Frank the opportunity to mount a more focused fight against Joel.

By the end of 1994, Frank Weber, Allan Mendelsohn, Anthony Conforti, and Joel's former accountants Berman, Shaffet & Schain had all settled with Joel. The agreement extinguished Weber's $15 million claim against Joel for post-termination management commissions. In return, Joel paid $562,500 to cover Weber's debts to creditors. From all the lawsuits, Joel would collect $8 million. According to Ed London (no relation to Rick London), Joel's business manager after Billy split from Frank Weber, it would have cost an additional $2 million to $3 million to pursue Weber in court.

Meanwhile, personnel changes in the federal prosecutors and FBI offices and a subsequent loss of interest in the case derailed any chance that Frank Weber might be criminally indicted.

Still, there was one holdout in the Joel/Weber war. It was Rick London. Frank Weber's brother-in-law had been Billy Joel's tour manager, the head of Weber's music video production company, and sole trustee of Billy's pension plan, to name a few of his Joel-related positions. During the Joel/Weber litigation, London had turned against Frank by trying to force him to indemnify London against Billy's claims.

Billy charged London with using the artist's pension plan funds to make secret loans to Frank, including for the horse partnerships. Joel also claimed that, without his knowledge, London "washed" the artist's pension money through London's company, Cash Digest, which served as Billy's bookkeeper. The "washed" $300,000 had allegedly been given as a loan to CBS Records senior executive Al Teller. (Teller denied knowing the money belonged to Joel.) Furthermore, Joel charged that London approved an unsecured $100,000 loan to Sunny Weather Horses, owned by Irwin Feiner, who had pleaded guilty in 1985 to running a multi-million dollar invoicing scam in the apparel industry.

Though he had no active counterclaims against Billy, London demanded at least $3 million dollars for his signature on the Weber settlement stipulation. London also insisted that any settlement he signed should bar Billy from later pursuing the pending claims against him. London even threatened to file a malicious prosecution suit against Joel. The case ended with a whimper instead of a bang, however, when Justice Lehner granted Billy's motion to discontinue the suit against London, while preserving Billy's right to pursue those claims in the future.

The successful end to the massive litigation to regain control of his money and career gave Billy Joel plenty of reason to celebrate. Though he had divorced Christie Brinkley—whom he credited with "trying to get me to look into my business long before I did"—Joel's popularity remained high, and so did his income. *Forbes* magazine estimated Billy's gross income for 1994-95 to be $33 million. As for Frank Weber, Joel had already declared, "There is no chance for reconciliation. I have absolutely no use for him."

A sobered Joel no longer used a manager to oversee his career. Instead, through his own company, Maritime Music, he contracted those services out to ancillary agencies. "Most of these agencies don't take a percentage of an artist's earnings or sign them to long-term contracts," Joel explained. "The assumption that artists need a 'personal manager' is a persistent myth based on misinformation handed down by generations of naive, exploited musicians."

In October 1995, Billy Joel threw a birthday party at a Manhattan restaurant for his girlfriend, Carolyn Beegan. One well-wisher who reportedly called during the festivities was English rock star Sting. Sting had a lot to discuss with Billy. Only a few days before, a London court had sentenced Sting's long-time accountant, Keith Moore, to six years in jail for stealing $9.4 million from his music client. Now Billy Joel obviously had a lot to tell Sting about finances, too.

George Michael:
Don't Let The Deal Go Down On Me

n the witness box, Sony Music Entertainment president Tommy Mottola defended himself against a claim that he had ties to the criminal underworld. The charge had been made by Rob Kahane, George Michael's personal manager, in a suit that Michael brought in London's High Court to be freed from a long-term recording contract with Sony. Kahane said that Mottola's tactics made him fear for his safety.

In addition to once being close to music industry *macher* Morris Levy, a Genovese crime-family associate, it had been said that Mottola was friends with Father Louis Gigante, the Bronx priest whose brother "Vinnie the Chin" was the Genovese family boss. Mottola had even played up his tough side by admitting to, in earlier days, "[g]oing in and pushing my way around . . . I was raging: *budda-bump, budda-bump, budda-bump.*"

As head of Sony Music, Mottola reportedly packed a 9-mm gun and rode in an armor-protected limousine. But when asked in court by Sony's English barrister, Gordon Pollock, about Rob Kahane's claim, the manicured executive with the thinning black hair denied any connections to "unsavory criminal organizations." "I was outraged by these statements," Mottola insisted.

Mottola said that Kahane's relationship with Sony had long been strained. "Mr. Kahane would always come in with a long list of complaints. There are times when a manager must know where to draw the line and when those actions won't be beneficial to his artist."

But the problem went deeper than that. George Michael "despises Tommy Mottola," said Michael's music publisher and confidante Dick Leahy. "He will not make an album and give it to him."

Mottola once worked as personal manager for acts like Hall & Oates, John Mellencamp, and Carly Simon, but George Michael now saw him as the embodiment of what he believed had gone wrong with the recording industry. Multinational conglomeratization had put most of the major U.S. labels in the hands of a few Japanese and European companies.

Even David Geffen—who gained hundreds of millions of dollars when Sony Corp.'s Japanese rival, Matsushita Electrical Industrial Co., bought MCA and Geffen Records in 1990—said, "It's starting to be like the movie industry now. All that's left in the movie world is a bunch of faceless conglomerates, and the result is that there aren't many good movies being made anymore, are there? I'm afraid it won't be long before the music industry ends up the same way."

"Most of the majors are in the fast food business and the artists are hamburgers," one-time CBS Records chief Walter Yetnikoff said. "Look what happened to George Michael."

CBS Records—to which Michael first signed in the United Kingdom in 1984, when he was a member of the butt-wiggling, teeny-bopper duo Wham!—had been a symbol of superstar stability. It was the perennial home of Bob Dylan, Billy Joel, Barbra Streisand, and Bruce Springsteen. George Michael's initial solo outing, the funk-inflected *Faith*, sold over 14 million copies worldwide and was the top-selling album in the United States in 1988. But after Sony bought CBS that year, Michael became convinced that he had lost his chance to fully establish himself as a mature artist with a serious musical message.

Sony's firing two years later of the swaggering Yetnikoff, who Dick Leahy referred to as "the last link in the chain of the pro-artist" CBS, didn't help. And when Michael refused to do interviews and appear in videos for his 1990 release, *Listen Without Prejudice Vol. I*, he was certain that Sony Music U.S. had retaliated by sabotaging its success. On top of that, Michael was potentially tied to Sony under his recording contract until the year 2003.

Accompanied by Rob Kahane and Dick Leahy, George Michael went to Sony's New York headquarters in October 1992 to plead for his freedom. At the meeting were Sony Music U.K. chairman Paul Russell, Sony Music Entertainment chairman Michael Schulhof, and Sony's international president Norio Ohga. "It was very strange," Kahane recalled. "Schulhof had no clue who George was. People were losing their tempers. And in the middle of this, Ohga starts taking pictures of George with a camera, supposedly to break the tension." Though he still owed Sony six albums, Michael said that he would never record for the label again. But Sony's executives weren't about to negotiate a settlement of Michael's contract. Instead, they played hardball and refused to let him go.

So on October 30, Michael filed a lawsuit that attacked his recording contract on a variety of fronts. Because similar provisions appeared in most record deals, the music industry immediately took notice. "Artists were glued to developments in the suit," said Michael's financial expert, London accountant David Ravden. "They were thinking, 'Great. If he wins, I'm next.'"

Lawsuits by artists trying to break free of record company shackles weren't unusual. But English courts had been more favorable to creative types than U.S. courts and had ruled in several cases that songwriters and recording artists could escape long-term agreements. U.S. law didn't give artists the ability to claim, as Michael had in his U.K. writ, that his recording contract amounted to an unreasonable restraint of trade. Still, "this is the first time a major artist has attacked a mainstream record deal on this basis," Michael's London counsel Tony Russell remarked.

If Sony lost, musicians would gain what their counterparts in the film business had for half a century: the right to free agency. It had been introduced into the motion picture industry in the 1940s, when actress Olivia de Havilland helped break the back of the studio star system—under which studios paid relatively low wages to talent they developed—by winning a suit over a long-term deal with Warner Bros. Pictures. But in 1992, record labels, which traditionally shored up their bottom lines with back catalogues of recordings of the artists they signed, weren't about to give up what George Michael described as "professional slavery."

"The case is a huge risk," Dire Straits manager Ed Bicknell said. "But if [Michael] wins, it could mean that for the first time the artists will have the record companies in a stranglehold."

George Michael was born Georgios Panayiotou in London in June 1963 to his English mother, Lesley, and his father, Jack, a Greek-Cypriot immigrant who arrived in England with little money and became a successful restaurateur. George was the third of three children and the only son. He set his sights on music early in life and began playing drums at age 12.

As a child, George wore thick-lensed glasses and was overweight. "People have no comprehension of what I looked like as a kid. I was an ugly little bastard," he said. Nevertheless, "I never really lacked confidence as an individual. I was always quite popular. I had this cockiness about me that had no real bearing in any particular attributes."

When he was 11, George's family moved from their London flat over a launderette to the middle-class suburb of Bushey, northwest of London. George soon became friends with schoolmate Andrew Ridgeley. They shared an affinity for Elton John records, soul and dance music, and began writing songs together. In 1979, Michael and Ridgeley formed a group known as the Executive. "We were terrible, but everyone loved us," George said.

Eager to get their recording career moving, in 1982 the two musicians signed as Wham! to Innervision, a new label distributed by CBS U.K. The ten-album contract gave the Wham! duo little to cheer about financially, however. Their first-album advance amounted to only 2,000 English pounds, and the royalty rates were relatively low: 8 percent for the United Kingdom and 6 percent for the rest of the world. Despite the success of their hit-ladden first album, *Fantastic*, Michael claimed he and Ridgeley earned only 100,000 pounds from it.

George Michael managed Wham! for a time. "It took me about two months to suss out that the business was full of assholes who didn't know what to do with me. And I knew better than they did in terms of what I should be doing," he said. "Once you've done it yourself, it's very hard to delegate responsibility. Professionally, I'm very wary of people."

In 1983, Michael and Ridgeley chose the flamboyant Simon Napier-Bell—who had managed the Yardbirds and glam rocker Marc Bolan—and Napier's partner, Jazz Summers, to manage their act. Wham! also retained London solicitor Tony Russell, an entertainment attorney with a reputation for being a tough negotiator. Michael believed that Innervision's founder, Mark Dean, was treating Wham! "very badly and dishonestly." The dispute turned into what Russell called "a bloody six months battle" during which Innervision filed suit to bar Wham! from signing with another label.

Despite negotiations filled with "acrimony and mutual suspicion, with no holds barred," the parties worked out a deal to sign Wham! directly to CBS. Under the March 1984 agreement, CBS would get the eight albums Wham! still owed Innervision. If Wham! disbanded, Michael and Ridgeley remained obligated to record individually for CBS. Wham!'s starting royalties rose to 13.5 percent for the United Kingdom and 10 and 11 percent for the rest of the world.

Wham!'s next album, *Make It Big*, which featured the hits "Wake Me Up Before You Go-Go" and "Careless Whisper," made stars of the golden-skinned, shorts-attired duo in the United States. But Michael had a self-image problem. He worried "[t]he minute you're lumped with teeny-bopper bands, no one listens to the music anymore."

"I don't know where I lost the plot and became that person with long blond hair, and the teeth, and the earrings," Michael said. "I don't know if I woke up one morning and suddenly *was* that person."

In 1986, George Michael left Andrew Ridgeley for a solo career. In June 1987, Michael released his first single, the Prince-influenced "I Want Your Sex," which became a worldwide hit. On *Faith*, Michael's initial solo album, the former Wham! man handled the writing, arranging, and producing chores and played many of the instruments. "People like Madonna and Springsteen and Prince—I've got to get into that league to satisfy me that my music is getting as far as it should," Michael said. But he had already formulated a long-range career plan. Profiling Michael in *Rolling Stone* shortly after *Faith* was released, Steve Pond wrote, "He even knows what he'll do once he reaches that level: nobody's going to believe it, but he plans to turn his back and walk away, putting his career into lower gear."

Walter Yetnikoff had worked his way up from CBS Records' legal department to run the music company. "Walter was a clever, sophisticated man—a good lawyer and quite a private person," Simon Napier-Bell said. "But when he was made head of CBS he suddenly found huge enjoyment in re-creating himself in the worst possible image. For fun, and to ensure corporate respect, he turned himself into a raging lion, drinking and swearing his way through a new career."

Napier-Bell claimed that Yetnikoff's posturing was "just bluff, and nearly all the artists spotted it and loved him for it, George Michael among them."

The Los Angeles-based team of Rob Kahane and Michael Lippman succeeded Napier-Bell as Michael's managers. Kahane had worked as a booking agent for Wham!; Lippman was a former entertainment attorney.

In November 1986, Michael said that he wanted a superstar deal from CBS. "All of us agreed that, because Walter was in the U.S. and George cared very much about making it in the U.S., that it was best to do the renegotiation here," Lippman recalled. CBS also signed its superstar deals in the United States. "Walter inferred that he'd be more comfortable dealing with [top U.S. music industry attorneys] John Branca and Allen Grubman," Lippman continued. Branca, in Los Angeles, had played a key role in CBS artist Michael Jackson's *Thriller* success. Grubman, in New York, had become an industry heavyweight after Yetnikoff sent several important CBS acts to Grubman's firm. "We asked both," but Branca declined, Lippman said.

Renegotiating recording agreements is a common industry practice initiated by artists once they have become successful. George Michael's hand was strengthened when the January 1987 single, "I Knew You Were Waiting (For Me)," a duet with soul queen Aretha Franklin for her label, Arista, landed at the top of the U.S. and U.K. charts.

But CBS decided it wanted Michael's renegotiation talks to take place in England, where he originally signed to the label. The discussions began in May, while Michael worked on *Faith*. CBS U.K.'s managing director Paul Russell believed, however, that Michael was "trying to get the best of all worlds"—both a higher U.S. and English royalty rate of 20 percent, and 16 percent for the rest of the world. (CBS gave its superstars a rest-of-the-world rate of 15 percent.) It would "be preferable to see a bit more of the apple before biting it all," the CBS U.K. record executive said. Unhappy with the progress of the talks, Michael decided to place the renegotiation on hold.

Faith's title track debuted in October 1987 and reached No. 1 in the United States. The album came out in November and sold four million copies in two months. It ultimately generated four No. 1 U.S. singles.

When contract renegotiations resumed, CBS mandated that the discussions be completed at one meeting. That meeting took place on December 1, 1987. Michael's camp was particularly unhappy with a contract clause that reduced his royalties for compact disc sales by 25 percent—a provision common to new and mid-level acts. Sony wouldn't budge. On December 17, Michael met with his advisers for 12 hours. During the meeting, Tony Russell told his client that they'd reached "take it or leave it time."

Michael, who had promised to deliver two albums to CBS in addition to the ones he still owed the record company, said, "I had little alternative but to accept CBS's offer, as I needed CBS's maximum support for my new album and I feared that I might antagonize Mr. Yetnikoff and put that support at risk if I made any further demands." Michael signed the renegotiated agreement in January 1988, just as Sony Corp. completed its $2 billion purchase of CBS Records.

George Michael spent 1988 outside of England, on his *Faith* concert tour. This allowed him to avoid U.K. taxes on his 1988 income.

To take advantage of this, Michael got from Sony that year: a $1 million nonrecoupable payment, $5 million in recoupable advances for *Faith*, $3 million for royalties already in the pipeline, and a $2 million prepaid advance for his next, yet-to-be started album. In addition, Michael's advisors convinced Sony to accelerate other monies promised him in the contract renegotiation.

In April 1988, CBS Records U.S. hired Tommy Mottola to replace its former president, Al Teller. Walter Yetnikoff trusted his close friend Mottola to keep an eye on Sony's record division while Yetnikoff pursued his interests in the film industry, including working on Sony's controversial purchase of Columbia Pictures in 1989.

George Michael named his next album *Listen Without Prejudice Vol. I* to reflect his desire to change his image. "For the first time in my career, my objective was actually to narrow my audience to some degree," he said. "I was aware that my promotion of *Faith* (and, in particular, the live performances and the videos) had further established my public image as a young man with a primarily young female audience and that this perception was likely to dissuade a more adult audience from listening to it objectively. Therefore I decided to remove my physical image from the marketing and promotion."

(Around this time, Michael also stopped dating women and began dating men.)

Michael's immediate order of business, however, was "whether or not my record company would support me through this transitional period. The Americans in particular," he said, "were of concern" because his decision "was likely to cause inconvenience to their traditional marketing methods," which Michael described as "hard sell."

In July 1990, Tommy Mottola and CBS's Columbia Records president Don Ienner flew to England to hear the new *Listen Without Prejudice* tracks. "I remember we had lunch with Tommy and Donnie and discussed George's change of direction," Michael Lippman said. "We presented it along the lines of Bruce Springsteen's [sparse, demo quality] *Nebraska* album. The record that followed that [*Born in the U.S.A.*] was the biggest Bruce ever had. We felt it was difficult for an artist to top his last big record, so let's try something new."

Michael said he explained to Mottola and Ienner, "that I considered that I could have a very long-term career if I was allowed to develop it as I felt necessary but that, if I had to continue along the same lines as before, my career would not last much longer." Michael said that Mottola and Ienner "just kind of accepted it all in a . . . 'Let's all be friends' manner, and I know more about the way that the American company works than to totally believe that things were going to be that easy."

Sony Corp. not only had a sensitive artist on its hands; it was every bit as image-conscious as George Michael. Walter Yetnikoff's substance abuse problems and his rocky relationships with industry executives worried Sony's leaders. Faced with this—and with fallout from the Columbia Pictures purchase and from a damning portrayal of Yetnikoff in Fredric Dannen's best-selling music industry exposé *Hit Men*—Sony forced out its CBS Records chairman in September 1990. Yetnikoff blamed Tommy Mottola and Yetnikoff's arch-rival, David Geffen, with helping bring about his downfall.

Dick Leahy insisted that George Michael's dissatisfaction with the post-Yetnikoff CBS ran deep. "George isn't the only one who believes it," Leahy said. "There are people within Sony who believe it, too." Several veteran Sony Music executives, some close to Michael, did leave after Yetnikoff's departure, but, in praising Yetnikoff, Michael and his advisors seemed willing to overlook the prominent role the former CBS Records chief played in bringing about Sony's purchase of the record company. "Because he initiated the Sony deal, had Walter stayed at CBS, he probably could have kept [the Japanese owners] more at arm's length," Rob Kahane claimed.

But "what fell apart between Tommy Mottola and George Michael was a lot more than the artist-oriented issue," said Michael Lippman, who soon split from Kahane. In addition, there was "a high degree of mutual antipathy" between Kahane and Don Ienner, a Mottola appointee.

Listen Without Prejudice Vol. I, released in September 1990, proved more popular than *Faith* in Britain but sold only a quarter of what its predecessor did in the United States. Michael blamed the album's relatively poor performance in part on "a deliberate policy decision to reduce [Sony's] efforts on the album because I had declined . . . to appear in videos for promotion of that album." Still, Andy Stephens, managing director at Sony's Epic U.K., which distributed Michael's recordings in the United Kingdom, warned Michael that his refusal to appear in promotional videos for *Listen Without Prejudice* gave "the competition an edge. Please, please don't hand it to them on a plate."

In a letter to the *Los Angeles Times*, Frank Sinatra chided Michael for shunning stardom. "Come on, George. Loosen up. Swing, man." But Sinatra also had once fought to transform himself from a bobbysoxer idol into a mature crooner.

In November 1991, George Michael again sought to eliminate the reduced compact-disc royalties rate from his contract. Sony asked Michael to in return appear in three promotional videos for the planned *Listen Without Prejudice Vol. II.* "He was totally depressed," Tony Russell said. "He expressed the view that it was clear to him that no one at Sony had listened" about his desired image change. According to Russell, this was "the straw that broke the camel's back."

Michael's counsel told him he could contest his recording contract on restraint of trade grounds. But the artist's concert duet with Elton John—a charity single of "Don't Let the Sun Go Down On Me" that Dick Leahy said Sony originally thought "was a bad career move"—hit No. 1 in 15 countries, including the United States and the United Kingdom. Though there was no album to back it, Michael felt his relationship with Sony was now "rescuable."

In early 1992, Michael donated three concert recordings to *Red Hot + Dance*, an AIDS charity album that Sony released. When the album sold poorly, Michael blamed Sony's promotional campaign. He also became angry because he believed the label had refused to allow one of his recordings to be included on Giant Records' soundtrack album for the popular TV show *Beverly Hills 90210*. Finally convinced that he wanted to leave Sony, Michael stopped working on *Listen Without Prejudice Vol. II*.

In August, his advisors returned a $1 million advance that the record company had given him earlier that year for the *Vol. II* project. Mark Schwartz, business affairs head at Epic U.K., called it "an historic first." "I am the last one to look a 'gift' cheque in the mouth," Schwartz wrote his boss Paul Russell, but "it feels like a case of 'What's wrong with this picture?'"

A month later, George Michael faxed Sony Music chairman Michael Schulhof: "Mr. Schulhof, you do not know me. But if you did, you would realize that these thoughts are mine, and that I do not come to important decisions lightly. As far as I am concerned, the question now is not whether I leave Sony, but *how* I leave Sony." Michael faxed Norio Ohga, too. "My relationship with the entire Sony Music Group is irreconcilable," Michael told the company's worldwide president.

When George Michael filed his 29-page writ against Sony in London's High Court on October 30, 1992, he insisted it wasn't a renegotiating ploy or a fight about money. Instead, he claimed it was about being treated like a piece of software by the electronics giant. To underscore the point, Dick Leahy said, "George has been with me ten years and I'm not exactly Warner Music. He made a new [publishing] deal with me at the beginning of the year and I didn't pay him a dime."

It's true that Sony had sought software content to foster sales of its hardware products ever since its Beta videocassette format had lost out to VHS in the 1970s. And Michael filed suit just as Sony was introducing its minidisc player.

One story circulating in the music industry, however, was that what put Michael over the edge was overhearing Don Ienner make an off-color comment about Michael's sex life. "George was staying at my home, as he often did when he was in Los Angeles," Rob Kahane explained. "I was on the speakerphone with Donnie, when George walks into the room. It was one of those phone calls where Donnie went nuclear. He was hostile and frustrated because George didn't want to promote [*Listen Without Prejudice*]. George asked, 'Is that what the climate's like at the record company?' But Donnie's comment wasn't why George filed suit."

What was clear was that Michael's suit came against a backdrop of seismic changes in record business economics. As multinational conglomerates rabidly paid top-dollar for record companies (PolyGram, for example, paid three-quarters of a billion dollars for A&M and Island), labels sought to anchor their assets by offering megadeals to artists with marquee value. Big-name artists had an advantage because record sales were sluggish in the early 1990s. That resulted in sweetheart deals in the tens of millions of dollars for artists like Janet Jackson, Madonna, Motley Crüe, and the Rolling Stones.

Among the many contract provisions Michael challenged in his suit were: a "seriously inequitable apportionment" of album revenues between the record company and himself; "free," non-royalty bearing product Sony gave to wholesalers and retailers as incentive bonuses; Sony's ownership of Michael's recordings, even though the costs of making them were recouped out of Michael's royalties; Sony's right to reject any recording as non-commercial; and Sony's obligation to release singles only in the United States and the United Kingdom, and no obligation to release albums at all.

Such provisions were standard in the industry because record companies insisted they needed to spread the risk of their investments in artists. Yet, these labels didn't band together over the George Michael matter. According to Dick Leahy, several of them contacted Michael's camp with signing overtures immediately after Michael sued Sony.

George Michael's suit against Sony Music represented a growing trend among performers—and entertainment lawyers—to try to escape what they considered to be punitive contracts, often signed early in artists' careers, with media giants. It was "basically a counterpart of what we've been doing all along" in the United States but "goes beyond anything I've seen here," said Los Angeles attorney

Don Engel, who represented such artists as Teena Marie, Olivia Newton-John, Luther Vandross, and Tom Scholz in record-company contract disputes. "But I hope it might rub off a little."

United States law didn't recognize restraint of trade in a contract between two parties. While George Michael fought Sony, however, Engel hurled an antitrust claim against Geffen Records on behalf of musician Don Henley. The crux of the claim was that Geffen Records conspired with other labels not to sign Henley, who was then involved in a contract dispute with Geffen. According to Engel, "David Geffen told us he spoke to two or three other record companies and asked them 'whether they would sign my artist while he was signed to me.'"

Geffen made the statement in a deposition in a $20 million breach of contract suit his label filed against Henley in Los Angeles Superior Court in January 1993. Geffen Records sued Henley after Henley, who was dissatisfied with the way Geffen Records marketed his product, said he wouldn't deliver any more albums to the label. At the time, Henley owed the record company two studio albums, plus a greatest hits package.

Henley had been associated with David Geffen since 1971, when his band, the Eagles, signed to Geffen's Asylum Records. Henley signed a solo deal with Geffen Records in 1984; the agreement was amended in 1988.

In March 1993, Henley filed a countersuit claiming that, under California's seven-year rule, his initial contract with Geffen Records had expired. The seven-year rule prohibited companies from signing artists to contracts for more years than that. From the record companies' perspective, a contract renegotiation started the seven-years running again. But California courts had never ruled on the issue because, to prevent a decision in favor of an artist, record companies invariably settled these suits.

Don Henley sounded a lot like George Michael. "David Geffen's company is no longer the one I signed with," Henley said. "It's been sold twice in the past couple of years, and I never even got so much as a phone call from [Geffen] about it. [MCA bought Geffen Records before Japan's Matsushita bought MCA. Several years later, Matsushita sold MCA to Seagram.] The entire thing is very dehumanizing. I feel like a commodity, like soy beans or pork bellies."

Don Henley's August 1993 conspiracy claim against Geffen named EMI, Sony Music, and Warner Music in court documents as the labels that Geffen had approached to deny offering Henley a recording contract. Don Engel deposed Allen Grubman, David Geffen's close friend and East Coast counsel. Grubman said that he had spoken to EMI's North American chairman, Charles Koppelman, about Henley on Geffen's behalf but denied participating in any conspiracy. Others set to be deposed in the suit were Sony's Michael Schulhof and Tommy Mottola.

"I'm about as concerned about this as I am about the baked potato I ate last week," David Geffen said about the conspiracy claim.

In February 1994, MCA Records sued Henley's Eagles cohort, Glenn Frey, for $5 million after Frey invoked the seven-year statute. Frey, whose solo career was languishing, was about to join the reunited Eagles.

In May 1994, the Eagles began their first concert tour in 14 years, but the Henley/Geffen trial was scheduled to start July 25. "Don Engel argued before the judge for a significant amount of time, explaining why that wasn't fair," said attorney Bonnie Eskenazi, who represented Geffen Records. "The judge said basically, 'This is my courtroom and Don Henley has obligations other than the tour.'" That made the Eagles reunion album, *Hell Freezes Over*, consisting of an MTV concert and four new studio songs, "a vehicle for settling the case," Engel noted. "Geffen claims two Henley solo albums are worth $20 million. So what is one Eagles' album worth?" Engel asked.

The answer was the two Henley solo albums because that summer Henley and Geffen Records settled their litigation, with Geffen getting the right to release *Hell Freezes Over* and a Henley greatest hits album. The Eagles reportedly got a $10 million advance. The settlement ended the Frey/MCA dispute, too. "Geffen was under pressure from the other labels to settle the case," Engel said. "Besides, it would have just been too embarrassing. [Warner Music Group chairman] Robert Morgado claimed he hadn't talked to Geffen in a couple of years."

On the surface, U.K. law appeared to be on George Michael's side. In 1974, songwriter Tony Macaulay, the composer of such pop hits as "Love Grows (Where My Rosemary Goes)," won a suit involving a ten-year contract under which his music publisher had no obligation to publish his songs. The House of Lords, England's senior court, based its decision on restraint of trade.

In 1988, the High Court ruled that a leaving member clause with ZTT Records that prohibited Holly Johnson, lead singer for Frankie Goes to Hollywood, from signing to another label constituted an unreasonable restraint of trade. (George Michael's counsel, Tony Russell, represented Johnson in the case, which the Court of Appeal affirmed.) Then in 1991, the High Court found the Stone Roses' nine-year record deal unreasonable because the rock group's label, Silvertone Records, had no obligation to either distribute product or release the band from its contract. None of these cases involved major label contracts, however, as did George Michael's suit.

High Court Justice Jonathan Parker scheduled the George Michael/Sony trial for October 1993. In English courts, each side's lawyers operate in two groups. Solicitors generally organize the case, prepare witnesses, and work directly with clients. Barristers, in traditional wigs and gowns, typically present arguments and question witnesses in court.

The Royal Courts of Justice in central London is a massive complex containing several dozen courtrooms. The small public galleries overlooking the courtrooms "usually are closed due to terrorist threats," George Michael's solicitor Cyril Glasser said. "But there was such huge interest in George's case, the court opened the gallery for the trial."

Fifty-five-year-old Justice Parker presided over few entertainment industry lawsuits, but he had recently heard a case between co-directors of a musical about Sigmund Freud. Opening arguments in the

Michael/Sony trial were set for Monday, October 11, but had to be postponed one week after Sony's barrister, Gordon Pollock, said he injured his back.

George Michael showed up in court looking more like a hip clerk than a pop star. In place of his earringed, bare-chested, and leather-jacketed *Faith* attire, he wore horn-rimmed glasses, a black Versace T-shirt, and a black Armani suit. Mark Cran, Michael's barrister, asserted in his opening argument that record companies used the complexities in record deals "to manipulate artists." In a detailed explanation, Cran discussed how record sale profits were apportioned. Justice Parker evoked laughter when he responded, "Well, that seems to be straightforward." George Michael stared silently at the judge.

Music industry executives and young female fans squeezed into the courtroom when Michael began his testimony on October 28 for the first of three consecutive days. Dressed now in a gray suit with a black velvet collar, a confident Michael read from a 66-page state-ment. He contended that Sony had "killed" *Listen Without Prejudice Vol. I* "in order to teach me a lesson," and that the dispute with Sony had left him "for the first time in my career, stifled creatively."

During questioning by Cran, Michael claimed that Don Ienner "felt that if he showed me what could happen, I might be scared into changing my ideas for the next album." In addition, Michael com-plained that he had been snubbed by Ienner and Tommy Mottola when they flew to an October 1991 concert Michael gave in Toronto. "They came on a private jet and my manager was due to go back to New York with them after the show, and then when I looked for my manager at the end of the show I was told that they had left halfway through so he'd had to go with them."

During cross-examination, the pugnacious Pollock suggested that Michael had manipulated his "sex-saturated" image. "Couldn't it be described as soft-core porn?" Pollock asked of Michael's "I Want Your Sex" video. The Sony barrister suggested that the artist had "made a virtue of the pelvic waggle."

"I'm perfectly aware of the importance of sexuality in my career," Michael responded. "I felt like doing that with my pelvis at the time. I don't think it was calculated." Michael revealed that a double had been used for the video's torso close-up shots. "I'm afraid my body's nowhere near as good as his. He was a lot larger than me and had no hair on his chest," Michael said to an amused courtroom crowd.

"Can you give us some idea of what you're worth?" Gordon Pollock asked.

"Do I really have to?" the pop star replied, admitting it was "more money than I know what to do with." Michael glanced up at his fans in the gallery and smiled as he wrote the number down. He handed the paper to Justice Parker, who smiled before handing it to Cran and Pollock. Pollock sparked laughter, too, when he asked whether he was looking at a decimal point.

When Tony Russell took the stand on the eleventh day of the proceeding, he claimed that, during the royalty renegotiation talks, Sony offered Michael "terms which were worse than had been offered to unknowns."

To establish that Michael had expert legal advice during the contract bargaining, Pollock said to Russell, "You were the John McEnroe of the legal profession, weren't you?"

Rob Kahane testified that Don Ienner went into a "rage" over the music video for *Listen Without Prejudice*'s "Freedom 90." The video symbolized Michael's image change by featuring a burning leather jacket and an exploding guitar. In his witness statement, Kahane described a meeting during which he charged that Tommy Mottola acted in a "corrupt and dishonest way." Kahane had gone to see Mottola at the record executive's Manhattan office. "Mottola's reputation preceded him," Kahane said. "He was very heavy-handed, the old-school approach."

During cross-examination, Gordon Pollock, who was using a shepherd's crook to help him walk, "beat the floor with it for theatrical effect, like it was Zeus's lightening rod," Kahane claimed. Pollock asked why Kahane hadn't complained to Tony Russell about the Mottola incident. "When something like this happens you just . . . you know, it scared me. I didn't really want to make it public. I mean, [Mottola's] a scary guy. I mean, we've all seen *The Godfather*."

Brian Howard, Tony Russell's law partner, gave the court an inside account of the interrelationships among Sony Music's executives. In a statement Howard obtained from Walter Yetnikoff, Yetnikoff said that when he found out about a proposal to let Michael Jackson have his own label and a stake in Sony's profits, "I was furious with Mr. Mottola, as I believed that if such an offer had been made, it was too much."

Yetnikoff noted that Mottola "advised me that the suggestion for the joint venture had come from [Allen] Grubman [who represented Jackson at David Geffen's behest]. It was my view that Grubman needed cutting down to size and that I would in no circumstances agree to the label deal. Mr. Mottola went berserk and eventually went over my head to Norio Ohga."

George Michael was in an unenviable position, Yetnikoff said, because, among other things, "The relationship between the U.S. and the U.K. CBS companies was not good from 1988 to when I left CBS. This was principally due to the relationship between Mottola and Paul Russell." Yetnikoff refused to testify at trial, however, or to sign the witness statement, which he called an "inaccurate interpretation."

Paul Russell testified for Sony that Tony Russell had a "ballistic fit" at the key renegotiating meeting on December 1, 1987. "He had lots of files," the Sony Music U.K. executive said. "I remember him slamming on the desk and saying, 'Well, if that's it, we're going to walk away. I'm fed up with this.' Words to that effect."

When Tommy Mottola came to the stand, he denied any campaign "to teach Mr. Michael a lesson" or to make Rob Kahane "fear for himself and his family." Mottola said that, rather than snubbing Michael when he and Ienner arrived at the artist's October 1991 Toronto concert, the Sony Music executives were told that Michael refused to see *them* because he was going to get a massage.

The High Court trial lasted 75 days in all. Marathon closing arguments began Feb. 21, 1994, and—except for a two-week Easter break—lasted until April 13. Justice Parker said that the lengthy proceeding had made him "punch-drunk."

But that didn't prevent Parker from issuing a lengthy 273-page ruling on June 21. In it, he found no deliberate policy by Sony to sabotage George Michael's career. Instead, Parker ruled that Michael's 1988 renegotiation was "reasonable and fair," a "substantial improvement" over his prior contract terms. In any case, Parker noted, by asking for an advance on his third album in February 1992, when he had been advised that he might be able to break his recording agreement on restraint of trade grounds, Michael affirmed the renegotiated CBS deal.

Justice Parker also concluded that Michael made no attempt to verify the information given him by his advisors about Sony. In particular, Parker cited Rob Kahane as "a thoroughly unreliable and untrustworthy witness" who was "motivated to an unacceptable degree by self-interest and a desire to protect his own position." Parker was especially troubled by two $500,000 loans that Sony made to Kahane Entertainment in 1990 and 1991. One witness testified that Kahane called Sony and demanded, "Where's my fucking money?"

"Parker didn't like me from day one," Kahane complained. "But I don't think he knows the way the music business works in the United States. What I said about Tommy Mottola sounded out of place in an English court. They wouldn't have taken as much notice of it in a New York court."

At a press conference held immediately after Justice Parker handed down his ruling, George Michael declared, "[T]here is no such thing as resignation for an artist in the music industry." Two days later, Parker ordered Michael, who had spent an estimated $4.5 million to pursue his case, to pay Sony's legal expenses, too.

Rob Kahane resigned as George Michael's manager in October 1994, saying he needed to concentrate on his new Trauma Records label. Meanwhile, Michael's appellate lawyer Charles Gray filed for an expedited appeal, worrying that his client's career was "a wasting asset." (Michael reportedly earned 16 million pounds in 1988, but only 400,000 pounds in 1993.) But in December 1994, the Court of Appeal said it wouldn't hear the case for over a year. That set the scene for a settlement of Michael's suit.

"The reality of the situation was that Sony had won but an appeal could have gone all the way to the European Court," Michael's solicitor Cyril Glasser said. "Sony had to face that possibility and an artist who would never record for them again." (In addition to unreasonable restraint of trade, Michael had alleged in his suit that his contract with Sony violated the European Economic Community's anti-competition treaty.)

The 400-page settlement deal was finalized in July 1995, when George Michael became the first artist signed to DreamWorks Records. DreamWorks—co-founded by David Geffen, Jeffrey Katzenberg and Steven Spielberg—and Virgin Records, to which Michael signed outside North America, were said to be obligated to pay Sony $40 million, plus a 3 percent royalty on Michael's future recordings. Sony got the right to release a George Michael greatest hits album containing several new songs and the costs of the Sony/Michael litigation were to be split. For his part, Michael received a reported $12 million for a short-term, two-album deal with a royalty rate of at least 20 percent—one free of many standard artist royalty reduction provisions. He would also own the DreamWorks recordings he made.

The same month he signed the settlement agreement, George Michael announced he had a new manager: former Sony U.K. music executive Andy Stephens, who Michael had considered one of his label allies. When Michael released his first DreamWorks single, "Jesus To a Child," in January 1996, Stephens admitted, "I think George is worried, especially having taken the stance that he took some time ago, that this record should be judged on its merits."

Older, Michael's first post-Sony solo album and his first in nearly six years, had him appearing more serious than ever. In the cover photo, he wore a goatee, his face half in a shadow. On the song "Star People" he anguished that fame was "a dream with a nightmare stuck in the middle." The album generated relatively lukewarm sales. Michael generated much greater attention when he was arrested two years later for committing a lewd act in a public restroom in Los Angeles.

George Michael's lawsuit against Sony certainly affected his career momentum. Did his litigation with Sony have an impact on the music industry, too? "Psychologically, the George Michael case affected the industry a lot," his former manager Michael Lippman observed. "It made artists see how costly such suits can be, both economically and to their careers. It also made record companies see their deals differently."

"The only thing exceptional about the suit was that it was the first time [in England] an artist failed to get out of a contract in a well-publicized case," Sony solicitor David Davis claimed—though he acknowledged that restraint of trade remained a strong claim in England and that record companies had responded by shortening contract terms and lowering the number of albums that artists must deliver.

"I hear the George Michael case mentioned with regular frequency," music accountant David Ravden said. "The business affairs reps at the record companies say, 'We'd better be careful about how we throw our weight around. We don't want another George Michael scenario down the road.'"

The Shirelles:
Will You Pay Me Tomorrow?

T he three surviving members of the Shirelles—Shirley Alston Reeves, Doris Coley Jackson, and Beverly Lee—flew into Nashville on the eve of trial. The first girl group to chart a No. 1 record in the United States—in 1961 with "Will You Love Me Tomorrow"—was suing G.M.L. Inc., one of the world's largest independent owners of hit sound recordings, for non-payment of royalties.

"We brought the Shirelles in from the airport separately because there had been so much discord between them," their Nashville counsel Sam Lipshie said. "But when we got them into the law-office conference room, they had a tearful, hugging reunion and sang 'Dedicated to the One I Love.'"

"Beverly and Doris had been fighting over the rights to the Shirelles name," recalled Chuck Rubin, who ran the Artists Rights Enforcement Corp. "But I said, 'It's like going back to 1960 all over again. You have to join forces and protect each other.'"

Along with pop singers B.J. Thomas and Gene Pitney, the Shirelles were seeking royalties in their July 1989 federal trial for recordings released on the Gusto Records label. Since moving to Nashville in the early 1970s, Gusto/G.M.L. owner Gayron "Moe" Lytle had amassed an inventory of tens of thousands of sound recording masters that included such influential labels as Starday and King/Federal. Many people in the music business had heard of Lytle, but he shied away from the Nashville social scene and remained an industry mystery. "I don't know anyone who's even seen him," Nashville music attorney J. David Wykoff observed.

But Lytle had become a familiar face to the Shirelles' lawyers. "He'd tell me he was in the dog food business," Sam Lipshie said. "His company sells that and farming equipment, too."

Chuck Rubin had almost accidentally become a champion for early rock recording artists who were long denied royalties on their hit records. He had known the Shirelles since he was a booking agent in the 1960s. The Manhattan-based Rubin started pursuing artists' royalty and copyright claims in 1977, after one-man band Wilbert Harrison, who Rubin once managed, called for help. Harrison hit No. 1 on the pop charts in 1959 with Jerry Leiber and Mike Stoller's blues-rocker "Kansas City," but said he wasn't receiving his recording royalties.

"We sued everybody who put out 'Kansas City,'" the tenacious Rubin said. "Arista Records, K-Tel, [Roulette Records owner] Morris Levy and Bobby Robinson [the owner of Fury Records, which originally released Harrison's record]. As it turned out, to get out of his contract with Savoy Records in Newark and onto Fury, Wilbert had paid for the 'Kansas City' session—the song was recorded in one take—so we made a claim that he owned the master."

While looking for albums that might contain the Harrison track, Rubin found hit recordings by many artists he had booked as an agent, including the Shirelles. "To determine how much Wilbert was owed, I figured I'd call and ask how much they were getting in royalties," Rubin remembered. "I found out that none of the artists were getting paid."

But the renewed popularity of classic rock recordings—through TV shows, movies, commercials, and later in compact disc repackagings—motivated these performers, many of whom had rarely or never before made royalties demands, to seek their monies. Before long, Rubin's Artists Rights Enforcement Corp. had a roster of over 100 clients, essentially a Who's Who of rock 'n' roll's early era.

The New York Times called Rubin "a white knight of rock." *GQ* described him as "more pit bull than Prince Charming." Rubin was "a guy who didn't happen in the business, and then he created a new business of harassing and suing people," the notorious record mogul (and close mob associate) Morris Levy said. "My personal opinion would be he'd sell his mother for a nickel."

"It took until 1980 or '81 to get the first payment," Rubin remarked in his West 57th Street office, overlooking Columbus Circle. "20th Century-Fox was putting together rock 'n' roll retrospective TV shows using film clips of various artists, such as the Del-Vikings and the Platters. In the end, they paid us triple rate. We went after Dick Clark, too."

The Shirelles originally formed in high school in Passaic, N.J., as the Pequellos. They began their recording career in 1958 with the group-penned "I Met Him On a Sunday" for the Tiara label, which Florence Greenberg, one of their friend's mothers, operated out of her house. The group followed its chart-topping Gerry Goffin-Carole King composition, "Will You Love Me Tomorrow"—released on Greenberg's new label, Scepter Records—with a series of Top 40 hits that included the No. 1 "Soldier Boy" and No. 3 "Dedicated to the One I Love."

But the Shirelles stopped recording in 1964, during a dispute with Scepter over the whereabouts of trust funds the group members were to receive when they reached age 21. The case was settled in 1965, but the Shirelles never regained their chart momentum. Shirley left the group in the mid-'70s and original member Addie Harris died of a heart attack in 1982, while on tour with Jackson and Lee in Atlanta.

Chuck Rubin went to see Harris, Jackson, and Lee at a 1981 concert in Manhattan. "[I]t was very difficult to track where everything went after [Scepter] went bankrupt," Doris Jackson said. So the trio of singers signed letters of agreement with Rubin's Artists Rights Enforcement firm. Shirley Reeves, B.J. Thomas, and Gene Pitney signed with Artists Rights around the same time. According to court documents, under its contingency deal, Artists Rights kept 50 percent of any sums it recovered but paid for accountants and lawyers out of that share. Few cases went to trial, however, because most music companies agreed to settle once confronted with proof of artists' claims.

CBS Records was among the companies from which Chuck Rubin sought royalties. The record company had advanced $500,000 to Springboard International Records, which bought up many significant oldies recording catalogues, in exchange for the right to license Springboard product. When Springboard fell into bankruptcy in 1978, the court permitted CBS to pick up ownership of Springboard's library. The deal involved more than 8,000 masters by over 200 artists, including B.J. Thomas, Gene Pitney, and the Shirelles.

"When we approached CBS, the company agreed to give us back-royalties and monies from third-party licenses," Rubin said. "We were going along fine and dandy when we heard that CBS was going to sell the masters."

Under the federal tax code in effect in the early 1980s, tax shelter promoters would acquire actual or purported rights to sound recording masters and sell them to one or more intermediaries at inflated prices (often covered by long-term promissory notes, rather than cash). The masters were then leased or sold to investors who sought federal investment tax credits and depreciation benefits.

CBS had sued the Koala Record Co., more a tax shelter conduit than a traditional label, for commercially distributing Springboard and other CBS masters. In part to settle its suit, CBS's Columbia Special Products sold the Springboard masters for $2 million on December 2, 1981 to the JEY Production Co., which was related to Koala. Koala bought the rights in the Springboard masters from JEY the same day. Koala then simultaneously leased to CBS the exclusive foreign and non-exclusive U.S. rights to distribute and license the Springboard catalogue for seven years. The $2 million dollars JEY paid CBS was allegedly provided by Koala's president and principal shareholder, Wesley Sanborn.

The deal, however, was looked on askance by the government. "There were federal investigations regarding the Springboard masters and the tax credits were disallowed," Sam Lipshie noted. Meanwhile, Koala quickly showed it would not be as honorable as CBS was when it came to paying royalties on the masters. "There were a few fumbling intros, a little dancing, time goes by and they fail to send two [semi-annual] royalty reports," Chuck Rubin said. "By the time I got the legal muscle to take action, Koala was no longer in the picture."

B.J. Thomas began his music career in Houston, Texas, where he parlayed his cover of Hank Williams' "I'm So Lonesome I Could Cry" from a regional into a national hit. Thomas had 14 Top 40 singles between 1966 and 1977, most of them on Scepter records, before he turned to Christian music. Five of his pop recordings placed in the *Billboard* Top 10. "Raindrops Keep Fallin' On My Head" and "(Hey Won't You Play) Another Somebody Done Somebody Wrong Song" both reached No. 1.

In 1977, Thomas re-recorded his hits for Louis Lefredo's Mandala Productions at Gusto Studios in Nashville. At the same time, Gusto Records bought the rights in the new masters. Thomas received $637.50 per cut and waived the right to receive any re-recording royalties.

Moe Lytle's Nashville lawyer, Grant Smith, described Gusto Records as "an after-market record company. Moe would re-record or sell the original old songs on budget labels to truck stops and [via TV]." "We were selling it to the average Joe in Iowa who still has an eight-track tape player," Gusto recording engineer, Randall Merriman, said. But Lytle achieved success in the new recordings market when Red Sovine hit No. 1 on the country charts in 1976 with his truckers' anthem "Teddy Bear" for the Starday label. In March 1984, Lytle spruced up his sound recordings inventory by buying the Springboard masters from Koala for $500,000.

Chuck Rubin already knew Moe Lytle. Rubin had approached Lytle in 1982 for royalties on behalf of Wilbert Harrison and other artists but said he was met with "stiff resistance." Lytle claimed Rubin never provided documentation to support his claims. Rubin said that Lytle told him, in effect, "We just don't pay artists' royalties."

B.J. Thomas, Gene Pitney, and the Shirelles (the Thomas plaintiffs) later joined together in suing Lytle's companies to save court costs and because, Chuck Rubin claimed, "We needed more than one artist to show this was not an isolated thing."

"We've all known each other for years and there's nothing secret in this business that we're in," the Shirelles' Doris Jackson said. "[W]e trust each other enough to go walk together in business and in our personal lives."

Gusto had been sued for artist royalties before, but "this was the first case of that magnitude," Grant Smith said. Given the animosity between Chuck Rubin and Moe Lytle, it would also be the first time that a royalties suit coordinated by Rubin would be fought all the way through trial.

Before the Thomas plaintiffs filed their December 1987 complaint in Nashville, however, Lytle struck at Rubin. In a 1986 federal suit, Lytle charged Rubin and Tony Williams, the original lead singer for the Platters, with infringing on Gusto's sound recording copyrights. The complaint challenged an agreement that Rubin brokered to require the U.K.-based MCR Productions, which Rubin believed had been selling pirated product, to pay royalties to release recordings the Platters made for Musicor, the same label for which Gene Pitney recorded his hits.

The suit charged Rubin and Williams with conversion and fraud. Rubin claimed the suit "was meant to harass and block our suit against Gusto to where we would settle with Moe."

The federal courthouse in Nashville stood on Broadway, halfway between the honky-tonks of downtown and the record industry suites of Music Row. Pursuant to their recording contracts, the claims of the Thomas plaintiffs would be considered under New York law, which allowed the artists to seek royalties dating back six years from the date their suit was filed.

District Judge Thomas Higgins oversaw the juryless trial, which began on July 10, 1989. A Nashville native of Irish decent, Higgins had been a civil litigator before being appointed to the bench by President Ronald Reagan in 1984. "Higgins is an activist, no-nonsense judge who likes to question witnesses himself," Sam Lipshie said. "But he lacked an understanding of what compact discs were and he called the Shirelles the 'Shirleys.'"

New York litigator Ira Greenberg presented the artists' opening statement. Greenberg represented large companies in business and product liability suits but had been working with Chuck Rubin on what would be Emira Lymon's successful claim to being the legal widow of Frankie Lymon, the lead singer of the 1950s hitmakers, The Teenagers.

Greenberg told Judge Higgins that B.J. Thomas, Gene Pitney, and the Shirelles sought three types of royalties: for their product manufactured and sold by Gusto; for their product sold by Gusto's licensees; and from fees for allowing the artists' recordings to be utilized in such formats as movies, TV shows, and commercials.

Grant Smith, whose clients included old-line country artists like Faron Young, said in his opening statement for Gusto, "I don't know where along the line the contracts between Scepter and the Shirelles and Mr. Thomas were lost, or where the contract between Mr. Pitney and Musicor was lost. But it never found its way to G.M.L., and we never knew that a contract existed to pay that royalty until this lawsuit was filed and the plaintiffs gave us a copy of the contract." Smith argued industry custom dictated that, because the artists' recording contracts were silent regarding royalties for third-party licensing, "they take nothing."

Gene Pitney appeared as the plaintiffs' first witness. The heart-throb singer from Rockville, Connecticut, had 16 Top 40 hits between 1961 and 1968. Four of them, including "I'm Gonna Be Strong" and "It Hurts To Be In Love," made the Top 10. Pitney's Musicor contract gave him an initial 3 percent royalty rate —low by today's standards, under which a new artist typically receives an 8 to 12 percent record royalty, but common for its time. Pitney got 4 percent the second year. (The Shirelles had a 4 percent starting rate, increased to 5 percent after the first year; B.J. Thomas got 5 percent the first year of his Scepter contract.) But Pitney had invested his music earnings into successful real estate ventures and continued to tour around the world.

"Now that I have heard the story unfold, heard all these different corporations, different companies where [my recordings] passed through, I don't even know what happened," Pitney confessed. "I gave a good part of my life for ten years during that period to create all these masters. I have to say it's tragic when this can happen, can get lost like that."

Moe Lytle had shut down Gusto's sales operations in 1986 and licensed his sound recording catalogue to the Highland and Richmond music companies in Dearborn, Michigan, and Toronto. The two outfits were controlled by Stephen Hawkins, an Englishman Lytle knew since the 1970s, when Hawkins worked for a company that sold records on TV. Pitney said that, six months before the trial began, he received two $400 checks from Hawkins' companies. "I didn't even know they were in existence," Pitney claimed.

"[I]t is your feeling that at some point in time the ownership of [your] masters would revert to the Shirelles?" Judge Higgins asked Doris Jackson when she testified. (The artists had amended their complaint to ask that they be given ownership rights in the sound recordings.)

"Well, when I think about when you're sitting there, you're listening to, or at movies, watching them, you hear your songs, your hard work that went into it, and you see that you're not getting a penny from them, somebody else is, wouldn't you, sir?"

Grant Smith tried to establish that the Shirelles had made four of their early recordings—leased by Florence Greenberg to Decca Records—without a contract.

"Let me think that through. I'm listening for the rock to splash at the bottom of the well," Judge Higgins said. "If they didn't have a contract, then they'd have no right to royalties. I suppose what you're saying, if I understand it, is four 15-year-olds walk into a Decca, to keep it simple, recording studio on Sunday and the man is there, he turns the machinery on and they start singing and then they walk out. You're saying Decca is free to exploit the recording of their efforts, and anybody else down the line?"

"If they recorded the song with the knowledge it was to be recorded for potential commercial purpose, yes," Smith replied. "If they were tricked or duped or something, that's different. But they were young people, young stars aspiring to fame, and I'm sure they were willing to take anything they could get."

Smith then argued that most of the B.J. Thomas product Gusto sold consisted of Thomas's royalty-free re-recordings. But, "I just wasn't satisfied with the sound, the quality of it," Thomas testified, "[and] the album cover is kind of awful . . . I've never seen this at a record shop, in truck stops, or any venue I've ever been in. I wouldn't think there's much demand for it."

Next, Ira Greenberg read excerpts from the deposition of Stephen Kountzman. Kountzman, who had worked for Moe Lytle since 1971, served as vice-president of Gusto Records, and now I.M.G., Lytle's distribution arm, running the day-to-day business operations. Kountzman had also been responsible for calculating the royalties Gusto owed. He said in his deposition that Gusto kept track of its unit sales by music publisher, rather than by artist. It did so on small slips known as "royalty pay cards." In addition, the company's customer invoices showed total sales, rather than how many units of individual items had been sold.

"Do you know or have any idea what amount of product embodying the works of the artists in this lawsuit were purchased in any given year?" Kountzman had been asked.

"No, I don't," he had answered.

In the company's mail order division—which the defense claimed generated minimal sales—Kountzman said, "There were no records compiled. The order was taken. The deposits were made. The orders were fulfilled. And orders were put in a box. They were kept for a certain period of time to make sure there [was] no customer service. And at the end of that particular time, they were thrown away."

B.J. Thomas's manager, Ted Hacker, started off the second day of trial testimony. Grant Smith asked about a visit Hacker made with Sam Lipshie and Lipshie's paralegal to Gusto's offices to examine company documents.

"Did you say, when I asked Mr. Kountzman—who was present and, of course, Mr. Lytle was also present—but I asked Mr. Kountzman to make photographs so that you wouldn't be able to come back and say we didn't tender these records. Do you remember that?"

"That's correct."

"And you remember saying, 'If you take my picture, I'm going to break the camera.' Do you remember that?"

"I don't remember saying that," Hacker insisted. "I might have been joking with you about that, but I don't remember making a threat of any kind."

Moe Lytle did not appear at trial. Instead, Sam Lipshie got on the witness stand to read excerpts from a June 1988 deposition that Lytle had given. Ira Greenberg read the questions.

"Do you make any effort to check whether royalties are payable to the artist?"

"Going back some years ago, I did a couple of times. I find out that if you go trying to run people down to pay them money, that people will take the money so that it don't really—some money that it don't really belong to, so I quit that."

"I believe you testified earlier . . . that if the artist had brought you the contract, to you in advance of the lawsuit, you would have sat down and figured out what you owed them. Right?"

"If they could have showed me that they had legitimate contracts, I would have figured out what I owed them and paid them."

"Is there a separate category or are there separate categories for the license income in your books?"

"Yes. Everything that comes from licenses would be totaled together in one lump sum."

"Are there entries in there that separate out the sources of license income?"

"No."

"How was that file cabinet organized?"

"It's really not. It sits there and I take and stick [the licensing agreements] in it."

"Is there any way to ascertain from documents what product [Gusto] has manufactured for Highland or Richmond?" (G.M.L. not only licensed masters to Highland and Richmond; Gusto and its successor division, Nashville Quality Duplicating, manufactured product for Stephen Hawkins' companies.)

"I don't know."

"Is it your company's practice to maintain correspondence in the ordinary course of its business?"

"No."

"Mr. Lytle missed his calling," Judge Higgins said. "He ought to be in the Cabinet in charge of reduction of papers. He's got this thing down to a science."

When Chuck Rubin took the stand, Grant Smith began, "Mr. Rubin, let's lay the cards on the table before we start so we'll know where we are and so the Court can understand and the record will show that there's a great deal of animosity that you have for me.

"First of all, on behalf of Gusto Records, I filed a lawsuit against you, did I not, and in that lawsuit I alleged fraud, did I not?"

"Yes."

"And that suit is still pending, is it not, and the judge has under advisement your motion to dismiss the lawsuit, is that right?"

"Right."

"Now, after the B.J. Thomas lawsuit was filed, you showed up at my office one day to look at some records of my client's, didn't you?"

"That's right."

"And I ordered you out of my office, didn't I?"

"That's right."

"We're not trying the lawyers here and suppose he dislikes you," Judge Higgins said. "I guess it might be an inference that that spills over against your client. I guess that's it."

"Absolutely, your honor."

"Let's go on."

The plaintiffs' chief expert witness, Fred Wolinsky, was a music industry accountant who had conducted over 100 record company royalty investigations. He came to court with a royalties estimate based on: sales data of artists similar to the Thomas plaintiffs in market, style, and degree of popularity; leasing and sales figures of licensees of the Springboard masters such as those from CBS; and industry custom and practice.

"We had no idea what monies Gusto had received because they stonewalled and I believe that was when the case shifted in our favor," Wolinsky later explained. "The law says that if a defendant withholds information over which it has control, the plaintiff has a right to make a reasonable estimate."

"Maybe two weeks before trial, I received thousands of documents from CBS, all totally disorganized," Wolinsky continued. "I spent July 4th weekend putting pages together that looked like they belonged in the same pile. When I walked into court with my report, Grant Smith's jaw dropped and he objected vehemently. Judge Higgins let the evidence in and asked me questions from the bench for an hour and a half."

The majority of the money the Thomas plaintiffs sought was from licensing income. Wolinsky testified that artists were entitled to 50 percent of that income because "the masters' owner (here G.M.L. or Gusto) need expend very little effort to earn the license fee as compared to the effort and related cost required to manufacture and sell phonorecords."

Wolinsky also claimed that Gusto should be responsible for licensing monies earned by Gusto's Springboard masters predecessor, Koala. "Your Honor, all I know is day one, we were receiving 50 percent of the net receipts that CBS Records licensed our product for. And then one day, the next day, all of a sudden there's this transaction [i.e., the sale to Koala]. CBS is in exactly the same position they were the day before [because it still has the right to license the recordings] except they got a million dollars more money.

"And now a company called Koala Records has the masters. . . . And now the [artist] is in a position where he gets exactly half of what he got the day before [because CBS paid licensing fees to Koala which was then to pay the artists]. . . . I think that's wrong. And I think that the people that make those kinds of arrangements have no concern whatsoever for artists' rights, and all they're doing is getting themselves richer and they don't care anything about the artist, and the artist has a right to 50 percent of it, regardless of who owns it."

"Mr. Wolinsky, what you're doing is generally passing judgment on the entire phonorecord industry, isn't that true," Grant Smith charged. "The industry is bad and the artist is good?"

"No. Absolutely not. The entire industry is not like this. If the entire industry was like this, I tell you right now, I wouldn't be in it. What I'm saying here is that whoever purchased the Koala, or 'business organization,' should have been well aware of what sham was set up and should have taken steps to indemnify themselves and to get themselves into a position that was legitimate whereby the artists received their fair share of the money. In this particular instance, I might add, they stepped into the position that they did and they kept the artists' share also."

"I tell you, my head is spinning on this business," Judge Higgins said. "I believe we better get a fresh start in the morning."

The defense led off its case by bringing Stephen Kountzman into court. Moe Lytle's general manager testified that Gusto didn't break down its distributor, retailer, etc., invoices by individual artists for two reasons. One, "to itemize the entire invoice when we were selling possibly two each of 150 different titles at any one time was just too laborious." Second, "85 percent of the product that we were selling was not royalty-related."

Kountzman said that Gusto had stopped selling albums "because of import competition, and [Lytle's] diversification into tractor equipment, tractors, dog food and everything else that he was getting into. He was getting involved with his farming. It was very difficult to explain why a record company was trying to sell tractors."

The main defense expert, Tom Bonetti, ran the Los Angeles-based Celebrity Licensing, which specialized in nostalgia recordings.

Bonetti claimed that artists didn't get half of licensing fees unless their recording contracts so stated. "Particularly with '50s and '60s artists," Bonetti said. "Frank Sinatra can get half of licensing income, but Frank Sinatra Jr. cannot."

An expert for the government in the Koala tax shelter litigation, Bonetti claimed that Gusto had taken in less money than it might otherwise have due to the large amount of illicit recordings on the market. "The licenses that were made by Springboard, and even to a greater extent Koala, were made to people who are generally known to be in the piracy business. They were not legitimate operators. They were not people who had rights to the majority of the masters that they claim to have rights to.

"And sadly, the Musicor and the Scepter [recordings], which of course include all the masters of the three plaintiffs, were among the most misused and abused masters of the '50s and '60s, both from the time that Springboard had them, and exacerbated when Koala took it over. They just were prostituted to an unbelievable extent, more than any other '50s and '60s masters of which I'm personally aware. . . . [T]he beast of Koala Records has 11 heads, and every time there's litigation or one dries up and goes out of business, two more pop up."

Judge Higgins asked, "Gusto can [nevertheless] acquire in good faith, bona fide fashion the masters to Mr. Pitney's work?"

"Yes, sir."

"And either inadvertently or because Gusto had been hoodoodled in some fashion, or some hoodoodling had gone on before back in the chain, they don't become aware of all the extant contracts that are out there that would result in royalties due to Mr. Pitney."

"It happens all the time, Your Honor."

"But that doesn't defeat Mr. Pitney's rights against Gusto."

"Not at all," Bonetti admitted.

Grant Smith then called on record producer Tommy Hill. Hill had coordinated the B.J. Thomas re-recording sessions. Portions of both the re-recordings and the original recordings of Thomas's hits, "I'm So Lonesome I Could Cry" and "Raindrops Keep Fallin' On My

Head," were played for Judge Higgins. Hill claimed that the re-recordings were better because they had been made on technically superior studio equipment.

"What is the purpose of—What am I to do in this exercise?" Higgins asked.

"They put on some witnesses like Mr. Rubin and Mr. Thomas who tried to project the image that this is a shoddy job, that it was cheaply done and that the product was no good," Grant Smith responded.

"Well, it doesn't really require any determination by the Court as the trier of fact, does it? This is not an issue in this lawsuit that I've got to make a determination of, whether the re-recordings are better than the Scepter masters, do I?" Higgins said. "You're lucky in this regard because you've got a judge with a tin ear."

The defense ended its testimony on the fifth and final day of trial with an appearance by Stephen Hawkins. An accountant by training, Hawkins had moved from England to Canada in 1975, and formed the Highland and Richmond music companies in the mid-'80s.

Hawkins told Judge Higgins in his clipped British accent, "I mean no disrespect to the plaintiffs, but the fact of the matter is their masters are a relatively insignificant part of the overall catalogue, and therefore my overall business."

Suggesting that G.M.L. licensed its masters to shell companies, Greenberg said, "Highland has no full-time employees, does it?"

"Other than myself, I use people on an as-needed basis," Hawkins replied.

"And G.M.L . . . is also, as of at least mid-1988, the source of about 99 percent of your outgoing product. Now, through the date of even your last deposition, you never paid to the plaintiffs a penny in royalties," charged Greenberg, who later claimed, "I've never seen a witness drink that much water in that short of time."

When Judge Higgins issued his decision in May 1990, he largely embraced Fred Wolinsky's royalties estimate formula and awarded the Thomas plaintiffs a total of $1.2 million, including interest. (Higgins found, however, that in their Scepter contracts, B.J. Thomas and the Shirelles waived the right to receive fees from TV, movie, and advertising licenses.)

"These artists, while perhaps not 'superstars' on the order of Elvis Presley, the Beatles, or the Rolling Stones, were nevertheless definitely 'stars' by most conventional standards," Judge Higgins wrote. "They are considered significant figures in the history of pop music, and there is considerable esteem and demand for their work among those interested in the music of their period."

The 6th U.S. Circuit Court of Appeals affirmed the decision in July 1991. "[T]he defendants claimed the rights to royalties earned before the date of [purchase from Koala] and the right to charge [artist-related] expenses of prior owners against the plaintiffs' royalties," the appeals court noted. "The implication of such broad rights is that Koala's sale included much more than the mere sale of the master recordings. Indeed, viewed in the light most favorable to the plaintiffs, the defendants' own expert explicitly testified that Koala's sale and Gusto's purchase included Gusto's obligation to assume the payment of accrued but unpaid royalties."

An unhappy Gusto asked the U.S. Supreme Court to consider the case. Oldies distributor Rhino Records argued in support of Gusto's petition that the successor liability ruling could chill, or even end, the sale and purchase of master recording catalogues. "Why don't artists come forward if they have a claim against a record company?" asked Rhino's in-house counsel, Bob Emmer. "Assuming they knew their masters were being exploited, where have they been for the last ten or 20 years?" But in December 1991, the Supreme Court declined to grant Gusto's request. And record companies faced a new wave of artist royalty claims.

One summer evening in 1997, Moe Lytle gave what he said was his first press interview ever. Red Sovine mementos adorned the lobby walls and Lytle's personal office in his brick-fronted warehouse in southeastern Nashville. A stocky, rawboned man, Lytle wore a casual blue sports shirt and low-hanging gray slacks that he hoisted up when he walked around his office. Lytle's Nashville litigator, Jay Bowen, sat in for the interview session.

Born in the small Western Tennessee town of Miston, Lytle migrated to St. Louis in the 1950s where he opened a nightclub named "Moe's Bootheel." "I booked mostly country artists," Lytle said in his Southern drawl. "Waylon Jennings, George Jones and Charlie Rich used to play my club. They'd do five 45-minute sets." Lytle began making trips to Nashville to record some of the artists who appeared at his establishment. He also bought a small mom-and-pop record store in St. Louis. "This real old couple owned it and they were paying $45 a month rent. I paid four thousand dollars for the business."

Lytle began distributing records to small convenience and grocery stores. With the start of Gusto Records in 1973, he invested in his first sound recording catalogue, the Stop country label, owned by former Starday producer Tommy Hill. In 1974, Lytle moved to Nashville and set up a custom tape manufacturing facility. For Gusto, "we started recording instrumental and concept albums," Lytle said. "We'd take studio pickers and come up with names like *The Nashville Harmonica Players Play Today's Hits* and they sold pretty well."

He also brought in numerous artists to re-record their hits. "We did all kinds," Lytle explained. "The music business was slow then and the artists wanted to work. We did Mary Wells, Sam and Dave, Gary Lewis and Jack Scott. Scott [whose 1950s hits included "My True Love" and "Goodbye Baby"] was working at a gas station and tickled to death to be able to re-record his records. The company that had the originals wasn't interested in putting them out."

But Lytle ran into legal problems when he released *Charlie Rich— The Silver Fox* in 1974, at the height of Rich's pop chart success. The album featured a recent picture of Rich but gave no recording date information. "They were masters he had recorded for [the Memphis-based 1950s label] Sun," Lytle recalled. "I leased them from Shelby Singleton, who owned them at the time. I get a subpoena from CBS at ten in the morning to appear in court two o'clock that afternoon. I only had four hours to get a local lawyer. Someone gave me Grant Smith's number." The court allowed Gusto to continue to sell the Rich album but ordered Lytle's company to place a prominent decal on the cover of each album copy indicating that it contained early, mono recordings.

Meanwhile, Moe Lytle acquired more sound recording catalogues. He bought gospel masters by the Stamps Quartet and the Blackwood Brothers. In 1975, he bought King-Starday—whose prior owners included songwriters Jerry Leiber and Mike Stoller and music publisher Freddy Bienstock. The largely rhythm and blues King/Federal catalogue contained master recordings by Billy Ward's Dominoes—featuring Jackie Wilson and Clyde McPhatter on lead vocals—Hank Ballard and the Midnighters, Little Willie John, and Ivory Joe Hunter. The Starday label had been a major force in country music, with George Jones, Cowboy Copas, and Moon Mullican on its roster. "There were probably 15,000 to 20,000 masters in that purchase," Lytle said. "Back then, people didn't think bluegrass and country were that big."

When Lytle bought the Koala masters, "there were 10,000 boxes with two to eight tapes in each box," he said. "Wes Sanborn [who owned Koala] decided to go out of business when he got into trouble with the government over the tax shelters."

But the more masters Lytle bought, the more difficult it became for him to keep track of the proliferating pirated product derived from his catalogues. Lytle battled especially hard against Marshall Sehorn. Sehorn was a white R&B entrepreneur who had worked as a promotion man for Bobby Robinson's Fire/Fury Records. In 1965, the burly Sehorn partnered with celebrated New Orleans producer Allen Toussaint to form Sansu Enterprises and, later, Sea-Saint Studios. Sehorn and Toussaint oversaw the production of Lee Dorsey hits like "Working in a Coal Mine," and recorded such local talent as Dr. John and the Meters.

By the early 1980s, Sehorn became involved in master recording tax shelter transactions. In March 1988, Moe Lytle sued Sehorn in

Nashville federal court. Lytle claimed that Sehorn had been illegally licensing Koala masters—including the B.J. Thomas, Gene Pitney, and Shirelles recordings. Sehorn insisted he had been granted a non-exclusive license by JEY in 1982. (However, JEY had already sold the recordings to Koala). Lytle claimed that Sehorn's JEY license was falsely backdated.

"We got a preliminary injunction against Sehorn and about a dozen other defendants," Lytle said. "But I agreed not to disagree with Sehorn's JEY contract if he did certain things, such as cutting off his rights in the year 2001. Sehorn also paid me $150,000 and gave me a license to some Chess and K-Tel masters."

But courts in California and Texas subsequently ruled that Sehorn had rights to neither the Chess catalogue—which included recordings by Chuck Berry, Bo Diddley, and John Lee Hooker—nor the K-Tel masters, which included Chubby Checker, Jan & Dean, and Little Richard recordings. "If I wanted to win a popularity contest, I couldn't," Sehorn admitted.

"It was the judgment in the B.J. Thomas case that probably forced Moe Lytle to settle with Marshall Sehorn," Celebrity Licensing's Tom Bonetti said. "The settlement was catastrophic for the record industry. It allowed Sehorn to continue to flood the market with licenses that mirrored the Koala catalogue."

MCA Records, which had beat Sehorn in the Chess case, now sued Moe Lytle's G.M.L. in California over G.M.L.'s use of the Chess masters. Lytle in turn moved to set aside his settlement agreement with Sehorn. But the day Lytle's lawyers were applying for a temporary restraining order against Sehorn on the Springboard catalogue, Sehorn filed for bankruptcy in New Orleans.

In October 1997, the bankruptcy court approved Sehorn's reorganization plan. Sehorn stipulated that the court could enter a judgment declaring that he never acquired rights to the Springboard masters.

Meanwhile, Moe Lytle continued to battle with the Thomas plaintiffs. Lytle had agreed on a schedule for paying the Higgins judgment and dropped his claims against Chuck Rubin. (In addition to the

Platters license dispute, Lytle sued Rubin over the issuance of a license for the British MCR Productions to use the Shirelles recordings. Rubin had argued the license was for the Shirelles' European vocal performance rights, not the group's master recording rights.) Then when Hank Ballard sued Lytle's companies in 1990 over his King/Federal royalty payments, Lytle settled by giving Ballard $150,000 and assuring him of future royalties income.

In April 1995, Ballard, Thomas, Pitney, and the Shirelles together filed a breach of contract suit alleging that Lytle failed to make full new royalties payments. The suit named Marshall Sehorn as co-defendant but charged that Lytle was ultimately responsible for Sehorn's payments, too.

"I guess the first time was so easy they thought they'd try it again," Lytle said that summer evening in his Nashville office. "Everywhere I go, they wave that thing [i.e., the Higgins and 6th Circuit judgments] around in court and try to use it to incriminate me. A real bad spot. I got outfoxed and screwed in the courts.

"Grant Smith didn't introduce the [full evidence] because he said there ain't no way the court is ever gonna believe Wolinsky's estimate. [Lytle successfully moved to quash the Thomas plaintiffs' attempt to obtain more extensive documents in the hands of Lytle's St. Louis accountants.] What they seen is, I didn't owe them near as much as they'd hoped. So they get this guy to come up with a fictitious figure."

"Moe Lytle once told me that people like me think he's a big shot, but that the big record companies think he's a little shot," Chuck Rubin said. " 'I just can't win,' Moe complained. '*You* should think I'm a little shot and *they* should think I'm a big shot.'"

The Beatles: "I Should Have Known Better"

On November 8, 1989, entertainment attorney Leonard Marks sat in a Beverly Hills hotel room taking the deposition of Phil Spector, the eccentric, legendary record producer who created the highly influential "Wall of Sound" in the early 1960s. At Spector's side, to support and advise him, was Spector's business associate, Allen Klein, the owner of the ABKCO music company. Spector had sued Marks's clients, Jerry Leiber and Mike Stoller, the writers of many early rock 'n' roll hits. At issue in the case was which of the parties' publishing companies should control the copyrights to a group of classic rock songs.

Across town that same day in Hollywood, Bhaskar Menon, the chairman of EMI Music Worldwide, announced that a decade-long legal battle between the record company and the most successful act in its history, the Beatles, had been settled. During the litigation, the Beatles accused EMI of cheating them out of tens of millions of dollars in record royalties.

It was fitting that Leonard Marks should be with Phil Spector and Allen Klein when Menon released his statement. Marks, a senior partner in the New York firm Gold, Farrell & Marks, had for the last seven years served as chief litigation counsel to the Beatles in the group's royalties dispute with EMI and its U.S. subsidiary, Capitol Records. Spector had completed the production of the tumultuous *Let It Be* album, the last one the Beatles released before the band officially broke up. Klein served as a primary catalyst that led to the Beatles' dissolution in 1971, when he managed the group. He also negotiated the recording agreement that was at the heart of the Beatles' fight with Capitol-EMI.

The Beatles spent more than $5 million in legal fees to pursue their royalties claims, but, in the end, the group had struck up the most lucrative deal of its career. It was also the largest settlement, or agreement of any kind, ever entered into between recording artists and a record label.

For dropping the litigation, the Beatles were to receive a cash payment from Capitol-EMI in the neighborhood of $80 million. They were also given the right to approve all commercial uses of their recordings and a significant royalty-rate boost to be monitored by the strictest accounting methods yet for artists. In addition, the settlement ended a series of related lawsuits the Beatles had filed against Capitol-EMI, and put to rest a legal challenge against Paul McCartney by George Harrison, Yoko Ono, and Ringo Starr. The latter dispute arose after McCartney secretly negotiated an increased royalty rate for himself on Beatles recordings when he re-signed with Capitol as a solo artist in the mid-'80s.

In many ways, the November 1989 settlement signaled the second coming of the Fab Four. Recordings tucked away in the vaults could now be readied for release and an authorized documentary in the works for two decades could be completed. "I think it was probably because the lawsuits were over," Beatles documentary producer Chips Chipperfield said. "They couldn't find anything to sue each other about." Even more amazing, Apple Corps Ltd., the clearinghouse for the Beatles' finances, had survived intact. This after Paul McCartney had threatened to shut down the company in anger over the business in-fighting among Apple's four principals.

The genesis of many of the Beatles' legal problems can be traced to the often-ludicrous business deals the group's manager, Brian Epstein, bound the band members to in their early days. When the Beatles signed as new artists to EMI's Parlophone label in 1962, Epstein and the four band members split one penny for each double-sided record release. For the United States, which would constitute 60 percent of the Beatles' record sales, Epstein and the group received half that amount. Four one-year options—covering record sales through 1966—called for an increase of only one-half penny for each option period. Unlike major label deals for even the newest bands today, the Beatles received no advance against royalties.

Epstein initially wanted the Beatles' song publishing to be signed to Hill and Range, which published the songs Elvis Presley recorded. But at the suggestion of Beatles record producer, George Martin, Epstein settled on a small publishing company run by Dick James, a former solo artist who Martin had produced. James formed a company within his publishing firm called Northern Songs Ltd. to handle the John Lennon-Paul McCartney song catalogue. Under the deal, James and his partner kept half of the songwriting income (a typical publisher's share), Lennon and McCartney each got 20 percent, with the other 10 percent going to Brian Epstein. James also took 10 percent off the top for the administration—the exploitation and overseeing—of the Beatles' music.

George Harrison said of the deal he signed with Dick James: "I always felt retrospectively that I was really ripped off. Now, nobody ever sat down with me, no manager or lawyers, and nobody ever gave us any advice, that was the thing. And in a way, Brian Epstein was slightly in cahoots with Dick James. But James never actually said, 'I'll publish your songs, and when you sign this piece of paper, I will be stealing your copyrights; I will own it for the rest of my life.' Which is what actually happened."

To represent the Beatles' legal interests, Epstein picked high-priced London solicitor David Jacobs, whose firm had represented several big-name entertainers, such as Liberace. For accountants, Epstein chose the Liverpool firm of Bryce, Hanmer and Isherwood, whose London office handled show business matters. Dr. Walter Strach, a senior member of the accounting firm, formed a company into which the Beatles' earnings went. The band members themselves got only 50 pounds a week. This would later be increased to just 100 pounds.

According to Paul McCartney, "We used to ask them, 'Am I a millionaire yet? . . . Are there more than a million of those green things in my bank yet?' And they'd say, 'Well, it's not actually in a *bank*. . . . We *think* you are.' It was very difficult to get anything out of them. The accountants never made you feel successful." McCartney further claimed that "the first time I actually saw checks was when I left Apple, and it wasn't me that saw them, it was [McCartney's wife] Linda because we'd co-written a few of our early things."

In a gesture of generosity—and perhaps guilt—Brian Epstein decided to give the Beatles 10 percent of NEMS Enterprises, the management company into which Epstein put his 25-percent management commission from the band. But when Epstein negotiated the Beatles' first film deal, with United Artists for *A Hard Day's Night*, he asked for only 7 1/2 percent of the film's profits. Walter Shenson, the film's producer, said that the film company had been prepared to pay Epstein and the Beatles 25 percent.

Perhaps the biggest business fiasco of all was the Beatles' merchandising deal. David Jacobs tapped London party-circuit fixture Nicky Byrne, who formed Stramsact and the U.S. subsidiary Seltaeb to handle the worldwide merchandise licensing. When Jacobs drafted an agreement for Byrne to sign, Byrne's lawyer told his client to write in whatever commission percentage he wanted. "So I put down the first figure that came into my head—90 percent," Byrne said. "To my amazement, David Jacobs didn't even question it."

NEMS later was able to increase its percentage with Seltaeb to 46 percent, but distrust between the parties damaged the merchandising campaign. For one thing, NEMS attempted to bypass Seltaeb by issuing U.S. merchandising licenses out of its London office. NEMS also filed suit in New York claiming that Seltaeb failed to pay it full royalties. Byrne counterclaimed for breach of contract, asking for $5 million in damages.

Brian Epstein asked Manhattan lawyer Nat Weiss, who became his U.S. business partner, for help. Weiss recommended well-known trial lawyer Louis Nizer. In 1967, Nizer settled the merchandising litigation with a payment of only $10,000 to Byrne. Despite Epstein's business naiveté, Nizer later described him as "very keen, able and well-spoken. I had a number of conferences with him, though I don't recall any of the group being up to my office." Of course, Nizer was likely to have nice words for Epstein: Epstein had given him a $50,000 retainer by personal check because, Epstein said, "The Seltaeb deal was my fault, and I don't want the Beatles to pay any further for my mistakes."

Depressed that his five-year management contract with the Beatles was set to end in October 1967, Brian Epstein believed he needed a business coup to keep the band in his hands. This he achieved to some extent when he renegotiated the Beatles' recording contract with EMI. The January 1967 agreement brought the Beatles the significant royalties increase the band deserved.

The nine-year deal called for the Beatles to deliver five albums during the first five years. For royalties, the group got—based on EMI's wholesale price to dealers—10 percent from the sale of the first 100,000 copies of each single and 30,000 of each album; an increase to 15 percent for sales above those amounts; and 17 1/2 percent in North America for sales of singles and albums in excess of 100,000 and 30,000 copies, respectively. The royalty provisions represented a significant breakthrough for recording artists. By comparison, U.S. artists in the 1960s typically received a royalty of from 3 to 5 percent. But Epstein made one important oversight during the contract negotiations. He failed to secure a cash advance for the Beatles. And the Beatles knew that Allen Klein, the Rolling Stones' manager, had obtained an advance worth more than one million dollars from the Decca label for his band. Within a year—after Epstein died from a drug overdose—the Beatles accountants, Bryce Hanmer, resigned with this warning: "Your personal finances are in a mess. Apple is in a mess."

Allen Klein, a tough, brash New Yorker who had managed soul singer Sam Cooke, began his music business career as an accountant who successfully pursued back-royalties claims on behalf of music publishers and songwriters. In May 1969, John Lennon, George Harrison, and Ringo Starr signed a management contract with Klein that entitled Klein to a 20 percent commission from his new clients' future earnings. "The first real sophistication came with Klein," admitted Nat Weiss. "But there were shadows attached to him."

Weiss was alluding to Klein's turbulent business background. This included Klein's dislodging of Rolling Stones manager Andrew Loog Oldham to make way for his own management deal with the group, and subsequent lawsuits between Klein and the Stones. Cynthia Stewart, Oldham's assistant and wife of Rolling Stones confidante Ian Stewart, said Klein looked to her like "a cross between a New York gangster and an undernourished wrestler."

Paul McCartney favored his father-in-law and brother-in-law-to-be, Lee and John Eastman, both Manhattan entertainment attorneys, as advisers for the band. McCartney deferred to Klein on a few matters, but never trusted or more than minimally accepted him.

Klein's major achievement for the Beatles was renegotiating the group's Capitol-EMI deal into a "buy/sell" agreement that gave the Beatles greater income than they could have earned from a conventional recording contract. Under the September 1969 buy/sell deal, Apple bought Beatles records that Capitol manufactured, then resold those records to Capitol for distribution and sale. As favorable as the buy/sell was, it wasn't enough to convince Paul McCartney that Klein should handle Beatles affairs over the long term. So McCartney sued his three band mates in the High Court of Justice in London on December 31, 1970 in a bid to eject Klein.

"And I got a lot of guilt off that," McCartney said. "But you tell me what you would have done if the entire earnings that you'd made—and it was something like the Beatles' entire earnings, a big figure, everything we'd done up to somewhere round about 'Hey Jude'—was about to disappear into someone's pocket. . . . Allen Klein had about 5 million pounds the first year he managed the Beatles. So I smelled a rat."

In his suit, McCartney acknowledged that "[a]s soon as the touring period ceased [in 1966], we began to drift apart socially." McCartney nevertheless claimed that the wedge he felt had been driven between them by Klein "was the first time in the history of the Beatles that a possible irreconcilable difference had appeared between us."

But, "Paul was the same with Brian in the beginning, if you must know," John Lennon insisted. "He used to sulk and God knows what." Lennon penned a series of cutting comments about McCartney in the margins of a copy of McCartney's suit that he reviewed. Lennon wrote such things as "never happened"; "Paul was guilty of this"; and "no one can ever get in touch with him" on his copy of the court document.

During the trial, Lennon, Harrison, and Starr sought to establish that Klein had taken just nominal commissions from the group. But calling Klein "a second-rate salesman," Justice Edward Stamp took the group's finances out of Klein's hands and appointed a receiver. In April, Lennon, Harrison, and Starr dropped their appeal of the High Court's ruling.

The Beatles partnership was formally dissolved in January 1975. By then, Lennon, Harrison, and Starr had become involved in their own litigation with Klein. Klein's management contract with the three artists expired in March 1973. In June, Klein sued John Lennon in England alleging non-payment of a $508,000 loan. Klein's former clients in turn sued him in High Court alleging misrepresentation; Klein countercharged for commissions and expenses. Klein lost the case but pursued the Beatles in a New York court. The litigation ended in 1977, in a deal reportedly midwifed by Yoko Ono at a reported cost of over $4 million to the Beatles to settle their differences with Klein.

George Harrison, however, continued to fight Klein in a separate suit until 1998. Harrison had been sued for copyright infringement in

1971 by Bright Tunes Music Corp., the holder of the copyright to the Chiffons' early 1960s hit "He's So Fine." In 1976, Manhattan federal Judge Richard Owen ruled that Harrison subconsciously infringed on "He's So Fine" when he wrote "My Sweet Lord." Owen decided that Harrison owed Bright Tunes $1,599,987 in damages. Klein bought the collection rights from the music publisher and songwriter's heirs for $587,000. He then asked the judge for the full damage amount. But Klein had been in touch with the Bright Tunes plaintiffs as early as the pre-trial settlement negotiations and had even offered them Harrison documents regarding the value of their claim. Owen awarded Klein only the $587,000 Klein paid Bright Tunes, concluding that Klein had breached his obligation to his former client. Klein later admitted, "I never did believe that George set out to copy 'He's So Fine.'"

In November 1990, Judge Owen handed down a ruling that divided up the songs' rights. Harrison lawyer, Joseph Santora, charged that Klein had been fully compensated under a secret 1980 deal Klein made, unbeknownst to Harrison, with Harrison's music agent. Klein nevertheless challenged a reduction in the price Harrison—who also had to make royalty payments to Klein for "My Sweet Lord"—would be required to pay for the Canadian, U.S., and U.K. rights to "He's So Fine." In October 1991, a New York federal appeals court sided with Harrison. The court also denied Klein a 20 percent administrative fee for overseeing the song copyright. Harrison and Klein finally settled their accounting differences in March 1998. "This is one of the few cases where a defendent found guilty of infringement ended up owning [the plaintiffs's] song," Joseph Santora said.

The lawsuits that the Beatles were frequently drawn into proved a boon to students of Beatles history. Paul McCartney's suit to dissolve the Beatles' partnership provided an inside look at the band's last days. Shortly before he was murdered by obsessed fan Mark David Chapman in New York in December 1980, John Lennon gave a deposition in a suit over the stage play and film *Beatlemania* that offered a glimpse of Beatles projects to come.*

In his deposition, Lennon stated that the Beatles were planning to perform together for an autobiographical documentary they were compiling. Lennon had previously blamed his rare concert appearances on his fight for permanent U.S. residency, which he won. During the four-year immigration battle in the 1970s, Lennon made frequent court appearances.

"I met with them [John Lennon and Yoko Ono] in their apartment at night and picked them up in the morning for hearings, literally dressing them for court," New York immigration attorney Leon Wildes recalled. "They were very nervous. For John, it was an emotional thing."

"[I]t just seemed like a toothache that wouldn't go away," Lennon said. He had been eager to tour with Elephant's Memory, the band that backed him up at the One to One benefit concert at Madison Square Garden in 1972. "But they kept pullin' me back into court!" Lennon complained. "Now, the last thing on earth I want to do is perform. That's a direct result of the immigration thing."

By the time of his *Beatlemania* deposition, Lennon and the other three Beatles appeared to be mending some of their interpersonal wounds. "Everybody's sued each other to their heart's content and now we're all good friends," George Harrison claimed.

Even so, the Beatles were preparing for what would be their most prolonged legal battle as a group. On April 30 and May 1, 1979, Apple Records filed complaints in state courts in Los Angeles and New York

---

*Chapman pleaded guilty to second-degree murder in June 1981 and was sentenced to 20 years to life in prison. "Chapman believes without question that God told him to plead guilty," defense attorney Jonathan Marks said after the hearing. "But it might better be called a delusion or hallucination." Marks noted that "Chapman's played me a tape of some of his original compositions. They're '60s songs, bittersweet, like the Beatles."

In 1986, Apple would win a $10.5 million judgment in Los Angeles Superior Court in the trademark and right of publicity suit against the producers of *Beatlemania*, which featured Beatles look-a-likes performing Beatles songs. The case would be the first in a series of such suits the Beatles would file.

charging Capitol-EMI with breach of contract for failing to pay the Beatles their full North American record royalties.

The group hired the accounting firm Satin, Tenenbaum, Eichler & Zimmerman to conduct a royalties audit of Capitol's books relating to Beatles product for 1969 through 1979. John Lennon signed the letter retaining the accountants. Satin Tenenbaum reported numerous inconsistencies in the way that Capitol-EMI accounted for Beatles' royalties.

According to Nat Weiss, although "Brian Epstein had problems with EMI over what kinds of records to put out, I don't remember any back-royalty complaints in the 1960s." But Capitol's lawyers later acknowledged that the Beatles had complained about royalty escalations as early as 1972. In June 1975, for example, the accounting firm Prager and Fenton concluded that Capitol-EMI underpaid the Beatles $3,206,312 between September 1, 1969—the day the buy/sell deal was signed—and the end of 1973.

The buy/sell agreement that Allen Klein negotiated with EMI contained a provision that entitled the Beatles to a 25 percent royalties increase if the last two Beatles recordings released before August 31, 1972, achieved minimum record sales of 500,000 units by January 26, 1976, the date the Beatles' recording contract with Capitol-EMI expired. The key issue in the Beatles' royalties suit was whether Capitol-EMI had properly deemed John Lennon's politically charged solo effort *Some Time in New York City*, which sold less than 200,000 copies, as the delivery of a Beatles album. If so, Capitol-EMI could deny the royalties escalation to the Beatles.

The *Some Time* album was released in June 1972. The two previous Beatles solo albums, Lennon's *Imagine* and McCartney's Wings' *Wild Life*, both quickly topped 500,000 in sales. George Harrison's *The Concert for Bangla Desh*, another bestseller, was released two weeks after *Wild Life*, but Capitol-EMI and Apple had agreed that the album, a charity project featuring numerous performances by other artists, wouldn't count as a Beatles release for purposes of the buy/sell contract.

That put the Beatles in the position of having to argue that *Some Time* shouldn't qualify as a Beatles album because John Lennon may not have appeared on every track. "There were several Yoko Ono songs on the album," said Joseph Wheelock, Capitol-EMI's lead litigator from Latham & Watkins in Los Angeles. "But it probably would have been musically embarrassing to Lennon if it turned out that he did nothing more than, say, use a drum stick as a baton during the session."

"That escalation clause was diabolical," Wheelock continued. "I've never faced an issue like it. At one point, I said to myself, 'Now you act like a judge and line up the facts on either side.' I couldn't decide it one way or the either. It was that close."

The Los Angeles entertainment firm Loeb and Loeb initially represented the Beatles in the California suit. Cleary Gottlieb Steen & Hamilton, which had handled many legal matters for the band, including the Allen Klein management litigation, served as New York counsel. Capitol-EMI counsel Wheelock previously helped the record company win a securities fraud suit brought by its shareholders. Daniel Murdock, who later headed up Capitol's New York legal team, had handled several artist royalties disputes for the label, starting with a $2 million claim by the band Grand Funk Railroad that was settled for less than $300,000.

The Beatles suit against Capitol-EMI moved slowly at first. As is often the case with such royalty suits, the Beatles may have filed their claims hoping that the record company would respond with a royalties offer. But Capitol-EMI had no reason to hurry the suit along. After all, it was to the company's advantage to maintain the status quo and pay the Beatles the lower royalty rate. According to Wheelock, the parties even agreed in writing that the case should proceed on a slow track.

By 1982, however, the Beatles became frustrated with the progress of their claims. In May of that year, the group decided to replace their New York counsel with Manhattan's Gold, Farrell & Marks. The latter firm's senior partner, Leonard Marks, had won a favorable settlement for songwriters Jerry Leiber and Mike Stoller in a royalties dispute with music publisher Hill and Range.

Marks's firm quickly amended Apple's complaint to charge that Capitol-EMI's alleged underpayment of royalties amounted to fraud, conversion, and breach of fiduciary duty. Then in December 1984, the Beatles won a judgment in a related suit Apple Corps filed in England over royalties owed the group outside North America, for the years 1966 through 1979. The High Court found no fraudulent concealment but ordered a new accounting of the royalties EMI owed. That accounting resulted in payment of over $4 million to the Beatles.

But friction among the Beatles increased as the New York case sped up. They were split as to whether it would be better to settle the case and take what they could get from Capitol-EMI or to confront the record company in court. Capitol-EMI had made the Beatles a settlement offer of about $8 million, and also offered to increase the Beatles' U.S. royalty payments to $1.20 per record. For the rest of the world, the record company would bring the old penny rate on the 1962 agreement up to the present contract.

Paul McCartney wanted to accept Capitol-EMI's offer, but George Harrison, Lennon's widow Yoko Ono, and Ringo Starr were against it. McCartney and his advisers, John and Lee Eastman, thought that a big problem with the Beatles going to trial was that Capitol-EMI held the better hand. The Beatles had been counting on Allen Klein's testimony, but John Eastman believed that Klein would testify instead for Capitol.

"We don't have a witness and how do you try the main part of your case without a witness?" Eastman pondered. "Here's a man who is your agent, who's Apple's appointed agent, he negotiated the deal and, um, here we are."

Joseph Wheelock confirmed that there was good reason to think that Klein might help Capitol's case. Said Wheelock, "One of the guys at Capitol told me that he talked to Klein and that Klein had tried to prevent the release of *Some Time in New York City*. Klein wanted the

Imagine and *Wild Life* albums to count as the Beatles releases to trigger the royalties escalation provision. But Lennon wouldn't listen. Now here was Klein's chance to say, 'I told you so.'" (Lennon jokingly referred to Klein as "Alice Klien" in the *Some Time in New York City* album notes.)

John Eastman nevertheless met with EMI chairman Bhaskar Menon to try to resurrect the record company's settlement offer. McCartney suggested that Capitol-EMI would be motivated to settle the suit because, "They don't want to damage their image sufficiently to say, 'We cheated the Beatles.'" But Eastman reported that "Bhaskar killed [the attempt to resurrect the settlement offer] sooooo fast—so politely and so fast. It's just amazing. In fact, I wondered why everyone had gotten together frankly. Bhaskar's just playing very tough right now."

John Eastman pointed out, "What they would say—it would become one of these fuzzy, funny fights in the press—is 'We've offered them eight million dollars, we've offered them the uplift which they're not entitled to because this one key album didn't meet the standard—and what are they crying over. What they're crying over is they want more, more, more, [that they're] certainly not entitled to under their contract, which this 'brilliant' Allen Klein negotiated for them, then the start-of-the-art man."

"And who cries for millionaires like the Beatles anyway?" Lee Eastman asked.

"Exactly," Paul McCartney and John Eastman agreed.

The Capitol-EMI litigation had other negative consequences for the Beatles. It had seriously damaged Apple's finances. John Eastman announced at an Apple meeting in London, "Here we are, directors of the company, going forward with this case that costs us as much in fees a year as our income is." Those costs, according to Eastman, were between $60,000 to $75,000 a month. At the time, Maclen [the Lennon-McCartney songwriting partnership within Northern Songs] had higher annual earnings than Apple. "About one million, four-hundred-thousand pounds," Eastman said, adding, "This is with Northern Songs' terrible accounting system."

"But what they intimated" at the Apple meeting, John Eastman later told Paul McCartney, "was that George [Harrison] thought you were so desperate to settle for some nefarious reason, that [you] would do anything to do it."

"Oh, there's never been any doubt of that," Paul responded. "For 15 years, it's all just me. You know what happens when you get playing monopoly or chess or whatever, you have to assume your 'enemy' might have something up his sleeve."

"Well you know why, they've had so much up their sleeves," Linda interjected. "Yoko's had so much up her sleeves she's bulging."

"Yoko, you know, is the general," added John Eastman. "She's always looking under the bed."

Harrison, Ono, and Starr were unwilling to settle with Capitol-EMI unless their royalty rate was "equalized" with Paul McCartney's. McCartney had infuriated the others when, after leaving the Columbia record label, he had negotiated a new solo deal with Capitol-EMI in 1985 that included an "override"—an increase for him on the royalties he would receive on Beatles product.

McCartney spent the first two or three hours of an Apple meeting "taking the bit between my teeth," explaining to them what the override was. "I'd come to the meeting for one thing. . . . I wanted Apple to be closed down that day, but I capitulated." Paul didn't "want his kids being hung up with Apple," Linda said. For another thing, he didn't want the override issue to be part of any royalties-suit settlement talks with Capitol-EMI; McCartney feared that the royalty increase on Beatles product he had gotten might be decreased to match what Capitol-EMI might offer Harrison, Ono, and Starr. As a compromise, Harrison, Ono, and Starr agreed to each give Paul a million dollars to help even up their positions.

Still, the three wanted to pursue McCartney in court. Their legal argument was that in signing the 1985 deal with Capitol, McCartney had diverted to himself an override opportunity to which Apple should have been entitled. Lee Eastman noted that Harrison, Ono, and Starr had already gone to English solicitors "who said they had no case." (A clause in the contract among the Beatles stipulated that all disputes under their agreement were to be decided under English law.) They then approached New York attorney Martin London of Paul, Weiss, Rifkind, Wharton & Garrison.

But "Martin London's letter [to the McCartney camp] did not mention a single English case," John Eastman said. "It was all based on New York cases."

McCartney said that he had told the Harrison-Ono-Starr camp at the Apple meeting, "You want to fight us, fine. We're ready for you."

What the Beatles needed in their fight against Capitol-EMI was a smoking gun. They would find it to some extent in an individual named Leonard Wolin. The Beatles' investigators had heard that Wolin claimed to have made irregular "back door" purchases of large amounts of records, including Beatles product, from a Capitol pressing plant. The investigators also heard that Wolin said he had sold the records to John LaMonte—a Philadelphia-area cutout records dealer with ties to organized crime. Unfortunately, Wolin had died. But Wolin's family allowed the Beatles' investigators to sift through his papers, stored in the attic of a Wolin family member's home. There the investigators found what they had been looking for: copies of Wolin's canceled checks written out to Capitol Records but deposited into the record company's employee recreation fund.

Now the Beatles asked the New York court for permission to supplement their royalties claims to include from 1979 to the present. The Beatles also asked for termination of Capitol's rights to manufacture and distribute Beatles product, and for a transfer of all sound recording rights to the group.

The revised complaint, which asked for $30 million in actual damages and $50 million in punitive damages, alleged that Capitol sold 19 million Beatles records that the label claimed it had scrapped. The Beatles also charged that Capitol had designated an excess number of Beatles albums as free, promotional records given away to wholesalers or used to obtain retail display space for other Capitol artists. According to the complaint, many of these promotional records were undrilled. (Promotional records are typically "drilled"— a hole is literally drilled through the sleeve—to prevent their sale.)

"That's just sheer nonsense, even more so than the normal stuff that Leonard [Marks] puts in his complaints," Capitol's attorney Joseph Wheelock countered.

In March 1986, however, the Beatles' lawyers deposed Capitol executives who confirmed some of the band's record-scrapping allegations. Dennis White, Capitol's executive vice president of Record Group Services, told Beatles' lawyer Alan Friedman that he knew of several instances in which records designated as scrap had been sold or stolen. In one case—in the mid-'70s at Capitol's Jacksonville, Illinois, plant—White said, "Our plant manager sold the product to someone . . . and the product being undrilled, that individual apparently sold it to other people who sold it to our existing customer base." White further stated that he had heard about the incident, which he said involved millions of records, from Don Zimmerman, then Capitol's president.

Walter Lee, vice president of marketing for Capitol, admitted that he knew of an incident in the early 1980s in which records that were to be melted into plastic coat hangers had found their way into the hands of John LaMonte.

Capitol-EMI issued a public statement admitting to an "isolated incident" at its Jacksonville plant but claimed the label had been "completely successful in correcting the situation." The record company also denied it had any dealings with LaMonte.

In July 1986, however, New York Supreme Court Justice Michael Donzin granted the Beatles' motion to serve Capitol-EMI with the revised complaint. Donzin acknowledged in an ominous warning to the record label that "if [the Beatles] claims are proven at trial, there should be no reason for them to be compelled to continue under the contract."

Meanwhile, the Beatles' lawyers made additional startling allegations. Leonard Marks claimed that Capitol had slated Beatles and other records for so-called "donations" to charities such as Boy's Town but instead sold the product without making any artist royalty payments. Capitol then claimed charitable tax deductions for these transactions, Marks alleged. For example, Marks said, a record wholesaler had informed Beatles investigators that he bought boxes of records from John LaMonte bearing shipping labels indicating the records had been "donated" to charities.

George Harrison concluded Beatles records were being given to "pension funds run by the Mafia. It's very dirty.

"They've all taken advantage of it because after the Beatles split up . . . they all came in, grabbing and plundering as much as they could. But now this is going to be pursued to the end, and even if we all die in the process, our children and our children's children will be after Bhaskar Menon and Capitol until he realizes he's just being a dong."

Despite these damning charges, Capitol-EMI won a significant court victory in April 1987 when it convinced Justice Donzin that the buy/sell agreement was a "fiction." Turning his earlier ruling on its ear, Donzin granted Capitol-EMI's motion to dismiss most of the Beatles' claims. "The purpose of the buy/sell arrangement is not readily apparent," Donzin wrote. "[T]he resolution of the [breach of] contract claims . . . will adequately resolve the rights and obligations under the contract." Donzin added that the buy/sell agreement looked to him "like a scam cooked up by the bean counters."

The Beatles launched an all-out litigation offensive in response. In 1986, Apple had filed suit against EMI in England over the use of Beatles audiocassettes in a Heineken beer pull-tops promotion. Now—in July 1987—the group filed a $40 million complaint against Capitol in New York federal court over the royalty rate and delay in the release of Beatles compact discs.

Bhaskar Menon blamed the delay on "insufficient manufacturing capacity." Plus, "it wasn't clear on what basis the Beatles' CD royalties would be computed and Capitol wanted that issue resolved before the CDs were released," Daniel Murdock, the record company's New York counsel, said. The Beatles, on the other hand, accused Capitol of withholding release of the CDs to force a settlement of the parties' disputes. Capitol had only begun to release Beatles CDs in February 1987. By comparison, Capitol began releasing CDs by artists like Kenny Rogers, Bob Seger, Tina Turner, and Sheena Easton in 1984 and 1985.

Apple also filed suit in Manhattan over Capitol's licensing of the sound recording of John Lennon's "Revolution" for a Nike sneaker TV commercial. The Beatles song "Help!" had been used in a Lincoln-Mercury car commercial sung by Beatles soundalikes. The Nike commercial, however, represented the first time that a recording featuring the Beatles appeared in a commercial.

Song rights are licensed from music publishers separately from rights in sound recordings, which are usually owned by record companies. Nike had obtained the song rights for "Revolution" from Michael Jackson, who bought the Beatles publishing catalogue from ATV Music for $47.5 million in 1985. Jackson compiled a list of Beatles songs he considered suitable for commercials, excluding personal favorites like "Eleanor Rigby" and "The Fool on the Hill."

In its $15 million false endorsement complaint, Apple claimed that the Beatles' recording agreement granted Capitol-EMI the right to use the Beatles' "goodwill and persona" only in connection with the sale of Beatles recordings and for no other commercial purposes. (Yoko Ono broke ranks with Apple by issuing a statement supporting the Nike commercial as a way to make Beatles music accessible to a new generation.) In February 1988, Nike decided not to exercise its option to use the "Revolution" sound recording.

In May, however, the New York federal court dismissed the Beatles' CD suit on the ground that England was the proper place to bring the claim. But the same month a New York appeals court decided that the Beatles had made sufficient allegations for the fraud and conversion claims in the group's original royalties suit to proceed to trial.

By this time, the Beatles' case had been significantly bolstered by a deposition the group's lawyers took from a former record distributor named Daniel Gittelman. In the 1960s and 1970s, Gittelman owned and operated the Somerset, Massachusetts-based U.S. Records, which distributed to department stores throughout the eastern half of the United States. Gittelman stated in his deposition that for years he received "side benefits" from Capitol in the form of a secret, 8 percent discount, usually as free salable records. Gittelman said that Beatles records amounted to 25 to 30 percent of this product. Asked if Capitol told him not to tell anyone about the arrangement, Gittelman said, "Definitely."

Gittelman later revealed, "A competitor of mine phoned Capitol one day and called their bluff on it. He asked for the discount and they said he could get it."

Settlement talks between Capitol-EMI and the Beatles soon resumed. The discussions were so serious that Leonard Marks announced that a moratorium had been placed on pre-trial discovery in the case.

The negotiations lasted for months. When the settlement came in November 1989, it ended all pending legal disputes among the parties. "What I think eventually broke the lawsuit was the CD issue," Joseph Wheelock said. "Everyone wanted the Beatles CDs out."

"Probably most determinative of the settlement was the adverse publicity that Len Marks was able to develop regarding John LaMonte," Daniel Murdock claimed. "For Capitol, that was very distasteful."

For the Beatles, the deal couldn't have been sweeter. Between November 1989 and early 1996—soon after the Beatles' official video documentary was first broadcast on ABC television and the three *Anthology* CDs of Beatles recording outtakes began to be released— the group reportedly grossed $300 million—far more money than the Beatles earned in all the years before.

EMI appeared to enjoy the settlement benefits, too. For the fiscal year ending March 31, 1996, the record company reported its profits rose 23 percent. What those figures didn't reveal was that EMI had not gotten what it thought it bargained for in the 1989 settlement deal. In 1991, an English High Court ruled that the Beatles could bar the record company from releasing CDs of two Beatles greatest-hits packages known as the *Red* and the *Blue* albums. The High Court also decided that the Beatles could prohibit the sale on CD, or in any new sound recording format, of previously released Beatles albums containing more than 12 songs.

The court's ruling meant EMI had to negotiate yet another agreement with Apple. This one, finalized in June 1993, required EMI to buy back its pre-existing rights to sell the two greatest hits packages in exchange for additional royalty payments to the Beatles of a steep $2.26 per CD. Hoping to recoup some of its costs, Capitol-EMI filed a malpractice suit against its New York counsel, Donovan Leisure Newton & Irvine. Malpractice suits by record companies against outside counsel are rare, but Capitol-EMI felt it had no choice. Capitol-EMI's complaint sought at least $11.6 million in additional royalties that the record company had been obligated to pay the Beatles as well as legal costs for drafting the 1989 pact and litigating against the Beatles over its interpretation.

In April 1996, New York Supreme Court Justice Herman Cahn allowed Capitol-EMI to amend its complaint to state that "at no time were [EMI] and Capitol advised by Donovan Leisure that their clear and unfettered right would be in any way diminished or otherwise adversely affected by their [execution] of the November 7, 1989 agreement." The case would go no further. Within weeks of the ruling, the record company and its outside counsel settled their differences, effectively ending the chain of litigation that had begun in the United States when the Beatles filed their royalties claims 17 years before.

While the Capitol-EMI settlement started money flowing into the Beatles' coffers in unprecedented amounts, it didn't prevent the same dollars from flowing out in large sums for George Harrison, however. Shortly after parting with Allen Klein in 1973, Harrison sought advice from Denis O'Brien, a U.S. trained lawyer who worked as a financial advisor in London.

"I was handling mostly corporate matters when I was asked to help [actor] Peter Sellers, who was in financial trouble," O'Brien recalled. "Peter and George Harrison were good friends. Both had an interest in India and Hinduism. It's through Sellers that I was asked to help George with his financial problems. This was within weeks of George leaving Klein." Harrison became so enamored of O'Brien's financial acumen that he made O'Brien his manager and gave him control of his business affairs—for the next 20 years, until 1993. That's when Harrison said he discovered his finances were in disarray.

O'Brien resigned as Harrison's manager in March 1993. He then supposedly warned Harrison's Los Angeles counsel Bert Fields "that, if Mr. Harrison sued [O'Brien] or forced him into bankruptcy, Mr. Harrison would be ruined."

Harrison nevertheless filed suit in Los Angeles Superior Court in January 1995. He charged O'Brien with being a "faithless and fraudulent manager." Harrison claimed that O'Brien had "enriched himself and lived on a lavish scale at Harrison's expense, buying yachts and villas in various parts of the world, while Harrison suffered enormous losses and liabilities as a result of O'Brien's improper and inept management and deceitful conduct." Harrison admitted in his complaint that the "complicated, Byzantine [business] structure, involving multiple off-shore corporations and other interrelated entities" that O'Brien had set up was "beyond Harrison's understanding."

What Harrison sought from O'Brien was recoupment of half of Harrison's payment of a $20 million-plus loan that the American Express Bank had made to HandMade Films—the languishing film company in which Harrison and O'Brien were partners. (HandMade Films successfully produced movies for the Monty Python comedy troupe but also the poorly received *Shanghai Surprise*, starring then-husband-and-wife Sean Penn and Madonna.)

Harrison said that he had invested in HandMade because O'Brien characterized the company as "essentially a risk-free venture."

O'Brien knew that Harrison could be generous with his money. In 1977, Harrison sent O'Brien a memo directing the distribution of Harrison's assets in the event of the musician's death. Harrison asked that all his copyrights, personal effects, Beatles performing outfits and other memorabilia, and stock he owned in any corporations be given to the Self-Realization Fellowship, a meditation institute in Los Angeles with which Harrison had long been associated. In a hand-written note dated October 5, 1980, Harrison directed that: $200,000 be given to Beatles publicist Derek Taylor and his wife, Joan, and $50,000 to each of the Taylors' children; $100,000 each to Harrison's maids, Mollie and Joan; $80,000 to Harrison's Friar Park, London, estate gardener, Maurice; $100,000 to Monty Python trouper Eric Idle; most of Harrison's song copyrights to his then two-year-old son Dhani; and the balance of any cash and future income to the Self-Realization Fellowship.

In his suit, Harrison alleged that O'Brien had promised to guar-antee half of what Harrison paid of HandMade's debts but avoided telling this to lenders or committing himself on any loan documents. As a result, Harrison had to pay $21,859,280.56, including interest, when the American Express Bank called in its HandMade loan.

O'Brien denied ever representing the film business as a no-risk investment to Harrison. "[H]ad I made such a statement he would never have believed me," O'Brien insisted, "as he personally produced in the early 1970s a film for the Apple Group called *Little Malcolm and His Struggle Against the Eunuchs* which lost 100 percent of its produc-tion costs."

O'Brien argued that HandMade had been structured as a tax vehicle that required Harrison's personal liability for Harrison to take advantage of the tax benefits. By doing so, "George saved himself $30 million," O'Brien claimed. "He didn't pay any U.K. taxes from 1974 through 1992. George may have lost money on the film company, but at the end of the day, he was millions of dollars ahead."

In 1988, HandMade experienced serious collection problems that resulted in the production company filing lawsuits seeking more than

$27 million from half a dozen film distributors. "[Harrison] was most unhappy regarding the litigation," O'Brien said. "Unfortunately, at the height of the problems, he abused with profane language the guests at a party celebrating the 10th anniversary of HandMade Films, attended by more than 240 people, including most of our bankers."

Then, according to O'Brien, Harrison sent termination letters to all of HandMade's employees. "[T]otal chaos resulted," O'Brien claimed, "with even more pressure by the banks to call in their loans." (HandMade Films was sold to the Toronto-based Paragon Entertainment Corp. in 1994 for $8.5 million.)

Harrison got more bad business news in the middle of his litigation with O'Brien. He learned he was in danger of losing the U.S. trademarks for the name and logo to Dark Horse, the record company that Harrison had founded in the mid-'70s.

The Dark Horse trademarks were owned by Loka Productions—the Panamanian corporation at the center of Harrison's business empire. Under U.S. trademark law, a trademark holder must renew a trademark registration every ten years. Harrison had to do so by October 31, 1995, but claimed he was powerless because O'Brien controlled Loka. Harrison's lawyers sought a court order to compel O'Brien to renew the trademarks.

O'Brien once again blamed Harrison for the shaky business affairs. O'Brien's Los Angeles lawyer, Daniel L. Germain, charged, "For some reason, Harrison has refused over the last few years to pay the out-of-pocket expenses for [the offshore] entities. . . . Indeed, many directors have threatened to resign as a result of Harrison's conduct. Harrison has no one to blame but himself."

O'Brien claimed that he lacked control over Loka because he had never been an officer, director, or shareholder of the Panamanian company. In fact, it seemed that neither Harrison nor O'Brien wanted to claim responsibility for Loka. On August 30, 1995, Germain wrote Harrison's Los Angeles counsel, Brian Edwards, "For nearly two years, Mr. O'Brien has attempted to give complete control of the 'offshore' entities to Mr. Harrison. All such proposals were rejected by

Mr. Harrison. . . . Mr. Harrison cannot have it both ways. He cannot force Mr. O'Brien to administer Mr. Harrison's offshore affairs in perpetuity and contend at the same time that he owns no interest in these entities for tax purposes."

Edwards responded on September 20, "We must reject Mr. O'Brien's illegitimate effort to condition a transfer of the marks on Mr. Harrison assuming the burden of dealing with the O'Brien-created offshore structure. As has been stated in rejecting other such proposals by Mr. O'Brien, Mr. Harrison has no duty to take over Mr. O'Brien's problems."

One week before the Dark Horse trademarks were to expire, Los Angeles Superior Court Judge Kathryn Doi Todd ordered O'Brien to either cooperate with Harrison or allow Harrison to proceed with the trademark renewal procedure himself. Judge Todd noted that the 1977 memo from Harrison regarding the distribution of his personal assets, as well as instructions from Harrison to O'Brien to incorporate Loka, demonstrated O'Brien's control over the off-shore company.

By the end of the year, the superior court granted Harrison's request to collect $11 million from O'Brien in the bank loan dispute. But the victory was largely Pyrrhic. First, there was the issue of the creative damage that Harrison suffered while wrapped up in the O'Brien suit. "I've hardly ever picked up the guitar," Harrison said after Judge Todd's decision. Then there was the problem of collecting from O'Brien. "We've got to follow him to the ends of the Earth," Harrison lamented.

At least Harrison knew where to find him. O'Brien, who had extensive experience dealing with banks, now had a new bank title of his own. He was vice-chairman of a division of the Union Bank of Illinois.

Michael Jackson: Dangerous Similarities

The song gave Michael Jackson trouble from the start. Jackson, who likes to record in the dark, was in a Los Angeles studio in September 1990, working on the vocal for the title song of his *Dangerous* album. To make room so he could dance, the normally agile performer tried moving a 7-foot-tall, 60-pound sound baffle. But "it started to wobble in the dark and he didn't know it and it fell over," Jackson recording engineer Bill Bottrell said. "We heard a large bang."

"I turned the lights on and saw Michael trying to get out from under this wall," assistant engineer Brad Sundberg recalled. "I went out to help him. He said he was fine."

Jackson continued to record, but when Sundberg drove him to the doctor the next day, Jackson found out he had suffered a mild concussion. Jackson didn't know it then, but the accident was a doubly bad omen. Two years later, Crystal Cartier, an aspiring singer/songwriter from Denver, Colorado, would file a $40 million copyright infringement suit alleging Jackson stole "Dangerous" from a song with the same title that she wrote. The case became so important to Jackson that when the trial was held, he would testify in court for the first time in nearly a decade.

That Cartier filed suit shouldn't have surprised Jackson, though. Not only was Jackson the frequent target of copyright infringement allegations, but by the 1990s, such claims against major artists had become rampant in the music industry.

The infringement-suit trend—which had been gaining momentum since the 1970s—turned a business created in large part by opening its arms to new, unsolicited talent into a closed shop in which only the most persistent and clever artists—or those willing to pay industry professionals sometimes a stiff fee to circulate demo tapes—could get their material heard by influential industry decision makers. The fear of expensive copyright litigation sealed off nearly every major label, many publishing companies, and numerous artist management firms to those wishing to break into the music business.

A copyright infringement suit involving Michael Jackson's song "The Girl Is Mine" played a significant role in closing the music industry's doors. In that case, Fred Sanford, an Illinois-based musician, had written a song titled "Please Love Me Now." Sanford charged in a $5 million complaint he filed against CBS in Chicago federal court (federal law preempts state courts from hearing copyright claims) that Jackson's song sounded "substantially similar" to his. Sanford had a strong financial incentive for suing: "The Girl Is Mine," a duet with Paul McCartney, had appeared on Jackson's *Thriller*, the best-selling album of all time.

"Substantial similarity" is the primary legal test in a copyright infringement case. Generally, an infringement plaintiff must demonstrate that the defendant had access to the plaintiff's song and that the two works sound legally alike. There is no bright line test, however, for determining what constitutes substantial similarity between song melodies. A copyright plaintiff may bring in music experts, and present song charts and audiotapes for the judge or jury to consider. Harmonies, rhythms, and other elements of the songs can be used for their probative value. But any substantial similarity ultimately is to be determined by a judge or jury based on how the songs impact upon the ears of the average, lay listener.

A copyright defendant can use songs written before either of the compositions in question to show that both the plaintiff's and the defendant's works were derived from a prior common source. That and proof of independent creation are a copyright defendant's main shields against an infringement claim.

Elvis Presley turns his G.I. pay over to his manager, Colonel Tom Parker, upon discharge from the Army in March 1960. (UPI/Corbis-Bettmann)

Film producer Hal Wallis (left) confers with Colonel Tom Parker. (Memphis Press-Scimitar Photo/ Mississippi Valley Collection/ University of Memphis)

Elvis Presley displayed special affection for his mother, Gladys, but he gave his father, Vernon (left), the power of attorney to handle his personal finances. (UPI/Corbis-Bettmann)

Billy Joel at a press conference with his then-manager—but ex-brother-in-law—Frank Weber (right). When Joel filed a $90 million complaint alleging Weber had used him as a "personal bank," Weber complained, "He's sued everybody who's ever had a drink with me." (Vinnie Zuffante/Star File)

Billy Joel and his then-wife, model Christie Brinkley, celebrate with entertainment attorney Leonard Marks (left) at Mark's 50th birthday party at the Tribeca Grill in Manhattan in January 1992. At the time, Marks was representing Joel in Joel's suit against former manager, Frank Weber. Marks also successfully represented the Beatles in their decade-long royalties suit against Capitol-EMI. (Courtesy of Leonard Marks)

Entertainment attorneys Arthur Indursky, Allen Grubman and Paul Schindler (from left to right) in their mid-town Manhattan office. (Carl Glassman)

George Michael (center) leaves the London High Court in October 1993 after observing trial proceedings in his suit to free himself from a long-term recording contract with Sony Music. (Glenn Harvey/Stills/Retna)

Singer B.J. Thomas (left) with his Nashville litigator Sam Lipshie in 1997. For the second time, Thomas—along with Hank Ballard, Gene Pitney and the Shirelles—had sued G.M.L. Inc. and Gusto Records for sound-recordings royalties. (Alan L. Mayor, Photographer)

Gene Pitney performing
in Italy, c. 1961.
(UPI/Corbis-Bettmann)

Chuck Rubin in Nashville
with three of the original
Shirelles—(left to right)
Beverly Lee, Doris Coley
Jackson and Shirley Alston
Reeves—during their
successful royalties trial
against G.M.L. Inc.
(Courtesy of Artists Rights
Enforcement Corp. All
rights reserved)

The mysterious Moe Lytle in
his Nashville office in the
mid-'70s. Lytle began as a
club owner in St. Louis and
became one of the world's
largest independent owners of
hit sound recordings.

Manager Brian Epstein and the Beatles arriving at Heathrow Airport, London, July 8, 1966. Epstein was not the most savvy manager, but after his death the Beatles were unable to manage themselves. (UPI/Corbis-Bettmann)

Linda and Paul McCartney on their wedding day; Linda's daughter from a previous marriage, Heather, is in the foreground. Linda's father and brother would become McCartney's closest business advisors. (Hulton-Deutsch Collection/Corbis)

A smiling John Lennon (back) and Yoko Ono (center right) look on as Allen Klein (center) signs the agreement settling his management dispute with his former Beatles clients Lennon, George Harrison and Ringo Starr. Klein negotiated the "buy/sell" arrangement that was at the heart of the Beatles' royalties fight with Capitol-EMI. (Photograph copyright 1977 Bob Gruen)

Crystal Cartier arrives at the Denver federal courthouse in her stage outfit for her copyright infringement trial against Michael Jackson. The judge ordered Cartier to go home and change her clothes but, she protested, "Michael could sit there wearing makeup, like a chocolate version of Boy George." (The Denver Post)

Dionne Warwick, Stevie Wonder, Quincy Jones, Michael Jackson, and Lionel Richie celebrating at the Grammy Awards, February 25, 1986. Richie and producer Jones would later be copyright suit co-defendants with Jackson. (UPI/Corbis-Bettmann)

Michael Jackson at court in Rome, Italy, in February 1997, after testifying in an infringement case brought against him by singer Al Bano. It would be the fourth infringement suit that Jackson won. (AP/Wide World Photos)

The members of Judas Priest left their trademark leather garb and metal studs at home when they attended the 1990 trial in Reno, Nevada, over alleged subliminal messages on their album, *Stained Class*. (Steve Joester/Star File)

Angry 2 Live Crew leader, Luther Campbell (right)—with group members
David Hobbs and Chris Wongwon (both center left)—on the steps of the federal
courthouse in Ft. Lauderdale, Florida, denouncing a ruling that found the
rappers' album, *As Nasty As They Wanna Be,* obscene. 2 Live Crew attorney, Bruce
Rogow (center), later presented the group's winning argument to the 11th U.S.
Circuit Court of Appeals as well its claim before the U.S. Supreme Court that a
parody of Roy Orbison's "Oh, Pretty Woman," constituted a fair use. (Copyright
The Miami Herald)

Roy Orbison works on a song
at the Nashville office of his
music publisher, Acuff-Rose,
in May 1961, during his early
chart success. Years later, Acuff-
Rose sued Orbison's estate
claiming that Orbison failed to
deliver the compositions
required under his last songwriting contract.
(Joe Horton Studio, Nashville,
Tennessee)

Fred Sanford alleged that he brought a tape of "Please Love Me Now" to a local CBS Records executive. Sanford's lawyer, Jerold Jacover, argued at the December 1984 trial that, despite the fact that CBS claimed to have discarded any tape of Sanford's it might have received, there was evidence from which it could be concluded that Sanford's song had been on the same floor at CBS's offices in Los Angeles at the same time as Michael Jackson. Jackson often visited the CBS building and, Jacover noted, was then behind on his *Thriller* album recording schedule.

Said Sanford: "[M]y tape was sent out by CBS after I'd given it to them. They called and asked if they could send it out to Johnny Mathis—whose office was on the ninth floor of CBS Records. And my tape was supposedly sent out March 11, 1982. And the first time anybody heard Michael's song was March 29, 18 days later. Mine is a duet, his is a duet. And I owned the copyright by six months. So I'm definitely convinced."

But a musicologist testifying on Sanford's behalf admitted that, while the Sanford and Jackson songs were similar, they could have been created independently. The turning point in the trial apparently came when Jackson took the stand. Jackson's general counsel, Los Angeles lawyer John Branca, said that "Michael wanted to show he couldn't be intimidated."

Jackson entered the packed courtroom under tight security. Wearing a yellow sweater pulled over a pin-stripped shirt, he spent four hours on the witness stand. Jackson testified that he woke up one morning, in London in November 1981, and sang the melody and other parts, such as the string arrangement to "The Girl Is Mine," into a tape recorder. Jackson said he was able to recall the time that he composed the song because his driver had been looking for a Thanksgiving turkey.

Clapping his hands and snapping his fingers, Jackson played his work tape for the jury. He sang the melody over some of his other songs to show it was part of his repertoire. Before Jackson left the courthouse, District Judge Marvin E. Aspen brought the entertainer into his chambers to meet Aspen's 15-year-old daughter.

To show prior common sources, CBS attorneys introduced into evidence the song "Longer" by Dan Fogelberg and the themes from the TV shows *Maverick* and *Cheers*.

The jury deliberated for more than 21 hours over two-and-half days before finding in favor of CBS. But according to attorney Jacover: "One of the jurors called me after the verdict was reached, which is practically unheard of. He said he had pangs of conscience, that he might have made a mistake and that he told this to the judge. Initially, the jurors were in favor of Sanford four to two. Then it was three to three. In the last hours of deliberation, Sanford lost. In my opinion, the jury wasn't prepared to make a statement to the world that Michael Jackson was a liar and a plagiarist. Fred Sanford would have won if anyone other Jackson had been involved."

The Sanford suit had a profound effect upon CBS Records. According to Robert Altschuler—then the record company's vice-president of public affairs—CBS in response instituted a strict company-wide policy directing all employees not to accept any unsolicited material. The CBS missive didn't protect Jackson from incoming suits, though. Eve Wagner, Jackson's litigation counsel, said that, at any time, Jackson was involved in at least three and as many as 15 litigation matters.

Wagner had literally gone to the mat for her client. That was in a suit brought by Hugo Zuccarelli, who claimed to have created a 3-D miking system. In his complaint, Zuccarelli alleged that Jackson hurt Zuccarelli's business reputation by giving him credit for use of the 3-D system on Jackson's *Bad* album, then removing the sound effects passages.

A Los Angeles Superior Court judge dismissed Zuccarelli's suit on statute of limitations grounds. "We had just left the judge's bench and were beginning to pack up," Wagner recalled, "when Hugo punched [Jackson lawyers] Larry Iser and Tim Alger in the face. Then he went after me. He shoved me through the courtroom doors and pushed me to the ground. He tried to play his 3-D demo tape for the marshal while he was being handcuffed and dragged away."

The lawyers filed a criminal complaint and Zuccarelli was found guilty of three counts of battery.

Jackson's 1991 *Dangerous* album created a cottage industry of its own in legal claims. According to Eve Wagner, after the album was released, "I believe that Mr. Jackson received over twenty-five demand letters, each of which threatened litigation and several of which demanded a large settlement offer."

Crystal Cartier filed her copyright infringement suit in Denver federal court in June 1992. In it, she named Jackson, his MJJ Productions, and his record company, Sony Music Entertainment (formerly CBS Records), as defendants. Cartier claimed to have written "Dangerous" in 1985 and recorded it at a Denver studio in January 1988 as part of her song "Player." But Cartier couldn't locate the 1988 master tape. The session engineer had not only recorded over it when working with other artists; the studio was no longer in business. Cartier contended that she distributed audiocassette copies of her recording in Los Angeles in July 1990. Then in October 1990, she recorded "Dangerous" in Denver once again, this time for her *Love Story: Act I* album.

Music expert Jim Mason confirmed to Cartier's lawyers that Jackson's song sounded "more than accidentally similar to Ms. Cartier's." Both songs were in D-minor, both recordings contained urban sound effects and rap passages, the bass and drum patterns were similar, and the word "dangerous" was repeated in the third measure of each song's chorus.

But Mason also admitted that "[Cartier's] song was similar to yet another song. [Santana's "Evil Ways," according to both Mason and a music expert for Jackson.] And I said, 'You know, if this whole thing keeps going, there could be a whole string of people because'—and I made reference to the fact that I think that every song is reminiscent of yet another song to somebody at some time."

Jackson's lawyers asked the court to dismiss Cartier's suit without holding a trial. They argued it wasn't until Cartier learned from court documents that Jackson's songs had been recorded in September 1990 that "she alleged, for the first time, that she had delivered demonstration tapes containing her song 'Dangerous' to various entities in Los Angeles, California in July 1990." But in November 1993, Denver federal Judge Edward Nottingham denied Jackson's summary judgment motion. He ruled that a jury should hear the case because "reasonable people could differ as to whether the two versions of 'Dangerous' are substantially similar."

Nottingham scheduled the trial for February 7, 1994. He had his own doubts, however, about Cartier's claim. Picking up on an analysis of the two songs in an affidavit submitted by defense expert D. Anthony Ricigliano, Judge Nottingham noted among the differences in the compositions that, while both Cartier and Jackson utilized high-pitched vocal patterns, the former used an "oooh oooh" while the latter employed an "ee hee."

Jackson's next legal maneuver was to try to have the Cartier trial delayed. On December 30, 1993, Jackson's Denver law firm, Holme Roberts & Owen, filed a motion for a continuance. The lawyers pointed out that a civil suit had recently been filed against Jackson in Los Angeles on behalf of a 13-year-old boy who alleged that Jackson sexually molested him. The molestation trial was set to begin February 21. In addition, criminal child molestation investigations involving Jackson were underway in Los Angeles and Santa Barbara counties. Jackson's lawyers claimed that the molestation matters would interfere with their ability to communicate with Jackson on the Cartier case and with Jackson's ability to appear at trial in Denver.

On January 6, Judge Nottingham turned down Jackson's continuance request. Nottingham said he wanted to await a determination of whether there would be a criminal molestation trial, too.

Meanwhile, "there was a press report that Michael offered Crystal a five-figure sum to settle," Jackson's Denver co-counsel Richard Gabriel said. "But the only offer we made was to waive the right to ask the court to award us attorney fees if she would drop the case, which she didn't." Jackson did settle the civil molestation suit in January, reportedly paying at least $15 million to end the action. California prosecutors later announced that no criminal molestation charges would be filed but left the case open pending the expiration of a six-year statute of limitations.

Jackson had an unrelated copyright infringement hurdle to overcome before the Cartier trial began. In a Los Angeles suit, songwriters Robert Smith and Reynaud Jones charged Jackson, his father Joseph, Jackson songwriters Rod Temperton and Lionel Richie, and record producer Quincy Jones with stealing musical motives—brief phrases—from six of the plaintiffs' songs. Smith and Jones alleged that these motives appeared on Jackson's recordings "The Girl Is Mine," "Thriller," "Another Part of Me," and "We Are The World." The latter was a superstar charity recording for the USA for Africa Foundation, to fight famine in Ethiopia. The foundation was also named a defendant in the suit.

Reynaud Jones had lived in the same Gary, Indiana, neighborhood as the Jackson family and claimed to have given songs to Michael as early as 1977. Co-plaintiff Smith contended that he put "the tape of my song in [Michael's] hand, after his father asked me to deliver songs to Los Angeles for a duet album for [Michael's brother and sister] Randy and Janet."

Smith's and Jones's Los Angeles lawyer, Howard Manning, said that profits on the songs in question could be "conservatively estimated at $750 million." Manning's clients wanted a whopping $250 million in damages. Defense lawyer Robert Rotstein, counsel to Jackson's insurer, the Fireman's Fund, said the plaintiffs wanted $20 million to settle the case. Jones claimed that Jackson offered the plaintiffs $100,000 to settle. Smith and Jones didn't accept.

The district court sided with Jackson in a pretrial ruling. The court found that Smith and Jones failed to present sufficient expert evidence to rebut a defense claim that several of the musical motives in question were scènes à faire, ones so common that they weren't copyrightable.

But this wasn't a garden-variety infringement action. Smith and Jones also charged Jackson with violating the federal Racketeer Influenced and Corrupt Organizations Act (RICO). The RICO statute requires plaintiffs to establish by a preponderance of the evidence that defendants have engaged in an illegal enterprise made up of a "pattern of racketeering activity." Smith and Jones claimed that the allegedly unauthorized dissemination and marketing of the musical motives at issue in their case constituted mail and wire fraud. The district court dismissed the RICO claim, however, on the ground that copyright infringement couldn't serve as a basis for establishing racketeering activity.

The Jackson defendants won the final phase of the case, too. In January 1994, a Los Angeles federal jury unanimously concluded that there was no substantial similarity between Jackson's songs and the plaintiffs' three remaining compositions. Reynaud Jones later complained that the judge's instruction to the jury "was worded in such a manner that they were asking did Michael fully take our entire song and that wasn't the issue. Michael took passages—several passages of our song." In June 1996, however, the 9th U.S. Circuit Court of Appeals affirmed the lower court ruling.

Jackson did not testify in person but did submit a deposition videotaped in Mexico City in November 1993. After finishing the deposition, Jackson had publicly stated that he was canceling the remaining dates on his international *Dangerous* tour to seek help for an addiction to medically prescribed painkillers.

Crystal Cartier grew up in Denver, where she sang in church and school choirs. A military services veteran with a college degree in marketing, Cartier formed the Love Story band in the mid-'80s and played the Colorado club circuit. A few days before her infringement trial against Michael Jackson began, she told the Denver weekly newspaper *Westword*, "I don't know if he knew it was my song at the time he made his decision to rape it, but he damn sure knew that it wasn't his."

Cartier was being represented in her case by Robert and Gretchen Eberhardt, a Denver-based father/daughter team who practiced estate, personal injury, corporate, and real estate law. Cartier hired the Eberhardts because—she said about Jackson's industry clout— "anyone connected with the music business was afraid to take my case." The elder Eberhardt, a tall, slender attorney with a narrow face, had served as a legislator in the Colorado House of Representatives. Gretchen Eberhardt, new to the legal bar, had a wholesome, farm-girl look that contrasted with the mechanical tone with which she spoke. Cartier apparently became dissatisfied with the Eberhardts' legal work prior to trial. "The weekend before, Crystal was quoted in the press as saying something like, 'Here I am, stuck with Ma and Pa Kettle,'" Jackson co-counsel Richard Gabriel recalled.

Judge Nottingham's courtroom was located on the second floor of the federal courthouse in downtown Denver. A former federal prosecutor with a quick temper, Nottingham ran a tightly controlled courtroom, and had a reputation for lecturing attorneys and witnesses who appeared before him. During the Cartier trial, he frequently lectured the Eberhardts on how to proceed with their case.

In his opening statement, Robert Eberhardt honed in on Michael Jackson's alleged access to Cartier's song. Eberhardt told the eight-member jury that, when Michael Jackson brought his *Bad* tour to Denver in the summer of 1988, Cartier and her sister, Antoinette Harris, got backstage and gave Jackson's road manager, Benjamin Collins, a copy of Cartier's "Dangerous" demo. Eberhardt also said that one of Cartier's stops on her July 1990 trip to Los Angeles included Warner-Chappell, the music publishing company that for many years administered Jackson's Mijac Music song catalogue. Cartier brought a promotion package of her "Dangerous" demo and "Queen Size Lover/Michael" single to Ed Pierson, in Warner-Chappell's legal department, Eberhardt claimed. Pierson had been a Denver music lawyer before joining Warner-Chappell and Cartier's package contained letters of reference from people in Denver who knew Pierson. "I think that's the key to the case," Eberhardt told the jury, "because Mr. Pierson runs the business office and the legal department for Warner-Chappell."

Jackson's lead counsel, Daniel Hoffman, a former University of Denver law school dean, told the jury in his husky voice that over 200 songs with the title "Dangerous" had been registered in the Copyright Office. Cartier registered her "Dangerous" in July 1991; Jackson his in February 1992. But Hoffman argued that the date of recording, rather than the date of registration, was more important for purposes of the infringement suit.

"Crystal Cartier has an obsession about Michael Jackson," Hoffman declared. "She fantasizes about Michael Jackson. These fantasies and obsessions relate directly to the case." Cartier had written a novel titled *Immortal Obsession* that featured a character named Michael the Meek (a vampire). Hoffman noted that Cartier proposed to cast a film of the book with Jackson in the Meek role and herself as high priestess.

Cartier was the first witness to testify at trial.

"Crystal, how many times have you been married?" Robert Eberhardt asked the heavy-set black woman with the sultry voice.

"Five," Cartier answered.

"I'll listen to background concerning her music. I'll listen to material relating to development of the song, but we're not going to have a life history," Judge Nottingham warned crisply.

"Your honor, I was going to bring out the fact that three of her husbands were named Michael," Eberhardt responded. "There were opening remarks that she was somewhat excited about Michael [Jackson]."

Cartier testified that during her July 1990 trip to Los Angeles, she stopped at Motown Records hoping to see Smokey Robinson—who she claimed she had met before—but he wasn't in. At Epic Records, the Sony Music label for which Jackson recorded, Cartier said she dropped off a copy of her demo tape and a letter for Jackson.

Ed Pierson was out of the office the day Cartier brought her demo package to Warner-Chappell, but she claimed Pierson subsequently called and said he would see if he could help her. Cartier said she gave her last copy of the "Dangerous" demo tape to Roger Christian, an A&R executive at WTG Records, another Sony Music subsidiary label. "That was the last tape I had. That was my personal master copy that I ran copies from," Cartier insisted, adding that she never received the tape back.

Cartier also testified that she first heard Jackson's "Dangerous" on the radio in the middle of the night in November 1991, while working on *Immortal Obsession*. "I was devastated," she said. "I couldn't believe what I was hearing."

"What were your feelings?" Robert Eberhardt asked.

"Hurt, really hurt. I mean, smashed. . . . And confused. Confused."

Daniel Hoffman asked Cartier during a heated cross-examination whether any pre-October 1990 version of her "Dangerous" existed.

"I said there's no version . . . on tape," Cartier answered. "Now, if you're talking about the chord charts, I can't attest to that without having those lyrics here in front of me. I'd have to see them, unless you want me to lie." (The defendants successfully blocked Cartier from introducing lyric and chord charts of her 1988 "Dangerous" recording and a 1992 re-creation tape into evidence.)

"I don't want you to lie. I want you to tell the jury the truth. The truth is, you don't know," Hoffman said.

"Your honor, she just answered the question," Robert Eberhardt objected. "Now he's putting words in her mouth."

"Objection's overruled," Nottingham decided.

When Hoffman posed the question again, Cartier admitted that she didn't know whether any prior identical versions existed. She also admitted that she didn't know whether there was any direct evidence that Michael Jackson or Jackson arranger Teddy Riley had heard her "Dangerous" demo before Jackson recorded his version.

Hoffman questioned Cartier about the letter she submitted to Jackson in July 1990. "Were you seeking money from Michael Jackson, as an investor?"

"Yes, I was. Support."

Hoffman read aloud from Cartier's *Immortal Obsession*. Like Jackson, Michael the Meek had a "private, sprawling, palatial and extremely eccentric estate. [His] many fabulous toys and pets rival even Disneyland."

"Isn't that what you said?" Hoffman asked.

"Taken in proper context, yes," Cartier replied.

"Did I read it incorrectly?"

"You're trying to take it out of context—as usual."

Hoffman noted that Cartier's proposed cast for turning *Immortal Obsession* into a movie included Diana Ross as the queen—"Billy Dee Williams, Mel Gibson, Denzel Washington, Madonna," Cartier continued.

"Look under directors and special effects. Does it say 'George Lucas, Steven Spielberg, John Carpenter, John Singleton' and then 'assistant director or consultant, Crystal Cartier'?"

"And above that, sir, it says, 'creative options are indicative of similar abilities desired,'" Cartier shot back.

"Fine. Below it says, 'Screenplay by Crystal Cartier and Stephen King'?"

"In question marks besides Stephen King, 'someone of Stephen King's stature,' 'cause I could never pull it off all by myself."

"And this was done before there was any dispute with Michael Jackson?"

"That's correct."

The next morning Hoffman probed what Cartier meant when, in a previous statement, she admitted about her 1988 demo, "When I heard it, I was like, 'Eek, this isn't what I had in mind.'"

Cartier insisted that she had meant the recording was not radio-play quality. Hoffman hammered in that, although Cartier had been dissatisfied with the tape, she nevertheless claimed to have used it to seek a recording contract. Hoffman also had Cartier acknowledge that the promotional letter she distributed to record companies in July 1990 (for her "Queen Size Lover/Michael" single) failed to mention her "Dangerous" demo.

Cartier's sister, Antoinette Harris, didn't help Cartier's case. Harris testified that she couldn't remember whether the Jackson road manager to whom Cartier claimed to have given the "Dangerous" demo at Jackson's 1988 Denver concert had been a man or a woman, Afro-American, Caucasian, or Hispanic. (Benjamin Collins, the *Bad* tour production manager, was a strapping black man with a gravelly voice who stood well over six feet tall.)

Kris Farris, Cartier's music expert, testified that rhythmic structures and melodies in the Cartier and Jackson songs were identical. Farris said he had once been an assistant to Paul Rothchild, who produced The Doors. Now, Farris was a construction worker.

Michael Jackson's counsel moved for a directed verdict after Cartier's lawyers finished presenting her case. A trial judge can grant a directed verdict if a party presents a case insufficient for a jury to consider. But Nottingham ruled the jury should hear the evidence Michael Jackson had to offer.

Jackson's lawyers called recording engineer Bill Bottrell, who had received co-writer's credit on Jackson's "Dangerous." Bottrell explained how he developed the song's musical bed by isolating a bass line in the composition "Streetwalker," which Jackson once planned to use on the *Bad* album. Jackson then wrote the "Dangerous" lyrics and melody, Bottrell said.

Bottrell testified that it was Jackson's policy not to listen to unsolicited tapes. To illustrate, he told how he had asked legendary Motown tunesmith Lamont Dozier—a co-writer of many of Motown's biggest hits—to send songs for Jackson to consider. The Jackson 5 had launched its career on the Motown label and Bottrell's idea was to re-establish those musical ties for Michael. When Bottrell brought Dozier's tape to the studio, Jackson "kept a wide berth around the tape. He wouldn't walk near it," Bottrell said. "I put the tape away and had an assistant call Mr. Dozier and say, 'Well, it probably isn't going to work out.'"

D. Anthony Ricigliano, head of music theory at the Manhattan School of Music, then testified that he believed the Cartier and Jackson songs had been created independently. During Ricigliano's testimony, Richard Gabriel complained that Cartier was distracting the jury. "She's shaking her head, doing all kinds of body language, making faces and shrugging, throughout the trial," Gabriel said.

Judge Nottingham told Cartier, "[I]f you can't control yourself any better than you're doing it, I'm telling you the next time you will be watching the proceedings—or listening to them—from the marshal's office upstairs."

The day the trial opened, *The Denver Post* quoted Michael Jackson's publicist as saying the proceeding "was not on [Jackson's] schedule." But Jackson flew into Denver on Sunday, February 13, on a Sony corporate jet. Cartier used the occasion to show up in court Monday morning dressed for the heightened media presence. Warner-Chappell's Ed Pierson was testifying at the time.

Pierson said he had been on his honeymoon when Cartier dropped her tape off at his Los Angeles office. When he returned, Pierson found Cartier's tape in his mail pile but claimed he threw it away without listening to it.

As Pierson spoke, Cartier bustled in, breasts protruding from the top of a low-cut, black-leather mini-dress. She sported fishnet stockings and spiked heels.

"That's the one day Crystal arrived in front of the courthouse in a limousine," Jackson litigation counsel Eve Wagner said. "And there we were, having to sneak Michael in through the judge's parking lot."

"When Cartier walked in, the whole jury stopped looking at me; I knew something was going on," Ed Pierson recalled.

Cartier admitted, "I didn't want to be totally upstaged by Michael or look like a frumpy old school teacher. I wore one of the costumes from my 'Dangerous' video, which had been playing on TV all week."

Judge Nottingham ordered Cartier to cover herself with a coat. Jackson then stepped into the courtroom. Some of his fans obtained seats in the spectator section by pretending to be lawyers or court staff. Judge Nottingham's teenaged son sat among them.

For his first court appearance since the 1984 "The Girl Is Mine" trial, Jackson wore eyeshadow, black pants, and a black shirt decorated with orange epaulets. His hair was in a ponytail, a trademark tendril brushing his face.

"Could you tell us [how old you were] when you started composing music?" Daniel Hoffman asked.

"Probably since the age of seven," Jackson softly replied.

"Could you tell us how old you [were] when you had your first song published?"

"Fifteen."

"Could you tell us approximately, Mr. Jackson, how many songs you've written to date?"

"In general, a couple of hundred," Jackson replied with a nervous laugh.

"And approximately how many of those songs have been released to the public?"

"Fifty, 60."

"How many songs, Mr. Jackson, were in the *Bad* album?"

"I think nine."

"And how many songs did you write for the *Bad* album that were not published?"

"I wrote probably 60, 70 songs for the *Bad* album that weren't published."

"How many songs did you write for the *Dangerous* album that were not released to the public?"

"[I] think 70 songs."

"Did your song 'Dangerous' evolve out of any previous song that you had composed?"

"Yes. I wrote a song for the *Bad* album called 'Streetwalker' and it had a strong driving bass lick. And that bass lick was taken by my engineer because I was kind of frustrated with the song in general. So he took the bass and put new chords to the bass melody, which is what inspired the song 'Dangerous.'"

"Could you describe for us, Mr. Jackson, the process and sequence of events which you use in composing songs generally?"

"Well, usually when I write songs I vocally, I orally use a melody into a tape recorder. For instance, with the song 'Streetwalker' . . . the base melody went [he sings while tapping his foot and snapping his fingers]. I take that bass lick and put the chords of the melody over the bass lick and that's what inspires the melody or the other sounds that I'm hearing in my head."

"You said you hear things in the song, the melody you hear in your head?"

"For instance, when creating the song 'Billie Jean,' I was riding in my car and it started with the bass lick again, which goes [he sings the bass part]. And on top of that I hear the chords. [He sings the chords.] Then the melody: [singing] 'She was more like a beauty queen, from a movie scene. I said, Don't mind if I do. You mean, I am the one.'

"And the lyrics, the strings, the chords, everything comes at that moment, like a gift that is put right into your head. And that's how I hear it."

"You just start singing the lyrics?"

"Absolutely. When I said, 'Billie Jean is not my lover,' I didn't think about it, it just came. It all dropped in my lap at once. And I loved it. So I drove home fast and I got on the microphone and put things down. Then I went into the studio, got the musicians over and gave them all their parts. That's how that was created. Same thing, you know, with other songs I create."

"By the way, do you read music?" Hoffman asked.

"No I don't. I don't think it's necessary."

"Did anyone in the world assist you in writing the lyrics to 'Dangerous'?"

"No."

"Mr. Jackson, who wrote the vocal melody to your song 'Dangerous'?"

"I did."

"Who named the song 'Dangerous'?"

"I did."

"Approximately how many hours, by the way, went into creating the song 'Dangerous' from . . . when Bottrell gives you the tape with the bass lick [with drum sounds and chords]?"

"For that one, I would say, maybe three weeks, just listening to it every once in a while and letting the melody create itself by hearing the chords and the bass lick, you know? And not dictating how it should be. Just letting it kind of form itself."

"Did you ever in your life hear of a person named Crystal Cartier before this lawsuit was filed?"

"No."

"Did you ever hear a song written by Miss Cartier called 'Dangerous' before this lawsuit was filed?"

"Never in my life."

Hoffman asked Jackson to recall the day he had recorded "Dangerous" in the studio.

"It was kind of a funny day," Jackson began. "Not really funny, but, I usually sing in the dark because I like to feel everything and I usually don't like people lookin' at me, unless I'm on stage. And so all the lights were off. And right before I started singing, this huge wall fell on my head. And it made a loud banging sound—it hurt. But I didn't realize how much it hurt until the next day. I was kind of dizzy. It's pretty much on the tape."

Hoffman instructed that the tape be played in court. Jackson shook and bobbed his head while he listened. Robert Eberhardt requested a bench conference. "That's what I call terrible body language, and to the jury," Eberhardt complained to Judge Nottingham.

"Well, what I observed was going to the rhythm. I didn't observe any kind of signaling or disagreeing." Nottingham said. "What I had reprimanded Ms. Cartier for is signaling the witness, which she did, and indicating disagreement with other witnesses' testimony."

Jackson continued by noting that he had asked arranger Teddy Riley to "update the sounds, to give it more of a, uh—hate using the word 'hip-hop'—but it had a hip-hop kind of modern feel where you could do all the new dances to." This included changing the sound of the bass and adding a "driving" snare that "had some anger," Jackson explained.

Jackson sang a section of "Another Part of Me," from his 1987 *Bad* album, to demonstrate how he had used the same melody for a section of "Dangerous."

Hoffman asked about Jackson's policy regarding unsolicited tapes.

"Well, I don't take any unsolicited tapes because I know the danger involved. I mean, what happens when you do something like that, it's this situation—"

"—Hold on," Hoffman interrupted, "Just answer my question. What is the policy?"

"The policy: I do not take unsolicited tapes. No way. Everybody knows that. That's the number one rule."

Gretchen Eberhardt asked Jackson during cross-examination to review the transcript of the deposition he gave for the case. Eberhardt wanted to establish that Jackson had then been unable to remember the name of the song from which he said that Bill Bottrell had taken the bass line for "Dangerous."

Eberhardt also questioned Jackson about who had access to his vault of studio tapes. When Jackson offered a detailed response, Judge Nottingham scolded, "Mr. Jackson, just answer the question."

"I'm just trying to tell her the situation—"

"—Just answer the question."

"I'm answering the question."

"You're not."

"Trying."

"You're failing."

Jackson let out a giggle. Gretchen Eberhardt then had both the Jackson and Cartier "Dangerous" choruses played in court.

"Now Mr. Jackson, do you hear anything similar in those four bars played together?" Eberhardt asked. (Both songs' choruses had strong similarities.)

"Well, we're both saying 'dangerous,'" Jackson replied, biting his lip.

"Do you hear any notes in common?"

"Not that I can think of."

"Does it sound to you, Mr. Jackson, like you're singing in harmony together?"

"Not to me."

When Jackson finished testifying, Judge Nottingham turned once again to Crystal Cartier. "Miss Cartier, your dress is inappropriate for court," Nottingham reprimanded. "Go home and change clothes. Right now."

Michael Jackson reportedly left the courthouse laying between the back seats of a gray van.

Outside the courtroom, Cartier complained, "For him this is a tax-deductible business expense. For me, it's my entire career on the line.

"The judge threw me out for the way I was dressed, but Michael could sit there wearing makeup, like a chocolate version of Boy George."

In closing statements the next morning, Robert Eberhardt told the jury that Cartier's "ultimate dream" was the release of her *Love Story: Act I* album. But, he said, "all her dreams were shattered" when she heard Michael Jackson's "Dangerous" on the radio.

Daniel Hoffman said, "You can decide, when she strolled in 20 minutes after court convened, in her entertainment outfit, if that wasn't an attempt to upstage Mr. Jackson and if that is part of her obsession.

"You must determine whether this represents fantasizing beyond all reality. She has every right to be a dreamer. But there comes a point at which you step out of reality."

Cartier stormed out while Hoffman spoke. She stayed away, too, when the jury delivered its verdict that afternoon. After deliberating less than four hours, the jurors decided that Michael Jackson hadn't infringed on Crystal Cartier's song.

"I just couldn't take it anymore," Cartier said. "One day it was David against Goliath. Then when Michael came to town, I went from being David to being the Wicked Witch of the West. They were starstruck. I had a nervous breakdown."

Cartier appealed to the 10th U.S. Circuit Court of Appeals with new lawyers, but the appeals court ruled against her. In 1997, Jackson again testified in a copyright infringement case, this time fighting a claim that his song, "Will You Be There"—also from his *Dangerous* album—infringed on singer Al Bano's hit "I Cigni Di Balaka (The Swans of Balaka)." In January 1998, a three-judge panel in Rome issued a ruling that absolved Jackson of the charges, which included criminal liability.

After her trial against Jackson, Cartier married for a sixth time and became a producer of public-access TV talk shows. She also continued to insist that Michael Jackson stole her song. "I'm not out to destroy Michael. I think he's a fabulous performer and I forgive him," she said, sobbing. "But until he does right by me, nothing will go right for him. That's not me. That's his karma."

The 2 Live Crew:
Nasty Accusations

nock. Knock.

A smiling Nick Navarro rapped on the door of the federal courtroom in Ft. Lauderdale, Florida, in a spirited mood.

"Open up. It's the sheriff," a television reporter chimed in.

Arriving for closing arguments in a suit filed against him by Miami rap group the 2 Live Crew, the dapper Broward County Sheriff was just where both critics and supporters said he wanted to be: at the center of a high-profile legal proceeding making front-page news around the world.

For the first time, a federal court was considering whether the lyrics of a music group met the legal test for obscenity. In 1966, the U.S. Supreme Court upheld obscenity convictions for the mail-order sale of a mostly percussion instruments album titled *Erotica* and a spoken word record of the works of French poet Pierre Louys. But in the spring of 1990, as rap music spread from urban black youth to mainstream, white America, police around the country were marching into records stores and warning retailers they could be arrested for selling the 2 Live Crew's misogynistic brand of party rap.

Drawn by the 2 Live Crew's graphic references to oral, anal, and sadomasochistic sex, law enforcement officials had turned the rap group's tall, black, gap-toothed leader, Luther Campbell, into the most high-profile entertainer to defend his work against recurring obscenity accusations in a quarter of a century—at least since comedian Lenny

Bruce had been prosecuted—and broken in spirit—for lacing his stand-up routines with profanities.

The 2 Live Crew sued Sheriff Navarro after Navarro's deputies took a copy of an order, issued by a Broward county judge, to local record retailers. The judge had concluded in an *ex parte* hearing (i.e., neither the 2 Live Crew nor their lawyers were present) that there was probable cause to believe the rap group's *As Nasty As They Wanna Be* album was obscene. Navarro's deputies then warned retailers that they could be jailed for selling *As Nasty* even to adults. The 2 Live Crew claimed this amounted to an unconstitutional prior restraint of speech and asked for a declaration that *As Nasty As They Wanna Be* wasn't obscene at all.

The Ft. Lauderdale trial wasn't the first over the 2 Live Crew's music. In June 1988, Tommy Hammond, the white co-owner of the record store Taking Home the Hits in Alexander City, Alabama—a religious, family-oriented town with a population of 14,000—sold an audiocassette of the 2 Live Crew's *Move Somethin'* to a police officer. (The album contained lyrics like "Open your legs, put 'em in the buck/'Cause that's the way I like to fuck.") Hammond kept 2 Live Crew tapes behind the counter and claimed he never listened to the album. But police seized all of Hammond's 2 Live Crew stock as well as recordings by other rap artists. Alexander City Police Chief Ben Royal then had Hammond charged with violating the city's obscenity ordinance.

Luther Campbell claimed the Hammond incident smacked of racism. "Royal was aware that the same tapes were available in the local black record stores, but . . . as long as the 'jungle' music stayed where it belonged, the chief was not interested in the least."

A municipal judge fined Hammond $500 at a brief hearing in a courthouse down the street from Hammond's store. The amount was small but the conviction set off alarm bells in the music industry. Hammond appealed the fine in a four-day jury trial.

The U.S. Supreme Court had said that, in obscenity cases, "the best evidence is the material, which 'can and does speak for itself.'" So the local prosecutor played the entire *Move Somethin'* album for the Alexander City jury.

To be obscene under U.S. Supreme Court guidelines, a work has to depict or describe patently offensive sexual conduct. And, looked at in its entirety, the work must: appeal to prurient interests (i.e., be capable of arousing lustful thoughts) from the perspective of the average person, applying contemporary community standards; and lack serious artistic, literary, political, or scientific value from the perspective of a reasonable person, applying a national standard. A work that withstands any part of this test is not legally obscene.

Tommy Hammond's expert witnesses, New York *Newsday* critic John Leland and Rhodes scholar and cultural influences expert Carlton Long, traced the development of rap music to show it had artistic value. In addition, Hammond's lawyers had police officers read sexually explicit excerpts from novels such as Philip Roth's *Portnoy's Complaint* that had been obtained from the public library.

Lyle Shook, a sexual crimes specialist who taught criminal justice at Auburn University, testified that the lyrics on *Move Somethin'* were too repulsive to be sexually exciting. "If the jury is aroused by these lyrics, then there probably are 12 sex offenders right here," Shook said.

On February 22, 1990, the jury deliberated just over an hour before voting to acquit Tommy Hammond. Alexander City may have been in the middle of the Bible Belt, but Hammond defense counsel Bobby Segall noted, "Conservative Southerners don't like a lot of governmental interference."

The 2 Live Crew controversy occurred during an upswing in obscenity prosecutions in general. "We're definitely in the middle of an anti-obscenity boom," observed Martin Garbus, who had been Lenny Bruce's lawyer. The political liberalism of the 1960s and the lifestyle excesses of the 1970s had given way to the Moral Majority agenda of the Reagan era. The growth of the home video industry in the 1980s reactivated antipornography advocates and, in 1986, the

Meese Commission—named for Reagan's U.S. Attorney General Edwin Meese—promised stricter enforcement.

The music industry became easy prey after the Parents Music Resource Center (PMRC)—whose founders included Susan Baker, wife of then-Secretary of State James Baker, and Tipper Gore—convinced the latter's husband, Senator Albert Gore, to hold hearings in Washington, D.C., in 1985 to examine music lyrics. The PMRC claimed it wanted to convince record companies to voluntarily sticker albums with content labels.

By 1989, Jean Dixon, a Missouri state representative, had introduced a mandatory labeling bill to require a prominently displayed sticker if an album mentioned bestiality, drug use, explicit sex acts, morbid violence, or suicide. Though Dixon's proposal was defeated, by the time she reintroduced it in 1990, similar legislation was being considered in over 20 states. To head off forced labeling, the major record companies agreed in March 1990 to voluntarily implement a "Parental Advisory—Explicit Lyrics" album sticker.

But rock albums began to be hauled into court as early as 1987. The opening volley took place in a Los Angeles Municipal Court, where Jello Biafra, lead vocalist for the punk rock group the Dead Kennedys, and Michael Bonanno, the former general manager of Biafra's Alternative Tentacles record company, were charged with distributing harmful material to a minor. The obscenity charges were filed over a poster of a painting by Swiss surrealist H.R. Giger inserted in the Dead Kennedys' *Frankenchrist* album. The poster depicted disembodied male and female sex organs engaged in intercourse. The charges were brought after a 14-year-old girl purchased a copy of *Frankenchrist* for her younger brother.

Nine police officers searched Biafra's San Francisco apartment for two hours and, according to Biafra's roommate, Suzanne Stefanac, a freelance journalist then researching the PMRC, "they tore the place apart." "I felt it was a DEA drug raid or something," Biafra said. "I was scared for my life."

Biafra claimed the poster's message—that people "were bent on screwing each other"—reinforced the album's social protest songs.

When the jury voted seven to five for acquittal, the judge dismissed the charges.

But the trial took its toll on the Dead Kennedys, which broke up in part due to the obscenity charges. Said Biafra, "What they're really trying to do with an action like this is not necessarily to send me to jail or fine me $2,000, but put my band and my label out of business so we can't make any more records like this. My punishment [was] being meted out even before the jury [made] any decision."

The 2 Live Crew's Luther Campbell grew up in Miami's Liberty City ghetto. The youngest of five brothers, Luther was born in December 1960 at Mount Sinai Hospital on Miami Beach. His father, Stanley, who was Jamaican, worked as a janitor; his mother, Yvonne, was a beautician who suffered from rheumatoid arthritis. Luther's father preached the need for his sons to get ahead. "There was no such thing as an excuse like I'm black, too poor or too large or too ugly or anything," Luther said. "We had to look my father in the eyes and say, 'I have tried my best. I can't do it but I will keep trying until I do, sir.'"

For his public education, Luther was bused to white, upper-middle-class schools on Miami Beach, though he admitted, "I didn't learn to read until I was a junior [in high school]." After graduating from Miami Beach High, Luther worked as a groundskeeper at a golf course and in the kitchen at Mount Sinai Hospital. But he already had his eye on the music business. After his mother bought a stereo system with money she won at jai-alai, Luther began entertaining neighbors by setting up the equipment in his backyard while his parents were at work.

"Luther used to shake up the neighborhood and have walls rattling all up and down the street, but nobody complained," his mother said.

Luther also sold audiocassettes that he made from his father's reggae album collection and hung around the popular urban-music radio station WEDR, studying the disc jockeys' colorful styles. While working at Mount Sinai, Luther spun records with the Ghetto

Style DJs at dances on weekends. Soon, he was booking gigs and promoting shows at area clubs, bringing in rap acts like the Fat Boys and Run-DMC.

The Ghetto Style DJs were fueled by a massive, bass-heavy sound system. Using prominent bass lines in the mix, Luther recorded the single "Throw the D"—based on a lewd dance—with the 2 Live Crew, a California rap group he had booked in Miami. He also adopted the nickname Luke Skyywalker, a play on a central character in the *Star Wars* films. Released in 1986 and sold from the trunk of Campbell's car, "Throw the D" sold over 200,000 copies without radio play or a major distributor.

The 2 Live Crew followed with the sexually explicit albums *2 Live Is What We Are* and *Move Somethin'*. Both sold more than 500,000 copies. With the release of *Move Somethin'*, Luther's Luke Skyywalker Records began stickering the rap group's recordings with "Warning: Explicit Language Contained."

On New Year's Day 1990, attorney Jack Thompson was having dinner at the Miami home of his friend, conservative radio talk-show host Mike Thompson. Jack Thompson—a Christian Evangelical who taught Sunday school at the same Key Biscayne church once regularly attended by Richard Nixon—had become an antipornography activist after helping get a divorce for a woman who was raped by her husband.

Mike Thompson had obtained a transcript of songs from the 2 Live Crew's *As Nasty As They Wanna Be* album from the American Family Association, a religious fundamentalist organization based in Mississippi. When he showed the transcript to Jack Thompson that New Year's Day, the Miami attorney saw the 2 Live Crew's lyrics as "a clarion call to the sexual brutalization of women."

Jack Thompson picked up the phone and called a local record store. "I was stunned that they were selling that trash to children," he recalled. The lawyer quickly set up a "sting" by accompanying a 16-year-old boy to three Miami-area record stores to purchase 2 Live

Crew product. Jack Thompson wanted to get officials in Dade County, which included Miami, to pursue Luther Campbell and his rap group.

Twenty years earlier, Thompson would have probably been hailed a hero by his home county. At that time, a Dade County jury found Jim Morrison, lead singer of the rock group The Doors, guilty of indecent exposure and using profanity at a Miami concert. In 1975, a Dade jury decided that the film *Deep Throat* was obscene. But by 1990—with its multiethnic mix of large black, Hispanic, and Jewish populations—Dade County had become Florida's most culturally sophisticated county. Jack Thompson had run as the Republican opponent against Dade County State Attorney Janet Reno, a Democrat, and lost by a wide margin. He was unable to get Reno to clamp down on the 2 Live Crew.

But Jack Thompson had already sent the 2 Live Crew's lyrics to law enforcement officials in 67 Florida counties and the governors in all 50 states. Luther Campbell claimed that Thompson was motivated by political retribution, though Thompson claimed otherwise. "A lot of people don't realize it, but all of this started a couple of years ago because one of my groups put out a record in favor of Janet Reno," Campbell said. "[Thompson] has been after me ever since."

In October 1988, on Florida's southwest coast, Lee County Judge Issac Anderson had ruled there was probable cause to believe the *Move Somethin'* album was obscene. Now, in February 1990, Judge Anderson responded to Jack Thompson's campaign by ruling there was probable cause to believe *As Nasty As They Wanna Be* was obscene. That didn't alarm Luther Campbell because, he claimed, Lee County was "a hick area where there were no sales going on anyway."

More troubling was a February 22 letter from Florida Republican Governor Bob Martinez, who was up for reelection, to statewide prosecutor Peter Antonacci. The letter asked for an investigation, as Thompson had demanded, of whether the lyrics of the 2 Live Crew or other groups violated state obscenity and racketeering statutes. "It is appalling to think that recordings that a judge has already determined may be obscene are readily available to minors throughout Florida," Martinez wrote.

Antonacci concluded in a March 6 letter to Martinez that any 2 Live Crew probes should be handled by local officials. But, according to Campbell, record stores throughout the state had already begun to pull the 2 Live Crew's records off the shelves.

Broward County Sheriff Nick Navarro had a reputation for seeking the spotlight. He even offered his department as the launching pad for the TV reality show *Cops*. Navarro, born in Cuba, moved to Miami in 1950 and worked as a Miami-Dade patrolman and a Federal Bureau of Narcotics agent. In 1971, he was appointed to head the Broward Sheriff's Office Organized Crime Bureau. He was elected county sheriff in 1984.

When Navarro received Jack Thompson's *As Nasty As They Wanna Be* letter, he gave it to his consultant, William Kelly. Kelly was a retired FBI agent who once specialized in obscenity matters under Bureau Director J. Edgar Hoover. Focus on the Family, a fundamentalist group based in Pomona, California, also had sent a set of *As Nasty* lyrics to Kelly in November 1989. But "[i]t was Thompson's complaint that caused the case to be opened," Kelly acknowledged.

With much of its growth resulting from white flight from Miami, Broward County was more conservative than its next-door neighbor to the south, Dade. William Kelly denied, however, that the decision to go after the 2 Live Crew was racially motivated. He noted that Judge Isaac Anderson, the Florida judge who first found the 2 Live Crew album obscene, was black. What couldn't be denied was that there had long been racial tension between South Florida's blacks and Hispanics. From the 2 Live Crew's perspective, it didn't help that Navarro was Hispanic.

The Broward Sheriff's Office sent Sgt. Mark Wichner, a detective in its Organized Crime Division, to make an undercover buy of an *As Nasty As They Wanna Be* audiocassette from a local Sound Warehouse record store. The double album, with already a million copies sold, featured songs like "Me So Horny," "Bad Ass Bitch," and "The Fuck

Shop." (By comparison, the 2 Live Crew's sanitized alternative, *As Clean As They Wanna Be*, had sold just over 200,000 copies. Luther Campbell liked to point to the *As Clean* album as proof that *As Nasty As They Wanna Be* was intended for adults.)

Wichner took the audiocassette, an affidavit, and a transcription of six *As Nasty* songs to Broward Circuit Judge Mel Grossman. On March 9, 1990, Judge Grossman issued a probable cause obscenity ruling for the 2 Live Crew album. In a reference to community standards, Grossman emphasized that "as avid a First Amendment proponent as *The Miami Herald* . . . stated in an article appearing in its February 28, 1990, edition that 'Many of 2 Live Crew's lyrics are so filled with hard-core sexual, sadistic and masochistic material that they could not be printed here, even in censored form.'"

Navarro's deputies brought copies of Grossman's order to area record retailers and told them they could be arrested for selling the 2 Live Crew album to either minors or adults. "It was like Mafia stuff," Campbell claimed. *As Nasty As They Wanna Be* soon disappeared from Broward County stores.

A week after Judge Grossman ruled, the 2 Live Crew filed suit against Sheriff Navarro in Broward federal court. But governmental obscenity warnings were already spreading across the United States. By April, a Pennsylvania county district attorney announced that *As Nasty* was harmful to minors; a Tennessee county district attorney declared *As Nasty*, and *Straight Outta Compton* by rappers N.W.A, may be obscene; and officials in a Georgia county warned retailers not to sell labeled albums to minors. Retailers in Ohio and Indiana were warned, too.

In Florida, Dade County State Representative Willie Logan introduced legislation to require Florida retailers to stock sound recordings that were harmful to minors out of customers' sights. Logan decided to push the proposal because "I heard my godson singing 'Me So Horny.' He was five years old."

The 2 Live Crew hired Bruce Rogow, a professor at Nova University Law Center in Ft. Lauderdale, to be its obscenity counsel.

Rogow once taught Campbell's entertainment attorney Allen Jacobi at the University of Miami. Tall and trim, with an Abe-Lincoln-like beard and a penchant for bowties, Rogow had represented black demonstrators in the deep South during the civil rights movement in the 1960s. A free speech specialist, he had also represented Nazis and members of the Ku Klux Klan. "The theme that runs through my cases is that the government is on the other side," Rogow said.

When Jacobi brought Luther Campbell to Rogow's house to talk, Rogow told Campbell "even if you lose [the suit against Navarro], you'll be so well known that you'll make a fortune." But Rogow also described the Broward Sheriff's use of Judge Grossman's probable cause order as "holding the record hostage. They've placed it in jail."

But Navarro's deputies had long been bringing similar probable cause orders to county pornography establishments. "We used to serve those orders every day," Navarro remarked.

Rogow saw political motivations in the obscenity charge as well. "The key to the 2 Live Crew thing was that there was a Republican governor—the first in the state for years—and a Republican sheriff—Navarro—outsiders looking for something to distinguish themselves."

This wasn't the first time Navarro and Rogow faced each other in court. When Navarro switched from the Democratic Party to the Republican Party shortly before the 1984 sheriff's election, Rogow represented the Democrats in an unsuccessful bid to force Navarro off the ballot.

After he filed suit for the 2 Live Crew, Rogow visited Navarro's office. "I told him, 'you better watch out, this could be trouble for you,'" Rogow said. "Navarro had the tape jumping out of his hand, joking 'It's hot!'"

Under federal law, a judge, rather than a jury, would hear the 2 Live Crew's suit. That's because the group asked for "equitable" relief—an injunction to stop the Broward Sheriff's probable cause practice—rather than for monetary damages. But Sheriff Navarro wanted a jury to decide whether the *As Nasty As They Wanna Be* album was obscene and, on March 27, he filed suit in state court against the 2 Live Crew.

Navarro may also have been hedging his bets in case he lost. "[He] may want the dispute in state court because, under Florida procedural rules, opposing parties can't request attorney fees," said Robyn Blumner, executive director of the American Civil Liberties Union in Florida.

The federal trial began in Ft. Lauderdale on May 14, 1990. Presiding U.S. District Judge Jose Gonzalez, Jr. was a moderate appointed to the federal bench by President Jimmy Carter. As the trial opened, Navarro's lawyer, John Jolly, called Sgt. Wichner to the stand to explain the chain of events that led up to Judge Grossman's probable cause ruling being brought to record retailers. Under cross-examination by Rogow, Wichner, who said he was a ZZ Top fan, claimed the Sheriff's Office had received numerous complaints about the 2 Live Crew. But Rogow noted the Sheriff's Office file contained only newspaper articles and a published letter from a Broward woman who stated that the 2 Live Crew was entitled to First Amendment protection. The only complaint came from Jack Thompson.

John Jolly then had the *As Nasty As They Wanna Be* album played in its entirety. While "Me So Horny," "Put Her In The Buck," and other album cuts blared through the courtroom, Gonzalez stared at the ceiling, took notes, and rubbed his eyes. He also studied the reaction of courtroom spectators, their initial giggles fading as the double-album set of songs played on. Afterward, Gonzalez said he had belonged to one of the college fraternities the 2 Live Crew made fun of on the album.

After a lunch recess, Jolly questioned the 2 Live Crew's gravelly-voiced David Hobbs (aka Mr. Mixx) about *As Nasty As They Wanna Be*'s liberal use of sound recording samples from artists like Jimi Hendrix, Kraftwerk, and Van Halen. Jolly's line of attack was that the 2 Live Crew did nothing more than record drum beats and obscene words over the samples to make the *As Nasty* album. "Anyone can sample 'Voodoo Chile' and add dirty lyrics, but that doesn't make Luther Campbell a Jimi Hendrix," Jolly said.

When Jolly asked Hobbs if the band obtained permission to sample the snippet of dialogue from the film *Full Metal Jacket* that formed the basis for "Me So Horny," Rogow objected. Sustaining, Gonzalez told Jolly, "You're saying that something borrowed from something else can't be art and that's not the issue here."

Crew member Mark "Brother Marquis" Ross testified that the rap group's lyrics were "telling the girls what I want to do with them . . . social science."

When Jolly asked Ross if he thought that the 2 Live Crew's lyrics were "knee-slapping stuff," Ross said yes. Ross also claimed "anything I do with my band is art because I am an artist."

Jolly then told Judge Gonzalez that "the hatred toward women on the tape offends community standards." But Rogow pointed out that Jolly produced no expert witnesses to show the 2 Live Crew album appealed to prurient interests. Without that, the album was "presumed to be art," Rogow said.

The 2 Live Crew's lawyers called on Emili Douthitt, who had conducted a survey of Broward record retailers on behalf of the ACLU. Douthitt testified that she contacted 42 Broward record stores and that only one continued to sell the 2 Live Crew album after receiving notice of Judge Grossman's probable cause ruling.

To paint a picture of community standards, the 2 Live Crew's lawyers handed Judge Gonzalez adult books and magazines with titles like *California Creamin'* and *Naked Stranger*. The materials were purchased in Broward County, some near the federal courthouse. The lawyers also played video excerpts from the raunchy comedy of Andrew Dice Clay and Eddie Murphy's *Raw*. Gonzalez then watched a portion of the locally obtained X-rated video *Teasers*. "It's made to turn you on," 2 Live Crew lawyer, Allen Jacobi, said of the X-rated film. "2 Live Crew does not turn you on." (The *Teasers* video would be missing when the rap group's lawyers retrieved their files from the court clerk.)

Clinical psychologist Mary Haber testified for the 2 Live Crew that patients she had asked to listen to *As Nasty As They Wanna Be* found the album boring, not sexually exciting. Or, as Luther Campbell put it, "She says that she has never had one patient tell her that he gets a stiffie from rap. . . . It's hard to laugh and get a hard-on at the same time."

To establish artistic value, Greg Baker, a music critic for the weekly Miami newspaper *New Times*, testified how hip-hop music, of which rap was a part, had started in New York 15 years before. It began as a subgenre of rock and entered the mainstream in 1979 with the Sugar Hill Gang's "Rapper's Delight," followed by "Rapture" by the rock group Blondie. Hip-hop emphasized lyrics and rhythm over melody and often used sampling, Baker noted. The 2 Live Crew's "Throw the D" was the first major rap record from Miami and the group pioneered the use of humor in hip-hop, Baker explained.

"Let me see if I understand correctly," John Jolly said on cross-examination. "The line 'Put your lips on my dick and suck my asshole, too/I'm a freak in heat, a dog without warning/My appetite is sex, because me so horny'—you consider that to be a significant artistic achievement, don't you?"

"Yeah, I think that's pretty good writing," Baker replied.

"You think it's the lyrical zenith of the album?"

"Boy, there's so many, I would hate to—"

"I don't have any additional questions," Jolly said.

The second and final day of trial opened with John Leland, the *Newsday* critic who testified on behalf of Tommy Hammond in Alabama. Leland discussed the history of hip-hop and rap and noted that Frank Sinatra arranger Nelson Riddle had said that "music is sex." Leland cited the Beatles' "Why don't we do it in the road?" and Jimmy Buffett's "Why Don't We Get Drunk and Screw" as examples. Leland said he believed *As Nasty As They Wanna Be* had serious artistic value because "I think that hip-hop represents a really strong musical revolution and that [by using heavy bass lines] 2 Live Crew have accomplished an innovation within the genre of hip-hop."

Carlton Long—another expert from the Hammond trial—was asked to give cultural and literary perspective to the 2 Live Crew's music. Long, who is black, explained how call and response—a back and forth chant between a leader and a group—dated back to West Africa. He also said that "doing the dozens"—a game of one-upsmanship developed during slavery—often contained sexually explicit words.

Outside the courthouse during a lunch recess, Luther Campbell headed up a parking ramp toward his car. Would he continue to record *As Nasty*-type lyrics if Judge Gonzalez found his album obscene? "It wouldn't affect the type of lyrics we use," Campbell replied. "We'll use them as long as our albums sell."

Sheriff Navarro made his first appearance at trial that afternoon, though he did not testify. In closing arguments, John Jolly character-ized the lyrics on *As Nasty As They Wanna Be* as an "abomination," "venom," and "dehumanizing." He quoted Bob Dylan's "Subter-ranean Homesick Blues" to defend the Sheriff's Office's lack of expert witnesses. "You don't need a weatherman to know which way the wind blows," Jolly told Judge Gonzalez. Navarro's attorney concluded by saying that the 2 Live Crew album had "a good beat, you can dance to it, but the court should give it a zero; it has no value whatsoever."

As Jolly concluded his summation, 2 Live Crew member Mark Ross appeared to be napping.

Bruce Rogow emphasized that adult materials could be bought "at the same place as *The New York Times* [which] should give you an idea of community standards." He added that Eddie Murphy's *Raw* could be obtained at the local Blockbuster video store. "[Y]ou don't have to be an adult. . . . If anything, the evidence in this case is overwhelming that the community standard of the average person in this community is a tolerant one."

Nick Navarro, Jack Thompson, and Luther Campbell all were present when Judge Gonzalez issued his decision on Wednesday, June

6, 1990. "He had the marshalls lock the courtroom doors, and he made us sit there and read the ruling," Bruce Rogow recalled.

Gonzalez sided with the 2 Live Crew on the prior restraint issue. The 18-day gap between Judge Grossman's *ex parte* probable cause ruling and the filing of Navarro's adversarial state court suit against the 2 Live Crew had left "the [rap group's] rights to publish presumptively protected speech . . . twisting in the chilling wind of censorship," Judge Gonzalez wrote.

But Gonzalez nevertheless found *As Nasty As They Wanna Be* obscene. Gonzalez claimed, "Neither the 'Rap' or 'Hip-Hop' musical genres are on trial" but he noted that "a central characteristic of 'rap' music is its emphasis on the *verbal* message.

"It cannot be reasonably argued that the violence, perversion, abuse of women, graphic descriptions of all forms of sexual conduct, and microscopic descriptions of human genitalia contained on [*As Nasty As They Wanna Be*] are comedic art. The specificity of the descriptions makes the audio message analogous to a camera with a zoom lens." Gonzalez's ruling made sale of *As Nasty* illegal in three south Florida counties: Dade, Broward and Palm Beach.

Rogow, who had been certain the 2 Live Crew would win, said, "It was the only time I've felt that a case has been taken from me."

On the courthouse steps, a furious Luther Campbell called Gonzalez's decision "toilet paper. He threw it to the ground and stepped on it," Navarro said. Campbell took a potshot at Jack Thompson, too, who was being interviewed nearby for TV. "He told me right on camera to go get some pussy!" Thompson said.

After midnight Friday, June 8, the 2 Live Crew defiantly sang songs from *As Nasty As They Wanna Be* at a concert the group gave at the trendy Club Nu on Miami Beach. Women from the audience joined the band onstage to engage in simulated sex. Luther Campbell squeezed one woman's breast in time to the music. The show ended when Campbell pushed a woman, who had begun stripping, to the ground, dumped water on her, and left the stage to a cheering crowd. Police in attendance made no attempt to arrest band members.

"So far I have yet to receive even one phone call from a citizen complaining about 2 Live Crew," Miami Beach Commissioner Bruce Singer said.

On Saturday afternoon, June 9, a group of protesters rallied briefly outside Jack Thompson's Coral Gables home, until police dispersed them because they did not have a permit. Inside, Thompson faxed U.S. Attorney General Richard Thornburgh for help. "I have had to stand alone on this for so long in the face of nonfeasance by state and federal law enforcement," Thompson claimed.

Thompson was fuming over the federal trial proceedings. Even though Gonzalez had found *As Nasty As They Wanna Be* obscene, "Navarro took a dive," Thompson charged. Thompson wanted Navarro and John Jolly to present expert witnesses at trial, but "Jolly wouldn't return my phone calls," Thompson said. "By not using expert witnesses, Navarro and Jolly made Gonzalez's ruling reversible on appeal."

Jolly, meanwhile, called Thompson's communications to him during the trial "hate faxes."

Charles Freeman owned the small E. C. Records store in Ft. Lauderdale. As soon as Judge Gonzalez handed down his ruling, Freeman announced to the press that he would ignore the *As Nasty* ban. On Saturday morning, Broward Sheriff's Detective Eugene McCloud, a black officer working undercover, purchased the *As Nasty* album in Freeman's store. He then handcuffed and arrested Freeman, who was also black, on a misdemeanor obscenity charge. A group of deputies rushed in and confiscated all of E.C. Records' copies of the 2 Live Crew album.

Freeman's friends bailed him out of jail on a $100 bond later that day. "As long as these hundred-dollar bills keep coming, I'm going to keep selling this record," Freeman proclaimed. "I'm going to sell *As Nasty As They Wanna Be* until the Supreme Court says I can't. I'm not being brave. It's just the same thing you would do if you went into a store, and they told you you can't buy underwear and socks."

On Saturday night, the 2 Live Crew performed two concerts at Club Futura in Broward County. Concertgoers were frisked, walked through a metal detector, and required to sign a document stating they were aware that explicit language would be used. The heavy police presence included City of Hollywood officers and Broward Sheriff's deputies.

During the early show, which had been advertised as "clean," the 2 Live Crew let the mostly teenaged audience shout the "dirty" lyrics. At the late show, the rap group performed the sexually explicit versions of songs from *As Nasty As They Wanna Be*. The rappers also led the crowd in chants of "Fuck Navarro" and "Fuck Martinez."

When Luther Campbell and 2 Live Crew member Chris Wongwon left the club after the concert, a dozen police vehicles followed and pulled the rappers' car over several blocks away. Campbell and Wongwon emerged with their hands in the air and were arrested for violating a ban on obscene performances. (An arrest warrant later was issued for the 2 Live Crew's Mark Ross. David Hobbs, who worked the turntables but didn't rap, wasn't charged.)

Campbell could be seen in TV coverage of the arrest wearing a Luke Skyywalker T-shirt. In May, a Los Angeles judge had ordered Campbell—in a trademark suit filed by *Star Wars* director George Lucas—to stop associating himself with the Luke Skyywalker name. "We were going to settle that case for $200,000," Campbell counsel Allen Jacobi said. "But when Luther was seen on national TV with that shirt, it cost us an extra $100,000."

Law enforcement officials acted swiftly in the wake of Judge Gonzalez's obscenity ruling. Within days, authorities in North Carolina, South Carolina, and Virginia declared *As Nasty As They Wanna Be* obscene. In San Antonio, Texas, vice detectives canvassed the city's record stores asking retailers to sign a statement that they would remove *As Nasty As They Wanna Be* from store shelves. On June 28, police arrested Dave Risher, the owner of Hogwild Records & Tapes in San Antonio. In Dallas County, the district attorney filed obscenity charges against Sound Warehouse, the first aimed at a corporate retail chain. And in Toronto, where in May police had monitored for lewdness—but not stopped—a Madonna concert, officers also told retailers to stop selling the *As Nasty* album.

"Record retailing has become a high-risk profession," the ACLU's Robyn Blumner said. "You do it now and you're on the edge of criminality."

On Monday, June 11, the 2 Live Crew filed an appeal to Judge Gonzalez's ruling with the 11th U.S. Circuit Court of Appeals in Atlanta. The same day, "Me So Horny" was mysteriously broadcast for the first of several days over the Broward Sheriff's Office radio band.

The record industry had historically been split between the smaller, independent labels that found and nurtured new talent and the major companies that often raided the independents' rosters. The music obscenity furor split the record industry even further. The major labels claimed they were too busy fighting mandatory record-labeling legislation to focus on the 2 Live Crew's obscenity concerns. The independent labels, the first to develop rap acts, charged the majors wanted no part of what was seen as a problem limited to a fringe of black rappers. And only a few artists, such as Sinéad O'Connor, spoke out in defense of the 2 Live Crew's free speech rights.

"The shame of it is that industry organizations have fallen far short of their responsibilities," complained Bryan Turner, president of Priority Records, the label that distributed N.W.A's "Fuck Tha' Police," also targeted by anti-rap reformers. "The majors have to realize they're not untouchables. They need government approvals for some of their [media] businesses."

It took Judge Gonzalez's ruling for the music industry's big guns to act. Soon after the decision was handed down, the Recording

Industry Association of America, an organization of the major labels, announced it would help with the 2 Live Crew's 11th Circuit appeal. The National Association of Recording Merchandisers offered some legal aid to retailers. And Bruce Springsteen gave Luther Campbell permission to use the melody from his song "Born in the U.S.A." for Campbell's *Banned in the U.S.A.* (prompting Jack Thompson to announce that "Bruce and Luther can go to hell together").

But these efforts paled in comparison to the resources of the highly organized conservative right. Wrote *The New York Times* music critic Jon Pareles, "In the end, it may not matter whether the cases against the 2 Live Crew hold up, because the machinery for restricting music is now in place. . . . [T]heir opponents have learned how to garner headlines, silence concerts and scare records off the shelves."

Charles Freeman's trial began on October 1, 1990. Freeman was represented by Bruce Rogow and ACLU lawyer Milton Hirsch. The six white jurors—five of them women and all over 40—had been chosen from a jury pool of 35 registered voters, of which only one was black.

Broward County Judge Paul Backman granted a defense request to bar assistant state attorneys Pedro Dijols and Leslie Robson from referring to the Gonzalez obscenity ruling. He did so because the federal trial involved a civil "preponderance-of-the-evidence" standard, a lower burden of proof than the "beyond-a-reasonable-doubt" standard in Freeman's criminal case.

Dijols and Robson had the *As Nasty As They Wanna Be* album played at high volume for the sullen jurors. Arresting officer Detective McCloud was the prosecution's only witness.

When Freeman's lawyers tried to introduce, for community standards purposes, locally purchased recordings by rap artists Ice Cube and the Geto Boys and pornographic videotapes and magazines, Judge Backman ruled the materials were irrelevant. The defense then brought in psychologist Mary Haber and music critics John Leland and Greg Baker, all who testified before Judge Gonzalez.

But on October 3, the jurors voted to convict Freeman. Never before had a jury found a retailer guilty of obscenity based on the sale of a music recording.

"They don't know a goddamn thing about the ghetto!" Freeman yelled when the verdict was read.

"This verdict sends a clear message to the record industry that they better stop distributing obscene records that degrade women," Jack Thompson warned. "If they don't, it will be a short trip up the distribution food chain to the board rooms of the major record labels."

Charles Freeman was spared a one-year jail sentence but fined $1,000. He closed E. C. Records after falling behind in rent. When a state circuit judge overturned his *As Nasty* conviction in 1993, Freeman had little to cheer about: He was serving an 18-year sentence in federal prison for selling crack cocaine.

Luther Campbell, Chris Wongwon, and Mark Ross arrived at the Broward County Courthouse less than one week after the Freeman obscenity verdict to face the criminal charges from the Club Futura show. The band members used the same legal team that had represented them during the federal trial: Bruce Rogow, Allen Jacobi, and Jacobi associate Randolph Strauss. Freeman prosecutors Pedro Dijols and Leslie Robson represented the government. The serious, intense Robson was born in Hong Kong and brought up in England; Dijols, a misdemeanor division supervisor accustomed to handling DUI matters, had volunteered to work on the 2 Live Crew case.

Judge June Johnson, who usually presided over DUI hearings, angered Luther Campbell by including *As Nasty* lyrics in the charges she read to potential jurors. Campbell burst from the courtroom, demanding, "What the fuck is this shit? What the hell is she doing, man?" But a kindergarten teacher in the jury pool claimed she frequently heard language worse than that.

The 2 Live Crew's lawyers attacked Florida's jury selection process. The use of registered voter lists, with a higher proportion of white than black residents, resulted in racial inequity, they claimed.

But with three defendants on trial, Judge Johnson utilized a pool of 70 potential jurors—twice that for the Freeman trial.

The racial bias issue resulted in a bizarre confrontation. When Dijols moved to keep a black truck driver who liked the 2 Live Crew's music off the jury, Rogow claimed, "[Dijols] wants him off the jury because he is black, knows his music and wears an earring."

"I am being accused of racism. That's unbelievable," Dijols exploded. "Let the record reflect that I am a black man from Puerto Rico!"

Judge Johnson allowed the exclusion.

It took a week to choose the two-man, four-woman jury. The jurors ranged in age from their twenties to their seventies. They included the mother of a condominium-crowd entertainer, a retired sociology professor, a diesel engine mechanic who liked The Doors, and a retired cook who was black. The 24-year-old foreman was an office clerk with a bachelor's degree in music who said he belonged to the same church as Jack Thompson.

The prosecution's chief piece of evidence was a poorly recorded audiotape of the 2 Live Crew's Club Futura concert that had been made by Detective Eugene McCloud. Further hindering the prosecution's case was a ruling by Judge Johnson that a transcript of the tape, which included detectives' comments about the show, couldn't be admitted as evidence. But Johnson did allow the prosecution to play songs from the *As Nasty* studio album. She also ordered that no one under age 18 be permitted in the courtroom.

Detective McCloud testified for five hours. While he did, Pedro Dijols positioned himself at a mixing board, starting and stopping the Club Futura audiotape for McCloud to explain what he heard and saw at the concert. The Broward County detective methodically and graphically offered testimony like "What the band is saying here is 'This is the way we like to fuck.'"

Robson asked McCloud to describe the women dancing on stage. McCloud, who said he was embarrassed, replied, "They were dancing like they were screwing."

When McCloud finished, the jurors asked Judge Johnson if they could laugh. "You can respond whatever way you want," Johnson answered. The jurors immediately burst out laughing.

"That's your verdict right there," Campbell said. "My music is supposed to make you laugh."

"I laugh when I convict people," countered Pedro Dijols.

Detective Debbie Werder, who had also been at the Club Futura show, tried to explain what was on the concert tape but had to ask for repeated replays because she was having trouble deciphering the words.

Mark Ross allegedly clutched a woman's breast on stage. Robson asked Werder, "What happened to the breast?" The jury responded with laughter and Robson had to ask for a recess when one of the jurors couldn't stop.

The defense called two witnesses to testify: music critic John Leland and Henry Louis Gates Jr., an English professor at Duke University whose *The Signifying Monkey: A Theory of African-American Literary Criticism*, had won an American Book Award.

Gates testified that "one of the sad things about black culture"—mirrored in many rap songs—was that it tended to be "sexist against women and homophobic." But Gates said that the 2 Live Crew's music had taken "one of the worst stereotypes about black men primarily, but also about black women"—"that we are oversexed and hypersexed individuals in an unhealthy way"—"and blown them up."

Prosecutor Leslie Robson collapsed at the end of the day but was released from a hospital that night.

On October 20, 1990, the jury unanimously acquitted Luther Campbell, Chris Wongwon, and Mark Ross of the obscenity charges. One reason was that the jurors believed the arrests had been made in retaliation for the 2 Live Crew's "Fuck Navarro" chant.

In addition, jury foreman David Garsow said, "We agreed with what [Gates] said about [the 2 Live Crew's lyrics] being like Archie Bunker making fun of racism."

"The big mistake we made was to let the jury get used to the 2 Live Crew's lyrics," Dijols admitted. "The shock value wore off real quick."

"Dijols and Robson weren't a team," Bruce Rogow said. "He had a sense of humor. She was like Marcia Clark in the O.J. Simpson case, unyielding and rigid. I think she lost the jury early on."

Dijols confirmed that he and Robson met with Sheriff Navarro before trial and considered dropping the charges, based on the poor quality of the concert recording evidence. Navarro was "no religious fundamentalist; he left it up to us," Dijols said.

Jack Thompson accused Dijols and Robson of "unethical conduct" and "intentionally throwing the case," though Dijols claimed "we ignored him." Thompson also sought a mistrial by accusing jury foreman Garsow of perjury for claiming "phony Christian affiliations and activities."

Garsow had said he was a member of the Key Biscayne Presbyterian Church, but Thompson charged that Garsow hadn't attended for two years. Garsow, who was HIV-positive, responded that he hadn't been to the church in several months because "there was a problem with the church wanting me not to be a member any longer due to my homosexuality."

But Jack Thompson's war over the 2 Live Crew's music was, in any case, beginning to lose steam. In November 1990, Dallas law enforcement officials dropped the obscenity charges against Sound Warehouse, though they did extract a promise that the record chain would no longer sell the *As Nasty* album. In December, prosecutors in San Antonio dropped the charges against record store owner Dave Risher.

In January, members of the rock group Too Much Joy were acquitted, after a two-day jury trial before Judge Johnson, of performing several *As Nasty As They Wanna Be* songs at an August show at Club Futura. Just before they were arrested, the band members had played the Bobby Fuller Four rock classic, "I Fought The Law."

The 11th Circuit overturned Judge Gonzalez's ruling in May 1992. Noting the 2 Live Crew had offered unrebutted expert evidence at trial, the appeals court said, "We reject the argument that simply by listening to this musical work, the judge could determine that it had no serious artistic value." The U.S. Supreme Court later refused to hear Navarro's appeal.

By then, Jack Thompson had turned his wrath from the 2 Live Crew to gangsta rap and participated in the fight against Time Warner over Ice-T's "Cop Killer." Sheriff Navarro ran into trouble when a Florida court ordered him to close a crack cocaine manufacturing facility he set up to help in reverse sting operations. Caught in a matrix of administrative problems, Navarro was voted out of office in a low-turnout election held the week after devastating Hurricane Andrew slammed into South Florida. But "the 2 Live Crew debacle created the atmosphere that ultimately brought Navarro down," Bruce Rogow said. "The adverse publicity was so bad; the press cut him no slack."

When Luther Campbell later threw a record company party aboard a rented yacht, the security coincidentally was provided by a service that Navarro founded after leaving the Sheriff's Office. "One of the security guys says, 'Let's take a picture and make sure to give a copy to Nick.'" Campbell smiled.

Judas Priest: Suicide Mission

Judge Jerry Carr Whitehead scheduled the pretrial conference at the Washoe County Courthouse in Reno, Nevada, to dismiss the suit. Judge Whitehead was about to rule that the freedom of speech provided by the First Amendment protected the heavy metal band Judas Priest and its label, CBS Records, from responsibility for the suicide deaths of two Reno youths. The youths' families had alleged that clearly audible lyrics on the Judas Priest album *Stained Class* prompted 18-year-old Raymond Belknap and 20-year-old James "Jay" Vance to each pick up a shotgun, point it at his head, and pull the trigger.

"The judge told the attorneys for both sides that he wanted to see us in his chambers at five o'clock on a Friday afternoon," Belknap family counsel Kenneth McKenna recalled. But when McKenna arrived, "it was like a wake for our case," he said. "It was obvious that Judge Whitehead did his research and that the free speech issue prevented us from going forward."

"But I had indications that week that there might be subliminal messages on the Judas Priest album," McKenna continued. "Earlier that day I called William Nickloff, our audio expert in Sacramento, and told him that I've only got a few hours to know whether there's subliminals on the album or not. Nickloff said he had found them and he faxed me an affidavit. The affidavit resurrected our case on the spot."

What followed—in the summer of 1990—was the first trial ever on whether rock lyrics could be legally liable for suicide. The subliminal message that Nickloff said he discovered was the bare words "Do it" on the *Stained Class* recording "Better by You, Better Than Me." But, "Do what?" asked Judas Priest general counsel Elliot Hoffman. "Even if the words *were* on the record, they never said what it was anyone was supposed to do."

Raymond Belknap and Jay Vance were the best of friends. They met in junior high school in the Reno suburb of Sparks and had lots in common. They both had unhappy home lives, grew up using alcohol and drugs, and quit high school after tenth grade. The pair also had frequent run-ins with police and dreamed of becoming mercenaries. They even talked about "obtaining semi-automatic or automatic weapons . . . and committing mass murder," Jay said.

Blond-haired Jay was an only child whose biological father refused to claim him as his own. Jay's mother, Phyllis Vance, underwent counseling for frequently hitting her son. Jay hit her, too. One time, he tried to choke his mother while she drove him in her car. Other times, he chased after her with a hammer or a loaded pistol and hit her with his fists. Jay ran away from home more than a dozen times. His stepfather, Tony, was a compulsive gambler with a drinking problem.

The gangly, red-haired Raymond had been physically abused by his stepfather, Jesse Roberson, one of four men Raymond's mother, Aunetta, a card dealer at a Reno casino, would marry. To toughen up, Raymond studied karate and collected weapons, including a sawed-off 12-gauge shotgun, a .22 rifle, and a pellet gun.

By their mid-teens, Raymond and Jay had become hardcore fans of Judas Priest. The music group formed in Birmingham, England, in the early 1970s and, by the early 1980s, worked its way to the center of the heavy metal movement. Heavy metal music drew an audience that was overwhelmingly white, male, and under 24 years of age. Judas Priest combined the wailing vocals and biting lead guitars of Led Zeppelin with the lyrical cynicism of heavy metal progenitors Black Sabbath. Dressed in leather, metal studs, and spiked armbands, Judas Priest laced its lyrics and videos with images of violence and destruction.

"Jay recited those lyrics like scripture," the short, stout Phyllis Vance said. "Me and Tony would be watching TV out in the living room and he'd be listening to Judas Priest in his bedroom so loud that *even through his earphones* we couldn't hear the TV. And if I'd go in and tell him to turn it down, he'd point that finger at me, just like [Judas Priest lead singer] Rob Halford, and scream, 'ON YOUR KNEES, AND WORSHIP ME IF YOU PLEASE!'"

In December 1985, Raymond Belknap was fired for refusing to work overtime on his production job at a Sparks printing shop, where he held the midnight to 8 a.m. shift. He had previously been fired from a job at a used-furniture store for stealing money to pay for a trip to Oklahoma to see his natural father. Raymond was currently on probation for that offense.

On December 23, Raymond accompanied his four-year-old sister, Christie Lynn, to the Happy Looker hair salon for her first haircut. While there, he had his long hair significantly trimmed for the first time in years. Aunetta Roberson then drove her son over to pick up Jay Vance. Jay had entered a drug and alcohol rehabilitation center that summer but failed to finish the program. He worked part-time as an assistant at a bindery but hated the job.

At Raymond's house, Raymond and Jay drank beer and listened to Judas Priest albums in Raymond's bedroom. This was a treat for Jay, whose girlfriend had talked him into getting rid of his Judas Priest records. Raymond and Jay then began arguing over some marijuana that Jay thought Raymond had stolen from one of Jay's friends.

Raymond decided it was time to give Jay his Christmas present— a new copy of Judas Priest's *Stained Class* album. Originally released in 1978, *Stained Class* was an album that Jay, who had several Judas Priest body tattoos, especially loved. The cover featured a metallic figure with a laser beam piercing its skull, with a dark substance flowing from one eye. The album contained songs like "Beyond the Realms of Death" and "Heroes End."

Jay became so engrossed with listening to *Stained Class* that when Raymond tried to play an album by Southern rockers Lynyrd Skynyrd, "I remember that there was a big, I think, exchange of—You know, we were yelling and screaming and arguing about it," Jay said.

When Jay's parents stopped by to pick him up for work, he refused to go and instead shouted after them as they left that he was quitting his job. Raymond and Jay then listened to *Stained Class* several more times, finished what was left of their dozen beers, and, as Jay later told his former high school guidance counselor, began chanting "Do it, do it."

By now, the two friends were "getting amped on the music and, when I say amped, we started getting this feeling of power," Jay claimed. "And I said this guy is saying, 'Leave this life with all its sin, it's not fit for living in' [a line from 'Beyond the Realms of Death']. I thought the answer to life was death and I reached that conclusion from my experience with Judas Priest." Raymond and Jay then "hugged each goodbye, let's see what is next, let's leave this world, let's go."

Flush with energy, they wedged a two-by-four under the bedroom door and trashed Raymond's room. When Aunetta Roberson knocked, Raymond grabbed his shotgun, jumped out the window and ran down the street, Jay following behind. By chance, they ended up in the playground of the Community First Church of God.

Dressed in a Miami Dolphins Super Bowl T-shirt, his belt-buckle in the shape of a marijuana leaf, Raymond stood on a merry-go-round and announced, "I sure fucked up my life." Then he balanced the stock of the gun on the ground, placed the barrel under his chin, counted to 20, and blew off his head.

When Jay picked up the weapon, "There was so much blood, I could barely handle the gun," he said. "And I reloaded it and then, you know, it was my turn and I readied myself."

But when Jay pulled the trigger, the shotgun slipped and, instead of killing him, the blast destroyed the bottom half of his face, leaving him unconscious on the ground. When he was asked the next day in the hospital what prompted the suicide pact, Jay wrote with one of his fingers, "Life sucks."

Kenneth McKenna was a personal injury attorney who had brushed up against the music business once before. In 1984, the pudgy, cherub-faced lawyer filed a half-million dollar lawsuit against Harrah's casino and '60s rock band leader Paul Revere. McKenna's client claimed she had been injured when a concertgoer fell on her from a balcony while trying to catch a trademark Revolutionary-War-style hat that Revere tossed into the audience. But a jury ruled Revere could not have foreseen the mishap.

Kenneth McKenna knew Aunetta Roberson on a social basis. When he read about the suicide shootings in the newspaper, however, he didn't connect them to her. Then, "she called me and said that her son had been involved. I assumed she needed consoling and help with things like funeral arrangements, but she came in the next day with the *Stained Class* album." The attorney had heard of a suit that blamed the music of former Black Sabbath lead singer Ozzy Osbourne for the suicide of a California teen. Still, McKenna said, "I expected that what I would do was scratch the surface, get back to Aunetta in a few days and say 'Get on with your life, there's nothing to blame the music for.'"

McKenna began making exploratory phone calls, including, he said, to the plaintiff's counsel in the Osbourne suit. He also discovered that suicide was a top cause of death among teenagers. Soon, McKenna prepared a lawsuit against Judas Priest and CBS Records. The May 1986 complaint targeted the lyrics to Judas Priest's "Heroes End": "Why do you have to die to be a hero?/It's a shame a legend big as that would sin."

According to the suit—which mirrored the allegations in the Ozzy Osbourne case—"the suggestive lyrics combined with the continuous beat and rhythmic nonchanging intonation of the music combined to induce, encourage, aid, abet and otherwise mesmerize [Raymond Belknap] into believing the answer to life was death." The suit further charged that the defendants "knew or should have known that this music has a certain cult like following and that there are persons such as the deceased who [were] susceptible to being influenced by this music and that it was foreseeable that persons such as the deceased would listen to this music and thereafter commit harm to themselves."

The complaint alleged that Judas Priest's lyrics had created an "uncontrollable impulse" to commit suicide, and that the defendants were negligent in disseminating the album, which should have included a warning of its "potential danger."

McKenna also got in touch with Jay Vance's family. They hired Reno attorney Timothy Post, who, like Phyllis Vance, was a born-again Christian. Post filed a companion lyrics liability suit against Judas Priest and CBS Records on their behalf.

Meanwhile, Jay began a series of painful plastic surgeries—over 140 hours in all—to reconstruct his face. Doctors used a piece of his shoulder to create a new chin. They took a section of his scalp to fashion a new nose. But Jay, who by now had sired a daughter out of wedlock, remained depressed and again began abusing drugs, both street and prescribed. In November 1988, he checked himself into the Washoe County Medical Center for psychiatric treatment. On Thanksgiving morning, he lapsed into a coma and on November 29, he died. The county coroner attributed Jay's death to an excessive amount of prescription drugs and a blocked breathing passage caused by the shotgun injury.

"The doctors told me James should have died immediately," Phyllis Vance said, "but I believe God allowed him to live as long as he did so that the truth about this case could be revealed."

On October 27, 1984, John McCollum, a 19-year-old Riverside, California, youth with drinking and emotional problems, had laid on his bed, put on a pair of headphones and begun playing Ozzy Osbourne albums. Osbourne's album covers featured demonic imagery, the singer posing with fangs, blood dripping from his mouth.

While listening to Osbourne's *Speaking of the Devil*, McCollum put a .22-caliber handgun to his head and fired once. He was still wearing the headphones, turntable needle treading the spinning record, when his body was found the next morning.

McCollum's parents hired personal injury attorney Thomas Anderson to file suit against Osbourne and Osbourne's label—also CBS Records—in Los Angeles Superior Court. Anderson, a born-again Christian, went to an Osbourne concert in San Diego.

"It was a frightening experience," Anderson remembered. "There were about 10,000 to 15,000 kids there. No one was smiling. Osbourne appears on stage and says, 'What do you fuckers want?' The kids were chanting 'Ozzy, Ozzy, Ozzy' with their second and fifth fingers extended. That's the sign of the devil."

Osbourne found out about the McCollum suit when he stepped off an airplane at the Los Angeles Airport. "There must have been 50 film crews waiting," he recalled. "I tried to get out of the way because I thought the cameras were there for some celebrity like Elizabeth Taylor. But they were there to get my reaction to the suit. I've never been so scared in my life."

The McCollum suit alleged, "[I]t is not just the words of Ozzy Osbourne's music which incited John, but his entire presence. Ozzy Osbourne's entire attitude, and even his album covers, demonstrate a preoccupation with death."

The suit claimed that Osbourne had a special relationship with his fans due to the first-person nature of his lyrics. "[I]t was actually as if Ozzy Osbourne was talking face to face to his listener or that decedent John McCollum was personally having a conversation with Ozzy Osbourne as he listened to the words of the albums," the complaint stated.

The suit described *Blizzard of Ozz* as "a progression of songs which lead down the path of emptiness to suicide" and focused on the lyrics to the album cut "Suicide Solution": "Made your bed, rest your head/But you lie there and moan/Where to hide, suicide is the only way out."

Osbourne said he wrote "Suicide Solution" as a protest against alcoholism, based on his own drinking bouts and the alcohol-related death of his friend, AC/DC lead singer Bon Scott. On August 7, 1986, Los Angeles Superior Court Judge John L. Cole sustained Osbourne's *demurrer* to the suit. (A demurrer is a pretrial challenge to the sufficiency of a complaint.)

But Judge Cole allowed the McCollum family to amend their complaint to allege that "Suicide Solution" contained masked words. Using an equalizer and a computer, the McCollums' experts said they had found in the instrumental break of "Suicide Solution" the masked words "Why try, why try/Get the gun and try it/Shoot, shoot, shoot." Not easily understood because they were sung at one and a half times normal speaking rate, the words became clear after repeated listenings, the plaintiffs claimed.

"I spent $30,000 to $40,000 to discover that message," Thomas Anderson said. "You can hear it once you it know it's there, but even if you didn't know, your mind would [subconsciously] pick it up."

Still, in December 1996, Judge Cole ruled that Osbourne's music was constitutionally protected free speech. The California 2d District Court of Appeal affirmed. In July 1988, the appeals court said that, under the First Amendment, Osbourne would have had to engage in an immediate incitement to violence to lose his free speech right. The court emphasized that the Osbourne albums that John McCollum had been listening to the night he died were recorded years earlier and that "musical lyrics and poetry cannot be construed to contain the requisite 'call to action' for the elementary reason that they simply are not intended to be and should not be read literally on their face. . . . Reasonable persons understand musical lyric and poetic conventions as the figurative expressions which they are."

The appeals court minimized the impact of the alleged masked words on *Blizzard of Ozz* by describing them as "unintelligible" and noting that McCollum had been listening instead to *Speaking of the Devil* when he pulled the trigger.

Osbourne's counsel Howard Weitzman said that the appeals court made it "very clear that a situation in which a fan commits suicide

cannot be the catalyst for censorship in the creative world of entertainment." Thomas Anderson insisted, "I don't see this as a freedom
of speech case anymore than is running a red light," though he
admitted that these types of suits were "dead in California."

At one of his concerts, Ozzy Osbourne taped a "Have a nice day"
sign to a broomstick and stood in line with religious protesters pick-
eting his show. "I was wearing jeans and a T-shirt. They didn't even
know it was me and they're carrying signs that said 'This man is Satan.'"

The Osbourne ruling presented the Belknap and Vance families
with a stiff stumbling block. "That lyrics were protected by the First
Amendment wasn't earth-shattering, but we were hoping the
Osbourne case would recognize there was a line you could cross,"
Kenneth McKenna said. Instead, the Osbourne decision forced
McKenna's clients to shift their focus from audible lyrics on *Stained
Class* to whether the album contained any subliminal messages that
may have prompted Raymond's and Jay's suicide pact. To accomplish
this, the plaintiffs needed to obtain the *Stained Class* master studio
recordings from CBS Records.

But CBS claimed it couldn't find the tapes and hired a former
Scotland Yard detective to help. In London, the detective went from
recording studio to recording studio, questioning tape librarians,
looking in log books, and searching shelves. Then, according to
Kenneth McKenna, "He finally went to CBS's London studio and,
when the librarian said they didn't have the tapes, the detective
simply left."

CBS said that it was able to locate one master tape from *Stained
Class*, that of "Better by You, Better Than Me." The song had been
recorded separately from the album's other tracks after CBS record
executives decided that *Stained Class* needed a cut with hit potential.
"Better by You, Better Than Me" was the only song on the album not
composed by Judas Priest's members. Written by Gary Wright, best
known for his mid-'70s solo hit "Dream Weaver," "Better by You,
Better Than Me" had originally been released in 1969 by the British
rock group Spooky Tooth, for which Wright played keyboards.

But Reno Judge Jerry Carr Whitehead wasn't convinced that CBS had lost the other *Stained Class* recordings. "Given their library, vault and security systems, it wasn't credible that those particular tapes all of a sudden couldn't be found." Whitehead fined the record company $40,000 over the incident, though he later said, "I might have given CBS too light a sanction."

Subliminal messages first gained widespread attention in 1957, when James Vicary, the president of the Subliminal Projection Co., announced the development of equipment capable of superimposing words or photographs for fractions of seconds over motion pictures. Viewers would not consciously see the quick images but could be subconsciously influenced by them, Vicary said. To back up his claim, Vicary noted that his company had superimposed "Drink Coca-Cola" and "Hungry? Eat Popcorn" for 1/3000th of a second every five seconds during a film at a New Jersey theater. According to Vicary, sales of both Coke and popcorn increased substantially.

The use of subliminal messages drew public criticism, however, and the major broadcast networks barred subliminal techniques from advertisements and radio and TV shows. The Bureau of Alcohol, Tobacco and Firearms and the Federal Communications Commission eventually prohibited such messages but no federal or state legislation was enacted to regulate them.

The plaintiffs in the Judas Priest case hoped that their subliminal message claim would turn their case into a strict liability suit. This legal doctrine required no proof that the defendants *intended* to place subliminal messages on *Stained Class*; the defendants would be liable simply upon a finding that the album was an "unreasonably dangerous product."

In addition, the Belknap and Vance families now claimed that Judas Priest had inserted backward messages on *Stained Class* that could be subconsciously perceived when the music was played forward. The phrase "Deliver us/from all the fuss" on "White Heat, Red Hot" really said "Fuck the Lord, fuck all of you," the plaintiffs alleged, while "Faithless continuum/into the abyss" on the song "Stained Class" spouted "Sing my evil spirit" when played backward.

Judge Whitehead was well-equipped to handle the First Amendment issues in the Judas Priest case. Before joining the bench, he had served as legal counsel to Nevada newspaper and TV companies. But in August 1989—in the first such decision by a U.S. court—Whitehead ruled that subliminal messages weren't constitutionally protected speech. Rather, the *privacy* rights of the individual being involuntarily subjected to the subliminal message outweighed the free speech rights of the subliminal messenger.

Wrote Whitehead, "The First Amendment right of an individual to be free from intrusive speech [is] paramount under circumstances involving subliminal messages where the individual has no knowledge that he is being bombarded by these messages, and therefore, has no means of making a conscious decision to either hear them or avoid them."

But citing Raymond Belknap's and Jay Vance's troubled lives, Whitehead expressed doubts that subliminal messages were a substantial factor in causing the youths to shoot themselves. Whitehead noted, however, that Nevada's liberal litigation policy required a trial where there was even the slightest chance that a plaintiff might prevail.

Judas Priest counsel Elliot Hoffman believed that Whitehead's decision to hold a trial was partly political. "He was reluctant to antagonize the local community, particularly because he was up for reelection," Hoffman claimed. "He wasn't prepared to deny local citizens the opportunity to seek what they thought was justice."

The Washoe County Courthouse was situated near the 24-hour neon-injected casinos of downtown Reno. On the morning of July 16, 1990, a small group of Judas Priest fans gathered outside the courthouse as members of the band arrived for the opening day of trial. The supporters, who grew in number during the proceeding, held signs with slogans like "Honk!! If You Rock!!"

Their heavy metal garb replaced by business suits, Judas Priest lead singer Rob Halford, guitarists Glenn Tipton and K.K. Downing, and bassist Ian Hill signed autographs for the fans. Some fans clutched copies of the *Stained Class* album. (During the four-week trial, the plaintiffs' constitutional law specialist, Vivian Lynch, even asked for autographs for her metalhead sons.)

Meanwhile, the music industry nervously watched. "If the lunatics prevail in this Judas Priest case, it opens up the possibility for medical malpractice insurance for musicians," artist Frank Zappa warned.

During pretrial preparation, the plaintiffs' lawyers communicated with PTA groups and the Parents Music Resource Center, a lyrics watchdog group. "We also heard from ad hoc religious groups fighting Satan and people who told us that they were getting alien messages coming out of their fillings," Kenneth McKenna acknowledged. McKenna said he hoped to prove his case through scientific evidence. However, for born-again co-counsel Timothy Post, the suit represented a question of good versus evil. "It's like chasing phantoms," Post said. "Sometimes the fact that you can't find it may be an indication that it's right in front of your face. It's like we're ghostbusters or something."

Yet, Judas Priest drew support from a surprising source. The Rev. Donald Wildmon—whose conservative American Family Association had been instrumental in igniting the nationwide rap obscenity prosecutions against the 2 Live Crew—surprisingly said, "It's not the subliminal that really concerns me. All this business of turning the thing backwards and all that doesn't amount to a hill of beans."

One week before trial, Judge Whitehead had accepted the parties' agreement that the case be heard without a jury. Finding impartial jurors could be a problem. According to local defense counsel in the case, Suellen Fulstone, "Due to the high level of interest in this not very big community, we might have had to move jury selection to an amphitheatre."

Judge Whitehead kept control of his courtroom by laying out guidelines for attorneys in chambers, then using a reserved, low-key manner during trial. At the defense table sat Judas Priest general counsel Elliot Hoffman, a New Yorker whose clients included Tony Bennett, Luciano Pavarotti, and the Who. With Hoffman was CBS in-house counsel Gail Edwin. To dispel the notion that the proceeding was about big-city lawyers and corporate conglomerates battling small-town families, Hoffman and Edwin rarely spoke to the court. Instead, Suellen Fulstone, a Nevada native, and her Reno co-counsels, Shawn Meador and Bill Peterson, handled the courtroom defense.

"This is a case about mind control. . . . This was not a suicide," plaintiffs' counsel Vivian Lynch argued in her opening statement. "This was an adventure, a journey to a better place. What they planned was good because Judas Priest said it was good." Lynch could relate to Raymond's and Jay's rough upbringings. She had lived in an orphanage until her teens and been sexually abused by a family member. She was once knifed in the back while pregnant.

"There is no subliminal content on the *Stained Class* album," Suellen Fulstone countered. "I say that unequivocally and we will prove that unequivocally. . . . There is a fascination with the possibility of mind control and manipulation. But this courtroom is no place for magic and experimentation."

The trial testimony began with Phyllis Vance. She was questioned by Timothy Post, who wore the suit that Jay Vance had planned to wear to trial. "They said I was the closest thing they had left to a son," Post claimed. Phyllis Vance testified that Jay stopped going to church after he started listening to Judas Priest's music. "He couldn't do both at the same time. He was either true to the God of our church or he was true to the god Judas Priest." But Jay's mother admitted under cross-examination that her son assaulted her twice following his suicide attempt—and *after* he stopped listening to Judas Priest's music.

William Nickloff, the plaintiffs' self-trained audio expert, used a computer and a tape machine to play slowed-down passages of "Better by You, Better Than Me" for Judge Whitehead. Nickloff once ran the now-defunct Secret Sounds Inc., which produced subliminal tapes. Nickloff claimed that Judas Priest had spread portions of the subliminal message "Do it" over 11 of the 24 tracks on "Better by You, Better Than Me" to make the words hard to find.

The plaintiffs also brought to the stand Eldon Taylor, a self-proclaimed minister from Las Vegas who claimed that his subliminal tapes could make breasts grow, and Wilson Key, an author of books about subliminal subjects who claimed to have discovered hidden messages on Ritz crackers and dollar bills.

Victoria Evans, a computer science professor at the University of Nevada, testified that she heard additional suicide messages on *Stained Class*. "This album is a time bomb waiting to go off," Evans insisted. But she also admitted that an innocuous phrase like "testing one" sounded like "no music" when played backward.

The one plaintiffs' witness Judge Whitehead said he did find persuasive was Howard Shevrin, a psychology professor at the University of Michigan. Shevrin testified that subliminal messages subconsciously received could later surface consciously as the recipient's own thoughts.

Next, the plaintiffs played a video that demonstrated how backward messages had been planted on recordings by the Beatles, the Electric Light Orchestra, Led Zeppelin, and Queen. When Andrew Jackson, an assistant engineer on the "Better by You, Better Than Me" recording session, admitted in court that he had worked on a backward message for a rock group just one month before his appearance at trial, "that let the cat out of the bag," Kenneth McKenna claimed. "Prior to that, the defendants insisted that backmasking was a figment of right-wing religious fanatic imagination."

Droopy-eyed lead singer Rob Halford was the only member of Judas Priest to testify. He denied using subliminal messages but admitted recording a phrase backward while working on the band's *Defenders of the Faith* album. Halford said he had done so by simultaneously combining the line "in the dead of night, love bites" backward and forward. The result was a garbled mess, Halford claimed.

"When you're composing songs, you're always looking for new ideas, new sounds . . . just as an artist would add another piece of paint to a canvas."

Defense counsel Suellen Fulstone asked Halford to sing a passage from "Better by You, Better Than Me." As he did, Halford noted how he typically highlighted a lyric line's last syllable with an audible breath. Defense expert Anthony Pellicano said that the alleged words "Do it" were really Halford's breaths combined with an electric guitar strum. Pellicano, a controversial entertainment industry investigator and president of the Forensic Audio Laboratory, claimed he worked on the 24-track recording of "Better by You, Better Than Me" for over 200 hours. "My opinion is there is no such thing as subliminal audio," Pellicano stated.

He then had Rob Halford sing the words "Deliver us/from all the fuss" from the song "White Heat, Red Hot" into a tape recorder four times. Pellicano played the tape backward to demonstrate that the result only remotely resembled the alleged message "Fuck the Lord, fuck all of you."

James Mikawa, a clinical psychologist who once headed Reno's suicide crisis center, later testified that Raymond Belknap decided to take his life before the December 23, 1985 shooting incident. "I concluded that Raymond Belknap was the one who was suicidal and James Vance was not," Mikawa said. (Vance originally told police that he shot himself for fear he would be charged with Raymond's death.) Suicide "is not something that happens overnight."

Rob Halford returned to the witness stand during the fourth and final week of trial. In the interim, he had gone to a Reno studio and recorded several lines from *Stained Class* backward. Played in reverse, the passages resulted in non-suicidal messages that sounded like "I asked her for a peppermint, I asked her to get one" and "Hey look, Ma, my chair's broken." Halford wanted to show that the alleged backward messages in the suit—including "Try suicide"—were "phonetic flukes."

In closing arguments, Vivian Lynch asked Judge Whitehead to award the Vance family up to $5 million for pain and suffering and medical costs. Kenneth McKenna asked for $1.2 million for the Belknap family.

When Judge Whitehead handed down his ruling on August 24, 1990, he said that "the plaintiffs have submitted a forceful argument that the backmasked messages are present." Whitehead had heard the words "Do it" on "Better by You, Better Than Me" and believed Raymond Belknap and Jay Vance heard the message, too. The judge decided, however, that any such message had been produced by accident. "Do it," he believed, had indeed been created by the coincidental combination of Halford's breathy exhalation and a Leslie guitar effect. In any event, the plaintiffs failed to establish that "Do it" was a proximate cause of the suicide-related deaths, Whitehead concluded.

Whitehead cautioned, however, that "the plaintiffs did not lose this case because defendants proved that subliminal stimuli have no effect on human behavior. . . . [I]t is unknown what future information, research and technology will bring to this field."

That prompted Vance family counsel Timothy Post to warn, "If artists who use subliminals don't develop more self-restraint and a concern for their consuming public, then a resentful public will turn on them. And then, it may turn out that there were actually three shots fired on the evening of Dec. 23, 1985."

A few minutes after receiving Judge Whitehead's ruling, Vivian Lynch wrote a country song titled "No More Deadly Music." "I won't sing of lust or violence/Talk of crack or speed or weed," the lyrics went. "I won't tell you death's the answer/Or sing of wicked Satan's creed." Lynch tried unsuccessfully to get Johnny Cash to record the composition.

When CBS Records advertised Judas Priest's new album, *Painkiller*, as "Awesome! Backwards or Forwards," Lynch blasted the ad as "almost criminally irresponsible." But Kenneth McKenna joked, "After I heard 'Better by You, Better Than Me' a thousand times, it grew on me."

By the time the Judas Priest trial wound down, McKenna was serving as a consultant in two suicide suits in Georgia federal court. The complaints were filed over Ozzy Osbourne's litigious "Suicide Solution." Sixteen-year-old Michael Waller and 17-year-old Harold Hamilton had shot themselves to death in separate incidents. According to plaintiffs' counsel Ben Mills, Waller said a few days before his death that "Ozzy had the solution." (The Waller case involved the *Blizzard of Ozz* album; the Hamilton case, Osbourne's *Tribute* album, which included a concert recording of "Suicide Solution.")

Mills initially filed suit over Osbourne's audible lyrics. Then, like the Judas Priest plaintiffs, Mills changed his clients' focus to subliminal messages. In May 1991, however, the Georgia federal court dismissed the Waller suit on First Amendment grounds, in effect ending the Hamilton case, too.

United States District Judge Duross Fitzpatrick agreed that, "In a world full of traps for the unwary teenager, such as rampant drug and alcohol abuse and a 'new morality' that stresses the importance of doing anything that feels good, an addiction to music of this sort could be another step in a path to self-destruction." But Fitzpatrick stressed that, "whether the defendants' album *Blizzard of Ozz* could fit this description, or whether the court approves of rock music in general or of this particular brand of it, is irrelevant."

For purposes of the First Amendment, Fitzpatrick said, "lyrics which are audible enough to make one consciously aware of their presence, though they may not necessarily be intelligible, do not qualify as a subliminal message." (The Wallers' audio expert had said he found "preconscious suggestions"—audible but mostly unintelligible words—on *Blizzard of Ozz*.) The 11th U.S. Circuit Court of Appeals in Atlanta upheld Fitzpatrick's ruling.

In May 1993, the Nevada Supreme Court affirmed Judge Whitehead's decision in the Judas Priest case. By then, Rob Halford had left the band. But artists making lyrical references to suicide continued to thrive. "Irresponsible Hate Anthem" from Marilyn Manson's best-selling 1996 album *Antichrist Superstar* contained the satirical line, "I am so all-American, I'd sell you suicide." In November 1997, the Manson band's "The Reflecting God" was blamed before a Senate subcommittee for the suicide of a North Dakota teenager.

"The backlash from the suicide suits has been that bands are more apt to use these types of lyrics to draw attention to themselves," Ozzy Osbourne claimed. "I never sat down to write lyrics with the intent that anyone should kill themselves. I feel very sorry for those kids. But why can't you sing about suicide? It's a thing that really happens."

The 2 Live Crew:
Supreme Highs and Lows

Perched in his front-row spectator's seat at the U.S. Supreme Court, Luther Campbell looked up at Associate Justice Clarence Thomas. Thomas and the high court's eight other justices were hearing arguments on whether a rap parody by Campbell's group, the 2 Live Crew—of the late Roy Orbison's rock classic, "Oh, Pretty Woman"—constituted copyright infringement or a permissible "fair use."

Justice Thomas had barely been approved for his high court appointment, following heated Senate hearings in which he was accused of sexually harassing lawyer Anita Hill, at the Department of Education and while he was chairman of the Equal Employment Opportunity Commission. Now Campbell—best known for the obscenity controversy over the 2 Live Crew's *As Nasty As They Wanna Be* album—was concerned with how a potentially oversensitive Thomas, the high court's only sitting black justice, might respond to the rap group's music. "Because of the Anita Hill thing, I thought he'd go totally against me or something," Campbell said. But, the worried Campbell continued, "There was no eye movement. He didn't ask any questions. I didn't know how to read him."

Most of the justices did grill the lawyers for Campbell and Acuff-Rose, the Nashville music publisher that filed the parody suit. Cases involving rock music had been to the Supreme Court before, but the 2 Live Crew case marked the first time rap music reached the nation's highest tribunal.

The case had serious free speech implications, too. Never before had the Supreme Court decided whether a parody could be a fair use. In typical fashion, the court chose to hear a case with consequences that reached far beyond the litigants themselves. "There's an important First Amendment issue here," said Bruce Rogow, who argued the case for the 2 Live Crew. "If you don't give parody room to breathe, creativity will be stifled."

Roy Orbison's "Oh, Pretty Woman" had offered up an idealized depiction of female beauty. The 2 Live Crew's "Pretty Woman" used the opening lyrics, vocal hook, and lead guitar riff from the Orbison song to taunt "bald-headed," "big, hairy," and "two-timin'" women. Luther Campbell described his group's recording as "a typical encounter in the hood."

Under the federal Copyright Act's compulsory licensing provision, once a song is published, anyone can record it—using essentially the original lyrics and melody—subject to payment of a statutory fee. (Permission of the copyright owner is generally required if new lyrics are used.) The numerous cover recordings of "Oh, Pretty Woman" ranged from a soulful version by singer Al Green to one by hard-rockers Van Halen. The song had also been featured in films like *Pretty Woman*, starring Julia Roberts.

Roy Orbison wrote "Oh, Pretty Woman" with Bill Dees, who sang harmony on the Orbison recording. The tune grew out of a flattering comment Dees made about Orbison's first wife, Claudette. "Oh, Pretty Woman" took less than one hour to write, including the machine-gun lead guitar line that has become one of rock's most recognizable riffs.

"Roy was playing guitar while he spoke to his dad on the phone," Bill Dees recalled. "His dad said something that made Roy stop and his finger slid up on the guitar neck. 'Did you hear how I played that?' Roy asked. That's how that lick was written."

Dees said of the 2 Live Crew recording, "At first, I think Roy would have liked the rap beat and the repeat of the guitar lick. What would have bothered him was that it's sung in one key and played in another. It's out of tune. After a few plays, he probably would have said, 'I hope they pay us.'"

The 2 Live Crew's cut was originally slated for the *As Nasty As They Wanna Be* album. But according to Luther Campbell's general counsel, Allen Jacobi, "I said, 'Don't put it on *As Nasty*. It'll been seen as a dirty version. You're better off putting it on [the 2 Live Crew's profane-less] *As Clean As They Wanna Be*.'"

Jacobi advised Linda Fine, the general manager of Campbell's record label, to send a copy of the rappers' "Pretty Woman" to Orbison's Nashville publisher, Acuff-Rose, to secure a copyright license. Weird Al Yankovic, after all, had been granted permission by music publishers to humorously rewrite the lyrics of many popular songs.

Continued Jacobi, "Acuff-Rose wrote back, 'We regret we can't allow you to use the *parody*.' As soon as I saw they used that word to describe our cut, I said to put it on the album."

As Clean As They Wanna Be credited "Pretty Woman" to Orbison and Dees and cited Acuff-Rose as the publisher, but Acuff-Rose was anything but pleased. On June 18, 1990—two weeks after a South Florida federal court ruled that *As Nasty As They Wanna Be* was obscene—Acuff-Rose filed suit against Luther Campbell, Campbell's record company, and the 2 Live Crew in Nashville federal court. Acuff-Rose charged the rap group's "Pretty Woman" with disparaging and infringing on the Orbison song.

Allen Jacobi said, "There's no question in my mind that they refused our request because these were black rappers and the version was thoroughly street."

"The timing of the suit had nothing to do with the Florida obscenity ruling," insisted Eddie Wayland, an attorney with Nashville's King & Ballow, which represented the Opryland Music Group, the owner of Acuff-Rose. "Acuff-Rose thought after the license was denied, that was the end of it. Then somebody bought a copy of the 2 Live Crew album in a store and that led to the suit."

Federal law gives copyright owners the exclusive right to control derivative uses of their works (e.g., a preexisting song with new lyrics) but tempers this by allowing other parties, in limited circumstances, to borrow portions of the original work without permission. The Copyright Act lists comment, criticism, news reporting, and scholarship among these permissible fair uses.

The Act provided a four-part test that courts historically utilized to decide fair-use suits. First is the purpose and character of a defendant's use, including whether it is commercial. Second is the nature of a plaintiff's copyrighted work; the more creative it is, such as a song compared to a phone directory, the more copyright protection to which it has been entitled (though this prong has become less important in light of the Supreme Court's ruling in the Campbell case). Next is the amount and substantiality of a plaintiff's copyright that a defendant has used. Finally, is the impact a defendant's use may have on the market for the plaintiff's work.

In August 1990, Luke Records deposited $13,867 in the Nashville federal court. This was the amount the record company calculated it owed in compulsory royalties had Acuff-Rose granted it a license. "It wasn't meant as an admission that the 2 Live Crew recording wasn't a fair use," the rap group's Nashville counsel, Alan Mark Turk, said. "It was meant, as a practical matter, to avoid years of litigation."

Acuff-Rose initially refused to accept the funds. Bill Dees said, "If I offered you money to rent your car and you said 'No' and I took it anyway, then paid you, the fact is, I still stole your car."

The 2 Live Crew also submitted an affidavit by folk humorist and music historian Oscar Brand. Brand acknowledged the substantial similarities between the Orbison-Dees and the 2 Live Crew songs. But he emphasized that the 2 Live Crew juxtaposed vocal keys for comic effect and added "scratching" (Brand called it "scraping")—the hip-hop technique of rhythmically creating sounds by maneuvering a vinyl record back and forth under a turntable needle.

The 2 Live Crew, like other rap artists, utilized its lyrics as protest, Brand said. "This antiestablishment singing group is trying to show how bland and banal the Orbison song seems to them. It's just one of many examples of their derisive approach to 'white-centered' popular music."

Nashville federal Judge Thomas A. Wiseman Jr. granted the 2 Live Crew's pretrial motion to dismiss the suit. In his January 1991 ruling, Wiseman observed that "a song is difficult to parody effectively without exact or near exact copying." He concluded, "The odds of a record collector seeking the original composition who would also purchase the 2 Live Crew version are remote."

"It's that Judge Wiseman didn't want to be the next one to censor the 2 Live Crew," Acuff-Rose's co-counsel, F. Casey Del Casino, said.

"I think that Judge Wiseman decided the case prematurely," Eddie Wayland claimed. "There were discovery disputes, documents we hadn't received yet. I believe a lot of the things the 2 Live Crew did were meant to go back after the fact to create an appearance that they were doing the right thing all along."

One disputed issue was whether the 2 Live Crew released its "Pretty Woman" before or after Acuff-Rose denied the license request. Another was whether the rap track had originally been intended as a parody. (One theory was that the 2 Live Crew—whose albums contained numerous initially unlicensed sound samples—was looking to associate itself, as other rappers did, with a well-known song to gain a larger audience.)

Acuff-Rose took Judge Wiseman's decision to the 6th U.S. Circuit Court of Appeals. Nashville was a songwriting Mecca, but the "Oh, Pretty Woman" case gave the appellate court its first chance to apply the fair use test to musical compositions.

Begrudgingly assuming for purposes of its opinion that the 2 Live Crew's recording *was* a parody, the 6th Circuit nevertheless reversed Wiseman's ruling. "[T]he factors involving the commercial nature of the use [i.e., to sell 2 Live Crew records] and the damage to the defendant are of particular significance," the 6th Circuit said in its August 1992 opinion. From this "blatantly commercial purpose," the appeals court "presume[s] that a likelihood of future [economic] harm to Acuff-Rose exists."

Conflicting federal court rulings in parody cases made the 2 Live Crew case ripe for U.S. Supreme Court review. The 9th Circuit in California, for example, found a parody of "When Sunny Gets Blue," a 1950s hit for Johnny Mathis, to be a fair use. The parody appeared on *Put It Where the Moon Don't Shine,* an album by disc jockey Rick Dees. Dees took the lyrics "When Sunny gets blue/Her eyes get gray and cloudy" and changed them to "When Sonny sniffs glue/Her eyes get red and bulgy."

The disc jockey's parody lasted only 29 seconds, but it used the main theme from "When Sunny Gets Blue." The 9th Circuit said that in making fun of the hit and "Mr. Mathis's rather singular vocal range," Dees had properly used enough of "When Sunny Gets Blue" to "conjure up" the song for his audience, then make his humorous point.

"Parodists will seldom get permission from those whose works are parodied," the 9th Circuit said of Dees' attempt to get a license from Marvin Fisher, the publisher and cowriter of "When Sunny Gets Blue." "Self-esteem is seldom strong enough to permit the granting of permission even in exchange for a reasonable fee."

That was certainly true for Fisher. He attributed his heart attack to the Dees parody.

Acuff-Rose's suit against the 2 Live Crew wasn't the only knotty affair the music publisher had over Roy Orbison's music. All was not well between Acuff-Rose and Orbison's estate. Orbison signed to Acuff-Rose as a songwriter in 1958, after the Everly Brothers scored with his "Claudette." Acuff-Rose president Wesley Rose also became Orbison's manager. But "Oh, Pretty Woman" in 1964 was Orbison's last major U.S. hit for years.

In 1965, he signed a new management and songwriting deal with Wesley Rose and Acuff-Rose—this time for a 20-year term. By 1979, "Roy had pretty much hit the bottom of the barrel in terms of his career, his finances and his personal life," entertainment attorney John Mason said. "He wasn't writing songs. And the deal with Acuff-Rose was pretty onerous." Under the agreement, Orbison assigned his royalties to the music publisher, which then agreed to pay Orbison $10,000 per year, plus any income over $200,000 that his songs earned.

Wesley Rose later signed Orbison to his Hickory record label and Orbison named Rose the executor of his estate. According to Mason, Orbison lost income because, among other things, the price Rose demanded for a license to use Orbison's songs in album compilations, films, and commercials put the music out of reach of most producers.

"I met with Roy and Barbara [Roy's second wife] at the Beverly Hilton for breakfast to see if I could help get Roy's career back on track," Mason recalled. "I felt he could untangle his contracts with Wesley based on undue influence and conflict of interest. Roy agonized over it because he revered Wesley. It was the way Elvis must have felt about Colonel Parker. Roy's respect for Wesley transcended what he knew was right in business."

According to Mason, when Orbison finally authorized him to approach Rose, "Wesley was polite, but not nice. He refused to terminate or change the agreements. He said, 'I brought Roy from obscurity to international fame.'"

The Orbisons hired Nashville litigator Jim Zwickel to file suit for them. The $50 million complaint—filed in Nashville Chancery Court in 1982—charged Rose with fraud. Orbison also claimed that he had lacked legal counsel when he signed his agreements with Rose. Rose responded, "I am shocked and hurt that Orbison has allowed himself to be influenced by others, as I believe is the case, to attack me in this vicious manner."

"Wesley wouldn't have settled the suit," John Mason said. "But he decided to sell Acuff-Rose to Opryland. Opryland went in and settled Roy's claim."

Under the June 1985 deal, Orbison ultimately would get back his shares of the copyrights in his prior Acuff-Rose songs, including his classic hits, plus a cash payment. "I'll end up with $2 or $3 million," a jubilant Orbison said. In return, he signed a new five-year songwriting contract with Acuff-Rose. The contract gave him a $70,000 annual advance to write ten songs each year.

"Roy delivered basically two songs under the agreement and Acuff-Rose put him on suspension [in June 1986]," Opryland counsel

Casey Del Casino said. "Then when the Traveling Wilburys album [the project Orbison recorded with Bob Dylan, George Harrison, Jeff Lynne, and Tom Petty] came out in 1988, he was listed as a co-writer on songs that Acuff-Rose had never heard of. The same thing happened when Roy's [posthumous best-selling] *Mystery Girl* album came out in early 1989."

"[W]e didn't ask any of the record companies or managers or attorneys or anybody, we just went ahead and did it and no one knew about it," Orbison said about the Wilburys project. "I think if we had tried to get together and told everyone that we were forming a little group, they would have told us that there were too many problems."

Orbison was also working again with his "Oh, Pretty Woman" cowriter Bill Dees. Dees had been a pallbearer at the funerals of Roy's then-wife Claudette, killed in a motorcycle accident in 1966, and two of the couple's three sons, who died in a fire at Orbison's Tennessee home in 1968. "I wrote ten songs with Roy that last year [i.e., in 1988]. He flew me out to Malibu three times," Dees said. "And he did something he'd never done before. He left the room while we were working on a song called 'The Way Is Love.' [Dees sings a portion of the tender ballad.] He came back 20 minutes later and said, 'I left the room because I didn't want you to see me cry.'"

After Orbison died of a heart attack in December 1988, "Barbara immediately called [Dees] and moved me out of the picture, giving me however much money it was for the publishing rights."

In May 1989, Acuff-Rose sued Orbison's estate. The complaint charged Barbara Orbison with inducing Roy to breach his Acuff-Rose deal. The Orbison estate argued that Roy had delivered the ten-song demo he recorded with Dees to the music publisher in February 1987, but that Acuff-Rose refused to pay Roy's contractual $70,000 fee. (The estate also claimed that Dees had signed his rights in the songs over to the music publisher in exchange for an advance.) The suit was settled in January 1991 with Orbison's estate giving control of Roy's share of the *Mystery Girl* copyrights to Acuff-Rose and Acuff-Rose assigning rights in the Traveling Wilburys songs to the Orbison estate.

. . .

In March 1993, the U.S. Supreme Court granted the 2 Live Crew's petition for *certiorari* (an appeal to have their case heard by a higher court). "Hip Hop Comes to the Hallowed Halls" announced the New York *Daily News*.

The Supreme Court grants only a small percentage of the several thousand *certiorari* petitions it receives each year. But the only parody case the Supreme Court had previously considered—a Jack Benny parody of the Ingrid Bergman/Charles Boyer film *Gaslight*—ended in a four-four tie after Justice William O. Douglas withdrew from the case. That let stand a 9th Circuit ruling that Benny drew too extensively from *Gaslight* to make his skit a fair use.

The Supreme Court had nevertheless issued a few fair use decisions. In 1984, the high court ruled—in a majority opinion by Justice John Paul Stevens—that non-commercial home videotaping of TV broadcasts constituted fair use. In 1985, the Supreme Court decided—in a majority opinion by Justice Sandra Day O'Connor—that *The Nation* committed copyright infringement when it published without permission the "heart" of the memoirs of President Gerald Ford—approximately 300 words describing Ford's Watergate pardon of President Nixon.

Among those filing *amici curiae*—friends of the court—briefs on behalf of the 2 Live Crew were the Comedy Central and HBO cable channels, NBC, and *Mad* magazine. Disc jockey Dr. Demento and political parodists Capitol Steps and Mark Russell claimed in their *amicus* brief that a ruling against the 2 Live Crew would "bring an end to musical political parody as it has existed since the time of the Revolution."

Songwriters Michael Jackson, Dolly Parton, and Mac Davis lined up on the other side. Their lawyer, Marvin Frankel, said his clients "would stand to lose millions of dollars in revenues" if Acuff-Rose lost its case. Joining them were the estates of Rodgers and Hammerstein, George and Ira Gershwin, Cole Porter, and Irving Berlin. "Would

Irving Berlin have had to stand by if 'White Christmas' was recorded and widely sold with lyrics referring to cocaine?" the estates' lawyer, Stephen Kaye, asked.

The 2 Live Crew were particularly concerned with how the Supreme Court would respond to rap music. Conservative Justice Clarence Thomas listened to Christian music. Justices Antonin Scalia, also a conservative, and Ruth Bader Ginsburg, a court liberal, were opera buffs. Chief Justice William Rehnquist, leader of the court's conservative wing, would add vivid gold stripes to the sleeves of his somber judicial robe, after seeing them worn by the Lord Chancellor in Gilbert & Sullivan's operetta *Iolanthe*.

2 Live Crew counsel Alan Mark Turk said, "I imagine most of the justices have watched *Saturday Night Live* or at least *Your Show of Shows* [the 1950s TV comedy program starring Sid Caesar and Imogene Coca]. So they're familiar with the concept of parody. But if we try to focus on the rap aspect of our song, we could lose. Rap music isn't something the justices are used to."

Luther Campbell put it more bluntly: "I think the Supreme Court justices'll be looking at it the same way people do who look at the news. All they see is negative things about rap. As soon as a rap group does a record, there's a problem, as if nobody wants to be affiliated with rap."

The 2 Live Crew chose Bruce Rogow, lead counsel in the rap group's obscenity cases, to present its Supreme Court argument. Rogow had appeared before the high court seven times and won the right for criminal suspects to be heard by a judge immediately after arrest. None of Rogow's Supreme Court cases involved copyright issues, however. "I'd never even read the copyright statute before the 2 Live Crew parody case," Rogow said.

Acuff-Rose hired New York attorney Sidney Rosdeitcher, who handled music industry copyright and antitrust cases and did legal work for the National Music Publishers' Association. Rosdeitcher previously had argued an insurance industry antitrust case before the Supreme Court.

The two lawyers faced off on Tuesday morning, November 9, 1993. The nine court justices sat behind their raised mahogany bench, against a backdrop of towering marble columns and gold-fringed, maroon velvet drapes.

The court allows one hour for each case it hears. As counsel for the petitioners, Bruce Rogow approached the lawyers' lectern first. He began: "Since the [English] Statute of Anne [the first copyright law] in 1709, through the Copyright Clause of our Constitution, through the copyright statute and until today, the purpose of copyright has been to encourage creativity. Parody is a creative force in our society and has historically been a creative force, and parody should be encouraged.

"The decision of the Sixth Circuit discouraged parody and we ask the Court today to reverse the decision of the Sixth Circuit. The rule that we suggest is that parody is a fair use unless it materially impairs the market for the original, and material impairment of the market for the original means supplant the original."

Rogow defined parody as poking fun at the original work or at society through the original work. "That's a little broader than it needs to be, isn't it, for this case?" court centrist Sandra Day O'Connor asked.

"Why shouldn't I be able to use any song that anyone's ever written in order to set patriotic lyrics to it? Isn't that something that's to be encouraged?" Justice Scalia postulated. "But one can criticize other things without borrowing the music from a tune. Unless you're willing to limit your proposition as much as Justice O'Connor just suggested, your argument doesn't hold."

"But we're in this narrow copyright area where we have on one side the private interest of the copyright holder, versus the public interest and the historical interest of promoting creativity," Rogow claimed.

"I don't think [that] is accurate," Chief Justice Rehnquist said. "I think the [Copyright Act] itself suggests there's a strong public interest in encouraging works that can be copyrighted."

"But a fair use is also good for the public and that's the point," Rogow responded.

Justice Ruth Bader Ginsburg noted that the 6th Circuit accepted the 2 Live Crew's "Pretty Woman" as a parody—as did the Supreme Court. Ginsburg wanted to know where Rogow thought the appeals court had gone wrong.

"By applying a presumption that if it is a commercial parody, then it is presumptively harmful to the market."

"Suppose there would be another rap version of this composition? Would that be a fair use?" Justice Ginsburg asked.

"Not if it was not a parody. . . . Just simply a rap version of 'Oh, Pretty Woman' would not qualify under the fair use doctrine."

Justice Ginsburg continued, "Suppose we have a rap version now that has different lyrics than the 2 Live Crew, slightly different in presentation of the music, and the claim is made this is a parody of the parody?"

"That would be entitled to a fair use claim," Rogow said. "There's nothing the matter with making fun of the people making fun of the original."

Rogow concluded, "The original does not hold the absolute right to preclude any other use of that original work. And the fact that 280,000 [the sales figure for *As Clean As They Wanna Be*] or 2,000 records were sold is not the decisive fact here. The decisive fact is that the court below applied a presumption that if it's commercial, it cannot be a fair use. That simply is wrong."

Acuff-Rose counsel Sidney Rosdeitcher pointed out when he stepped to the lectern that the 2 Live Crew had claimed it was selling its rap album to disaffected black urban youth. "We dispute that . . . rap music is so limited," Rosdeitcher said. "Rap music is danceable music. . . . What I'm saying in this case is it's not just that they profited from the parody. They profited here, in addition, because they needed music and they needed dazzling, good music, and they took one of the great rock and roll classics."

"If you're going to have parody as a fair use at all, it seems to me you might be much more effective using the whole thing than just a phrase," Justice O'Connor noted.

"[But] the copyright protection itself is an engine of free expression and is designed to encourage dissemination of ideas and creativity," Rosdeitcher responded.

Rosdeitcher then explained how Run-DMC had worked with Aerosmith to remake the latter's hard rock song "Walk This Way" into a rap hit. A few minutes later, Justice Anthony Kennedy queried to laughter, "In your example, I think it was Aerosmith progressed, or regressed, to rap?"

Rosdeitcher quoted from an article in the *South Atlantic Quarterly* by music critic Alan Light: " 'Rap was established as a viable pop form, at least as long as its connections to the traditional rock and roll spirit were made explicit.' "

"Now, that's what happened here," Rosdeitcher continued. "[T]hey took our music in order to have a free ride."

Justice Stevens suggested that Acuff-Rose turned down the 2 Live Crew's offer to pay for a copyright license because "you really wanted to prevent this music from being distributed at all."

"And if it is not a fair use, we had a right to say no, that this wasn't the way to best exploit the rap market," Rosdeitcher replied. "When they sold the record, they didn't put 'parody,' they didn't give it another name. They called it 'Pretty Woman.' . . . They then say, it's written by Roy Orbison and Bill Dees, it's published by my client."

That the 2 Live Crew "offered to pay you royalties and the fact they were candid about the true origin of the work tends to cut in their favor, rather than the other way," Justice Stevens said.

Rosdeitcher pointed out that Acuff-Rose had turned down a request from the rap group Brother Makes 3 to use the vocal hook from the Orbison-Dees song. "And so there's evidence, plain evidence that there's a rap market for our song."

But "there's nothing to keep them from licensing a rap version," Bruce Rogow insisted in his four-minute rebuttal. "['Pretty Woman'] is one cut out of ten on the record. . . . The 2 Live Crew album was not named *Pretty Woman*, it was named *As Clean As They Wanna Be*." But if the 2 Live Crew had released its parody as a single, "[W]e would still argue fair use," Rogow said. "But the truth is, [Acuff-Rose doesn't] want to license this as a parody."

By the time the oral arguments ended, seven of the nine Supreme Court justices had joined in the questioning. Only Justices Harry Blackmun, the court's oldest member, and Clarence Thomas remained silent. But neither asked questions often, the latter almost never.

Outside the Supreme Court, a gaggle of fans awaited Luther Campbell from behind police barricades. As Campbell strode down the courthouse steps to face reporters, the fans shouted, "Over here! Over here!"

The Supreme Court justices meet on Wednesdays and Fridays to review the cases they hear each week they are in session. No one else, including court staff, is allowed to attend the conferences. "[It] is not a bull session in which off-the-cuff reactions are traded," Chief Justice William Rehnquist said. "The truth is that there simply are not nine different points of view in even the most complex and difficult case, and all of us feel impelled to a greater or lesser degree to try to reach some consensus that can be embodied in a written opinion that will command the support of at least a majority of the members of the Court."

The majority-opinion writing assignments are doled out evenly among the justices. "If I had to guess from the oral arguments who would write the 2 Live Crew opinion, I would have thought it would be Justice Ginsburg," the rap group's Nashville counsel, Alan Mark Turk, said. "She asked a lot of the questions and her daughter teaches copyright law."

Chief Justice Rehnquist instead chose liberal justice David Souter to write the 2 Live Crew majority decision. During 1990 Senate hearings for Souter's high court confirmation, it had been revealed that the then-New Hampshire Supreme Court justice "lived alone in a dilapidated farmhouse, ate cottage cheese and an apple for lunch and watched television on a black-and-white set." But a close friend had told *New York Times* reporter David Margolick that Souter "has that British satirical sense of humor [and] does wonderful impressions."

In what turned out to be a 9-0 vote, Justice Souter's March 7, 1994 opinion held, for the first time in Supreme Court history, that a parody *may* qualify as a fair use. The determination would be made on a case-by-case basis.

Souter looked first at the purpose-and-character-of-use prong of the Copyright Act's fair use test. He wrote, "[T]he more transformative the new work . . . [whether the parody] adds something new, with a further purpose or different character . . . the less will be the significance of other factors, like commercialism, that may weight against a finding of fair use." Souter continued: "While we might not assign a high rank to the parodic element here, we think it fair to say that 2 Live Crew's song reasonably could be perceived as commenting on the original or criticizing it, to some degree" by taking "the naiveté of the original of an earlier day" and rejecting "its sentiment that ignores the ugliness of street life and the debasement that it signifies."

To do this, Souter said the 2 Live Crew could fairly use the "heart" of the original—the opening lyrics and guitar riff—from the Orbison-Dees song. "If 2 Live Crew had copied a significantly less memorable part of the original, it is difficult to see how its parodic character would have come through." Moreover, Souter noted, the 2 Live Crew "thereafter departed markedly from the Orbison lyrics for its own ends."

Some music publishers were shocked by Souter's opinion. Martin Bandier, chairman of EMI Music Publishing, said the Supreme Court's decision took "free speech to an absurd level." But Justice Kennedy expressed doubts in his concurring Supreme Court opinion that the 2 Live Crew recording was a legitimate parody: "As future courts apply our fair use analysis, they must take care to ensure that not just any commercial takeoff is rationalized *post hoc* as a parody." Sidney Rosdeitcher claimed that the Supreme Court had "made absolutely clear that the burden of proof remained on the party asserting fair use and that there was no presumption in favor of parody."

"We're still undefeated," Luther Campbell declared. But Souter's decision didn't end the "Oh, Pretty Woman" litigation. Instead, he sent the case back to Judge Wiseman in Nashville to determine whether the rap group's repeated use of the Orbison guitar riff throughout its recording was excessive. Souter also wanted the lower court to examine whether the 2 Live Crew had hurt Acuff-Rose's ability to license non-parody rap versions of "Oh, Pretty Woman."

Luke Records and Acuff-Rose immediately launched into settlement talks. But Luther Campbell's financial problems would stall resolution of the "Oh, Pretty Woman" case.

The 2 Live Crew was a group in name only when the Supreme Court heard the parody suit arguments. Since December 1991, Luther Campbell had been defending a lawsuit filed against him in Miami by 2 Live Crew members David Hobbs and Mark Ross. Hobbs and Ross charged in their Dade County Circuit Court complaint that Campbell, the sole director and shareholder of Luke Records, underpaid them at least $1 million in recording, merchandising, and publishing royalties, and had taken unauthorized concert commissions. Despite sales of millions of 2 Live Crew records, Hobbs and Ross claimed they were broke.

"Neither has enough money to fly to Miami to attend hearings," their lawyer Richard Wolfe said.

"They go and spend their money stupidly—buying cars, going partying, squiring girls all around the United States," Campbell retorted. "I'm not responsible for no grown man or what he does with his money."

In a related suit, Hobbs and Ross alleged that Campbell fraudulently obtained a federal trademark for the 2 Live Crew name. The suit claimed that Campbell had written in his trademark application that his record company began using the 2 Live Crew name in August 1985, the month Campbell first booked the group to appear at a Miami skating rink and a year before Campbell incorporated his label.

"I was the producer and had the musical ideas and Mark did the lyrics," Hobbs said. "Luke is what you would call in the rap industry a 'hype man,' a person that comes on stage and motivates the crowd."

Campbell admitted that Hobbs founded the 2 Live Crew but claimed it had been his idea to reconfigure the group into a successful, sexually explicit rap act. To settle the suits, Campbell nevertheless paid Hobbs and Ross $600,000 for the 2 Live Crew name.

Hobbs and Ross weren't the only artists angry at Campbell. Peter Jones—as M.C. Shy-D, the first successful solo act on Campbell's label—sued him in 1990. Jones claimed that Campbell underpaid him royalties for the Shy-D albums *Gotta Be Tough* and *Comin' Correct in '88*. Jones's depositions had to be taken at a correctional facility in Georgia, where he was imprisoned for shooting off an adversary's testicles during a fight in a club. In October 1994, the Dade Circuit Court ruled that Campbell owed Jones a total of $1.6 million in royalties, interest, and punitive damages.

"Luther agreed to give us $1.25 million to settle the case," said Richard Wolfe, also Jones's lawyer. "He paid about $900,000, then defaulted by [among other things] failing to return the Shy-D master tapes and to make one of the payments."

It turned out that Campbell had serious cash flow problems. Luke Records' distributors claimed Campbell's label owed them a combined $1.8 million, based on returns from retailers and unrecouped advances. "Luther's created a lot of bad blood. He's pissed off a lot of people," said James Leshaw, a Miami attorney for one of the distributors, Sony Music's RED.

In March 1995, a recording studio, a record manufacturer, and a production company forced Luke Records into involuntary bankruptcy. They claimed that the payments Campbell made in the Shy-D case had interfered with Campbell's ability to pay them. According to court documents, Luke Records had $6,005,588 in assets but owed $6,063,243 to a total of 199 creditors. Faced with a public auction of a piece of prime land he owned and an attempt by Peter Jones to seize Luke Records' stock, Campbell filed for personal bankruptcy, too, in June 1995.

James Feltman, a court-ordered accounting examiner, observed that Campbell had "tremendous talent in the areas of artist and product development, as well as promotion" and should continue to run Luke Records because "[s]imply stated, Campbell is the business." But Feltman also said that Luke Records "has historically proven itself to be ineffective, if not incompetent, in the areas of finance, contract administration, and accounting." For example, Feltman noted, Luke Records gave "significant" advances to artists but had failed to produce any royalty statements since mid-1993. That year Luke Records grossed over $14 million.

Campbell also had rocky relations with his lawyers. Allen Jacobi was Campbell's general counsel when the 2 Live Crew obscenity and parody cases began. Campbell fired Jacobi during the Shy-D settlement talks. According to Jacobi, "I figured out what Peter Jones's royalties were, chopped that into a quarter and wanted to give him $100,000 to go away. Luther said, 'Whose side are you on, anyway?' He told me to take a hike."

Campbell claimed that Jacobi had taken an illegal fee when he negotiated a $5 million record distribution deal for Campbell with Atlantic Records in June 1990, at the peak of Campbell's obscenity-controversy notoriety.

Campbell used New York attorney Stuart Silfen "to review the Atlantic paperwork. Jacobi did the broad strokes. It took one night," Silfen said.

"Jacobi was probably only the second lawyer I had in my life," Campbell acknowledged. "I had a problem with Allen's fee [a 10-percent commission]. That was pretty much why I got rid of him."

Miami litigator Nick Manzini filed suit for Campbell against Jacobi. The complaint alleged that Jacobi took an excessive fee and improperly shared it with a non-lawyer, Campbell consultant David Chackler.

Manzini also filed a complaint against Jacobi with the Florida bar. Richard Wolfe explained, "We end up representing Jacobi and the Florida bar rules it was a finders' fee—reasonable and customary in line with industry standards—not an attorney's fee, so it was legal."

Around this time, Campbell hired his tax lawyer, Joe Weinberger, to be Luke's in-house counsel. "Joe wanted to get into the record business and I always had this thing about being taken down by the IRS," Campbell said. "So I thought I could have this tax guy be general counsel." Weinberger worked at Luke Records through 1994. "When gangsta rap became more popular than booty rap, I lent Luther $1 million to keep his label running. He paid back $600,000, then asked for more. Without getting security for the loan, I refused."

One day, Weinberger arrived at Luke Records' Liberty City headquarters to find Campbell had changed the locks on the doors. "He said he did it to stop Richard Wolfe from executing on the Shy-D judgment," Weinberger said. "Then Luther accused me of embezzling the money I lent him. He sued me, saying I was trying to get his creditors to put him into involuntary bankruptcy—which was true."

"I suspected Weinberger of doing something wrong because he had some kind of involvement with Richard Wolfe, the guy who's always suing me," Campbell claimed. "I found out they went to the University of Miami together. Who knew more about my business besides me than Weinberger? So why does Wolfe have all this information?" (Wolfe acknowledged "the seating was alphabetical in law school, so Joe and I sat one after the other in class. But I never got any information from him about Luther's business. In fact, Joe was the bitterest of legal adversaries.")

In March 1996, the bankruptcy court in Miami okayed Luther Campbell's complex reorganization plan. Under it, the majority of Luke Records' sound recording, publishing, and merchandising assets, including the 2 Live Crew properties, were sold for $800,000 to Lil' Joe Records—a label Joe Weinberger founded after being fired by Campbell. Joe Weinberger also obtained the rights to the 2 Live Crew name, and signed Mark Ross and David Hobbs, now rejoined by 2 Live Crew member Chris Wongwon, to a new recording contract. Campbell paid $500,000 to retain the rights to the Luke Records name.

Bruce Rogow and Sidney Rosdeitcher had negotiated a settlement of the "Oh, Pretty Woman" litigation soon after Justice Souter remanded the Supreme Court case to Nashville. Under the agreement, Acuff-Rose gave the 2 Live Crew what the rap group wanted in the first place: a compulsory license to use the Orbison-Dees song. (Roy Orbison's share of the "Oh, Pretty Woman" copyright was now in the hands of his estate; Acuff-Rose still owned the publishing rights to Bill Dees' share.)

Still, with the band broken up, "there was a delay in getting the settlement signed," Bruce Rogow explained. "Finally, I said there's nothing more I can do."

Opryland in-house counsel Sarah Nordlund complained to Judge Wiseman, "First, Mr. Rogow advised us that he could not locate one of his clients. Thereafter, we have been shunted from one new lawyer for defendants to another."

Nordlund was protesting a motion by Alan Mark Turk—now a creditor in the Luke Records bankruptcy proceedings—to withdraw from the "Oh, Pretty Woman" case. But once Luther Campbell, David Hobbs, Mark Ross, and Chris Wongwon all signed the Acuff-Rose settlement agreement, the Miami bankruptcy court gave its approval and, on May 15, 1996, Judge Wiseman entered an order in Nashville formally ending the rap parody litigation.

When he emerged from bankruptcy, Luther Campbell set up his new Luke Records incarnation in Miami Beach's Art Deco district. On display in the record company's otherwise bare storefront window was a "Censorship Is UnAmerican" poster that had served as a freedom-of-speech badge during the 2 Live Crew's obscenity skirmishes.

Upstairs in his office, Campbell sat behind a desk, brushing his closely cropped beard. A few days earlier, Louisiana prosecutors had dropped a criminal charge alleging that Campbell tossed a woman from a concert stage. This was the latest in a series of criminal counts, ranging from disorderly conduct to weapons possession, that Campbell had managed to dodge.

He had also just wrapped up a legal round from his post-bankruptcy proceedings. Richard Wolfe, Campbell's nemesis, and Frank Terzo—the liquidating trustees—had sued Campbell for, among other things, allegedly diverting Luke Records fan club merchandise—valued at $100,000 during the bankruptcy—and instead turning over only "two plastic bags filled with approximately two dozen baseball caps, one dozen bandannas and three dozen T shirts," all worth "less than $350." In addition, Wolfe and Terzo claimed that Campbell convinced a halfway-house resident to cash a $9,999 check from a restricted $10,000 Luke Records bank account. Then, the trustees charged, the man turned the funds over to Campbell for $20.

"Frank Terzo froze my accounts and we'd already written out business checks—for insurance and salaries—that were going to bounce," Campbell claimed shortly after ironing out his differences with the trustees. "So I told this halfway-house guy, 'We'll pay you to do some painting.' He signed the check and I took the cash to cover the outstanding checks."

A wily record industry player who turned First Amendment issues into a cash cow, Campbell nevertheless paid a high price for fighting the law. Not only had he lost the rights to the lucrative 2 Live Crew recordings, he also dropped a good part of his fortune on lawyers. Trying to jump-start his career through TV projects, as a solo artist, and through a softening of his raunchy image, Campbell estimated in his South Beach office, "I'll bet I've spent a third of all the money I've earned in legal fees alone."

Endnotes

Chapter 1

p. 1 "It's crazy": Author conversation with Jack Soden, August 1997.

p. 1 "It's really giving Elvis back": Dirk Beveridge, "A Kingly Decision," *Las Vegas Review-Journal*, March 20, 1997.

p. 1 "Practically non-existent": Bill Ellis, "Sensible Elvis Inc. aims to grow rock-solid empire," Memphis *Commercial Appeal*, August 17, 1997.

p. 2 But it wasn't until 1977: *Zacchini v. Scripps-Howard Broadcasting Co.*, 433 U.S. 562 (1977). This case involved the TV broadcast of footage of a human cannon-ball's act. Right of publicity suits, which are decided under state law, are usually determined under the law of a celebrity's state of residence or, in some cases, the law of the state that has the most contacts to the circumstance from which a suit arose.

p. 2 Since Elvis's death, the entertainer's estate: Elvis Presley's estate legally closed in February 1993, when his daughter, Lisa Marie, inherited it on her 25th birthday. This chapter uses the word "estate" generically for events that occurred after February 1993.

p. 2 "You know, the other day": Edwin Howard, "Interviews Over Course of Elvis' Career Show His Evolution as Superstar," *Memphis Business Journal*, August 10-14, 1992, p. 19.

p. 2 "In the '50s, we had to drive": Author interview with Frank Glankler, April 1990.

p. 2 "Elvis had access to": This and subsequent Beecher Smith quotes from August 1997 author interview, unless otherwise indicated.

p. 3 Elvis Presley earned an estimated $79 million: Stephen G. Tompkins, "Elvis's share: not a king's ransom," Memphis *Commercial Appeal*, February 7, 1988. At times, Elvis was in the 90 percent tax bracket. His tax bills were always high; he utilized no significant tax deductions.

p. 3 "From 1973 on": This and subsequent Barry Ward quotes from July 1997 and August 1997 author interviews.

p. 4 "Elvis said, 'Maybe'": Author interview with Jack Soden, April 1990.

p. 4 "Elvis told a lot of people": Author interview with Beecher Smith, October 1997.

p. 5 "I'd be damned if I'd let Mr. Presley": "Elvis Freed From Jet Contract," Memphis *Press-Scimitar*, May 9, 1975.

p. 5 "Absolutely running him ragged": Bill Hance, "Presley Comes To Town, But It's 'No Show' At Studio," *The Nashville Banner*, January 28, 1977.

p. 6 "The most unbelievable thing": This and subsequent Blanchard Tual quotes from June 1990 author interview, unless otherwise indicated.

p. 7 "Colonel Parker can kiss my ass": Author's confidential source.

p. 7 "Payoff" and "for keeping Elvis under control": Blanchard Tual's guardian *ad litem* report, July 31, 1981.

p. 7 "Never hid anything" and "to suggest that I ever attempted": James Kingsley, "The Colonel Speaks," Memphis *Commercial Appeal*, August 16, 1981.

p. 7 "Wanted it, he got it" and "Sometimes it was such a heartache": Randell Beck, "Suspicious Minds," Memphis *Press-Scimitar*, September 8 and 9, 1981.

p. 7 "They say Presley is" and "And all this security mumbo-jumbo": Hance, *The Nashville Banner*, January 28, 1977.

p. 8 "I hope the tax bills": Randell Beck, "Taxes, Legal Fees Drain Presley Estate," Memphis *Press-Scimitar*, February 8, 1982.

p. 8 The 1983 settlement agreement severed: In 1990, the estate acquired 35 tons of Elvis Presley memorabilia from Colonel Parker.

p. 8 "A couple of weeks after we opened": This and subsequent Jack Soden quotes from August 1997 author interview, unless otherwise indicated.

p. 9 "At all times, Elvis knew": Affidavit of Colonel Tom Parker, September 3, 1977, in *Factors Etc. Inc. v. Wild Side Inc.*, 77-4705 (S.D.N.Y.).

p. 9 For example, Elvis's talent agent, the William Morris Agency, protested: William Morris Agency memo to Hal Wallis and Wallis's associate, Joseph Hazen, June 5, 1962; *Ladies' Home Journal*, June 1962, p. 3.

p. 9 "I had my Midget Fanclub there": Colonel Parker letter to Hal Wallis, April 15, 1959.

p. 9 "Presley products sold more than $30 million": William D. Laffler, "Elvis-Named Products Sold $30 Million First Year," Memphis *Press-Scimitar*, November 5, 1965.

p. 10 "I knew it was illegal": William Thomas, "When It's Merchandising A Celebrity, 'The Bear' Is There," Memphis *Commercial Appeal*, December 18, 1977.

p. 10 "We felt that the Elvis merchandising": This and subsequent Lee Geissler quote from September 1997 author interview.

p. 10–11 "For the purpose of knocking out": Thomas, Memphis *Commercial Appeal*, December 18, 1977.

p. 11 The New York right of privacy statute: New York Civil Rights Law Secs. 50 and 51.

p. 11 But Judge Tenney ruled: *Factors Etc. Inc. v. Creative Card Co.*, 444 F.Supp. 279 (S.D.N.Y. 1977); *Factors Etc. Inc. v. Pro Arts Inc.*, 444 F.Supp. 288 (S.D.N.Y. 1977). In 1984, the New York Court of Appeals ruled that the right of publicity was subsumed in the state's right of privacy statute. *Stephano v. News Group Publications Inc.*, 64 N.Y.S.2d 174. As a result, New York has no descendible right of publicity. *Pirone v. Macmillan Inc.*, 894 F.2d 579 (2d Cir. 1990).

p. 11 When Pro Arts appealed: *Factors Etc. Inc. v. Pro Arts Inc.*, 579 F.2d 215 (2d Cir. 1978).

p. 11 It earned about $125,000: Deposition of Rob Russen in *Estate of Elvis Presley v. Russen*, 80-0951 (D.N.J.).

p. 12 "Was unimpressed by the fact": Deposition of Rob Russen, October 1, 1980, in *Estate of Elvis Presley v. Russen*.

p. 12 In 1981, U.S. District Judge Stanley Brotman: *Estate of Presley v. Russen*, 513 F.Supp. 1339 (D.N.J. 1981).

p. 13 "Nobody says I can't wear sideburns": Michael Lollar, "Great Pretenders— Imitators Compete In Reverence For Elvis," Memphis *Commercial Appeal*, August 10, 1990.

p. 13 The district court...but in March 1980: *Memphis Development Foundation v. Factors Etc. Inc.*, 616 F.2d 956 (6th Cir. 1980).

p. 13 In June 1981, the appeals court decided: *Factors Etc. Inc. v. Pro Arts Inc.*, 652 F.2d 278 (2d Cir. 1981).

p. 13 "Like standing in the middle": Author interview with Jack Soden, April 1990.

p. 14 "Glankler Brown got in touch": Author interviews with Mack Webner, May 1990 and October 1997.

p. 15 "The public is likely to believe": Reply Memorandum of Elvis Presley Enterprises Inc., September 4, 1985, in *State of Tennessee ex rel. The Elvis Presley International Memorial Foundation v. Crowell*, in the Chancery Court of Davidson County, 85-1355.

p. 15 "[N]o one, not even EPE, has raised any objection": Supplementary Affidavit of Cheryle Smith, November 8, 1985, in *State of Tennessee ex rel. The Elvis Presley International Memorial Foundation v. Crowell.*

p. 15 "It would be difficult for any court today": *State of Tennessee ex rel. The Elvis Presley International Memorial Foundation v. Crowell,* 733 S.W.2d 89 (Tenn. App. 1987).

p. 16 "Graceland was the exclusive buyer": This and subsequent Sid Shaw quotes from October 1997 author interview.

p. 17 "Neither Elvis nor I": Affidavit of Colonel Tom Parker, June 11, 1985, in *Elvis Presley Enterprises Inc. v. Elvisly Yours Inc.,* 85-2211 (W.D. Tenn.).

p. 17 In April 1987...the 6th Circuit ruled in favor of the estate: In July 1985, the district court had denied the Presley estate's motion for a preliminary injunction in the Elvisly Yours case.

p. 17 "Shaw admitted using": *Elvis Presley Enterprises Inc. v. Elvisly Yours Inc.,* 817 F.2d 104 (6th Cir. 1987).

p. 17 "Has no other purpose in mind": Affidavit of Priscilla Presley, November 30, 1987, in *Elvis Presley Enterprises Inc. v. Elvisly Yours Inc.*

p. 17 The 6th Circuit later narrowed: *Elvis Presley Enterprises Inc. v. Elvisly Yours Inc.,* 936 F.2d 889 (6th Cir. 1991).

p. 18 "Even if Elvis Presley was still alive": *In the Matter of Applications Nos. 1371624, 1371627 and 1371637 by Elvis Presley Enterprises Inc.,* CH 1996 E No. 1337 (1997).

p. 18 "My mouth dropped open": Author interview with Jay Cooper, July 1997.

p. 18 "Elvis Presley has a reputation": Daniel Fisher, "Graceland Sues as Bar Owner Links King To Kitsch," Memphis *Commercial Appeal,* November 24, 1996.

p. 19 "All Shook Up": This and subsequent Judge Gilmore quotes from ruling in *Elvis Presley Enterprises Inc. v. Capece,* 950 F.Supp. 783 (S.D. Tex. 1996).

p. 19 In May 1998, Judge Carolyn King: *Elvis Presley Enterprises Inc. v. Capece,* 1998 U. S. App. Lexis 9012.

p. 20 According to EPE's Memphis litigator: Author interview with Bill Bradley, October 1997.

p. 20 Through 1985, estate income: Affidavit of Joseph Hanks, August 8, 1985, in *State of Tennessee v. Crowell ex rel. The Elvis Presley International Memorial Foundation.*

p. 20 Between 1991 and 1996, it was more than $20 million: *Elvis Presley Enterprises Inc. v. Capece,* 950 F.Supp. 783 (S.D. Tex. 1996).

p. 20 "We're not even flexible": This and subsequent Carol Butler quotes from August 1997 author interview.

p. 20 The estate's typical deal: Based on author's reading of an Elvis Presley Enterprises merchandising license.

Chapter 2

p. 21 "She was sort of secretive": This and subsequent Frank Weber quotes from February 1992 author interview, unless otherwise indicated.

p. 22 "I trusted him": Billy Joel comment submitted to author, February 1992.

p. 23 "He sent a check": Timothy White, "Billy Joel Is Angry," *Rolling Stone*, September 4, 1980, p. 37.

p. 23 "He never had enough money": Tony Schwartz, "Billy the Kid," *Newsweek*, December 11, 1978, p. 68.

p. 23 "Dittyboppers" and "kick over garbage cans": Ibid.

p. 23 "The loudest thing": White, *Rolling Stone*, September 4, 1980, p. 38.

p. 24 "I love this guy": Fred Goodman, "An Innocent Man," *Spy*, March 1991, p. 73.

p. 24 Netted only $7,763: White, *Rolling Stone*, September 4, 1980, p. 37.

p. 24 "I've got lawsuits": White, *Rolling Stone*, September 4, 1980, pg. 38.

p. 25 "The reader should be put on notice": *Powers v. Joel*, 83-1929, in the Second Judicial District of the State of Nevada in and for the County of Washoe, April 29, 1988.

p. 25 "Now I see somebody coming": WPLJ-FM May 16, 1996 broadcast of Billy Joel's "Questions, Answers and a Little Music" from Town Hall in New York City.

p. 25 "Her function as my manager": Anthony DeCurtis, "The Rolling Stone Interview—Billy Joel," *Rolling Stone*, November 6, 1986, p. 80.

p. 25 "I had questions": Deposition of Billy Joel, March 3, 1988, in *Weber v. Joel*, 5030/87, in the Supreme Court of the State of New York, New York County.

p. 25–26 "Because she had brought Frank in": Billy Joel deposition.

p. 26 "If you want this marriage to work": Billy Joel deposition.

p. 26 "Great errors he claimed": Billy Joel comment submitted to author, February 1992.

p. 26 "I met him at a party": Billy Joel deposition.

p. 26 "I don't know where he is": Billy Joel deposition.

p. 28 "I may not be rich": David Wild, "The Rolling Stone Interview—Billy Joel," *Rolling Stone*, January 25, 1990, p. 36.

p. 28 "A fire hydrant": Giles Smith, "Playing piano until the fingers get burnt," *The Independent*, July 8, 1993.

p. 29 "Weber repeatedly has abused": *Joel v. Weber*, 20702/89, in the Supreme Court of the State of New York, New York County.

p. 29 "We found that": Author interview with Leonard Marks, February 1992.

p. 29 About to obligate Joel to a $6 million loan: Affidavit of Leonard Marks in Support of Motion to Discontinue Action (Marks Affidavit), April 13, 1995, in *Joel v. Weber*.

p. 30 Billy Joel managed to collect only $250,000: Ken Schlager, "Inside Track" column, *Billboard*, May 25, 1991, p. 80.

p. 30 Frank's May 1990 bankruptcy petition: Marks Affidavit.

p. 31 "I've been paid": Stan Soocher, "Bitter Battle Over Billy Joel's Business," *Entertainment Law & Finance*, June 1991, p. 6.

p. 31 "They've tried to intimidate me" and "I get five pounds of paper": Soocher, "Bitter Battle Over Billy Joel's Business," *Entertainment Law & Finance*, June 1991, p. 6, and author interview with Anthony Conforti, February 1992.

p. 31–32 CBS Records chairman Walter Yetnikoff: Fredric Dannen, *Hit Men— Power Brokers and Fast Money Inside the Music Business* (New York: Times Books, 1990), p. 151.

p. 32–33 "Harbored ill feelings" and "did wrongfully, knowingly, intentionally": *Frank Management Inc. v. Joel*, 20702/89, in the Supreme Court of the State of New York, New York County.

p. 33 In one, Sandy Linzer: Dannen, *Hit Men*, p. 151.

p. 33 In the other suit, an independent record label: James Kaplan, "The Rock 'N' Roll Consigliere," *Vanity Fair*, October 1991, p. 114.

p. 33–34 Grubman's insurance company settled: Stan Soocher, "Madonna Bruce & Grubman Indursky," *The National Law Journal*, November 18, 1991, p. 31.

p. 34 "In many cases, it exists": Author interview with Freddy DeMann, November 1991.

p. 34 "We are a league unto ourselves": This and subsequent Arthur Indursky quotes from June 1991 author interview, unless otherwise indicated.

p. 34 "Relentless and tenacious" and "negotiating my *tuchus* off": Author interview with Allen Grubman, September 1991; shirt ripped to shreds: Dannen, *Hit Men*, p. 152.

p. 34 But Yetnikoff disliked Tannen: Dannen, *Hit Men*, p. 155.

p. 35 "Weber represented": Affidavit of Arthur Indursky In Support of Motion for Consolidation, July 8, 1991, in *The Union Savings Bank v. G&I Equities*, 6158/91, in the Supreme Court of the State of New York, County of Suffolk.

p. 35 Grubman complained: Details of Weber/Grubman relationship from Leonard Marks Memorandum of FBI meeting with Grubman and Indursky on May 21, 1992, attached to Affidavit of Alan R. Friedman In Opposition to

Defendants' Motions Regarding Discovery (Friedman Affidavit), June 23, 1993, in *Joel v. Grubman*, 26155/92, in the Supreme Court of the State of New York, County of New York.

p. 36 "Burn horses" and "crazy": Marks Memorandum of FBI meeting with Grubman and Indursky.

p. 36 "Desperate for money": Friedman Affidavit.

p. 36 Totaling over $180,000: Affidavit of Billy Joel attached to Friedman Affidavit.

p. 36 "Financial consulting and tax planning": Invoices in Exhibit "O" attached to Friedman Affidavit.

p. 36 In 1985 alone, the payments amounted to $100,000: Invoices in Exhibit "P" attached Friedman Affidavit.

p. 36 "Nothing that would take more": Marks Memorandum of FBI meeting with Grubman and Indursky.

p. 37 "Kickbacks": Friedman Affidavit.

p. 37 "So they were paying less" and "something was wrong": Jane Cohen and Bob Grossweiner, "Bulletin" column, *Performance*, October 2, 1992, p. 5.

p. 37 "A contrived and libelous attempt": Defendants' Verified Answer in *Joel v. Grubman*.

p. 38 "Not a single one" and "When your defense is weak": Kim Neely, "Joel Sues Lawyers," *Rolling Stone*, November 26, 1992, p. 21.

p. 38 "Confused as to whether": "Bit Parts" column, *Entertainment Law & Finance*, March 1993, p. 8. (Bert Fields interviewed by Steven Jay Gabe.)

p. 39 Frank Weber, Allen Grubman and Arthur Indursky were present: Marks Affidavit.

p. 39 "Sabotage," "knew nothing about" and hid in the bushes: Jane Cohen and Bob Grossweiner, "Bulletin" column, *Performance*, August 27, 1993, p. 4.

p. 39 "It's done": "People" column, New York *Daily News*, October 26, 1993.

p. 39 "Totally defeated" and "virtually every settlement agreement": Marks Affidavit.

p. 39 Sony Music Entertainment chairman Michael Schulhof: Jeffrey A. Trachtenberg, "Lawyer for Billy Joel Discloses Payments by Sony to End Conflict-of-Interest Suit," *Wall Street Journal*, May 3, 1995.

p. 40 "Pivotal" point: Author interview with Alan Friedman, July 1996.

p. 40 In return, Joel paid $562,500: Marks Affidavit.

p. 40 An additional $2 million to $3 million: Author interview with Ed London, August 1996.

p. 40 From all the lawsuits, Joel would collect $8 million: Reply Affidavit of Leonard Marks in Support of Motion to Discontinue Action, May 2, 1995, in *Joel v. Weber*.

p. 41 During the Joel/Weber litigation, London had turned against Frank: Marks Affidavit.

p. 41 Billy charged London with using: Ibid.

p. 41 "Washed" the artist's pension money: Ibid.

p. 41 Allegedly been given to...Al Teller: Ibid.

p. 41 Teller denied knowing: Fred Goodman, "A Matter of Trust," *Entertainment Weekly*, October 9, 1992, p. 8.

p. 41 Irwin Feiner: Marks Affidavit, p. 30, and Rich Wilner, "Feiner gets jail term, probation," *Women's Wear Daily*, April 18, 1988.

p. 41 "Trying to get me to look": Wild, *Rolling Stone*, January 25, 1990, p. 36.

p. 41 "There is no chance": Billy Joel comment submitted to author, February 1992.

p. 41–42 "Most of these agencies" and "The assumption": "If I Knew Then What I Know Now," *Musician*, April 1995, pp. 25 and 26.

p. 42 One well-wisher: "Page Six" column, *New York Post*, October 23, 1995.

Chapter 3

p. 43 "Going in and pushing my way around": Robert Sam Anson, "Tommy Boy," *Vanity Fair*, December 1996, p. 317.

p. 43 Mottola reportedly packed: Anson, *Vanity Fair*, December 1996, p. 290.

p. 44 "Despises Tommy Mottola": David Sinclair, "He's A Loser, Baby—Court rejects George Michael's plea to break his contract with Sony," *Rolling Stone*, August 11, 1994, p. 28.

p. 44 "It's starting to be like the movie industry": Robert Hilburn and Chuck Philips, "Rock's New World Order," *Los Angeles Times*, November 29, 1992.

p. 44 "Most of the majors are in the fast food business": Paul Gorman, "Industry's foremost dealmaker prepares for life with the indies," *Music Week*, November 30, 1996, p. 10.

p. 44 "The last link in the chain": This and subsequent Dick Leahy quotes from November 1992 author interview.

p. 45 "It was very strange": This and subsequent Rob Kahane quotes from July 1997 author interview, unless otherwise indicated.

p. 45 "Artists were glued to developments": This and subsequent David Ravden quote from July 1997 author interview.

p. 45 "This is the first time": Author interview with Tony Russell, November 1992.

p. 45 It had been introduced into the motion picture industry: *De Havilland v. Warner Bros. Pictures*, 67 Cal. App. 2d 225 (1944).

p. 46 "This case is a huge risk": Simon Garfield, "The machine that ate George Michael," *The Independent*, November 11, 1992.

p. 46 "People have no comprehension": Rob Tannenbaum, "George Michael—Artist Or Airhead?" *Musician*, January 1988, p. 30.

p. 46 "I never really lacked confidence": Ibid.

p. 46 "We were terrible": Tannenbaum, *Musician*, January 1988, p. 31.

p. 46 Earned only 100,000 pounds: Tannenbaum, *Musician*, January 1988, p. 32.

p. 46–47 "It took me about two months to suss out": Ibid.

p. 47 "Once you've done it yourself": Tannenbaum, *Musician*, January 1988, p. 98.

p. 47 "Very badly and dishonestly": Justice Jonathan Parker in *Between: Panayiotou and Sony Music Entertainment*, High Court of Justice, Chancery Division, [1994] EMLR 229.

p. 47 "A bloody six months battle": Tony Russell letter to Allen Grubman, December 19, 1986.

p. 47 "Acrimony and mutual suspicion": Justice Parker in *Between: Panayiotou and Sony Music Entertainment*.

p. 47 "The minute you're lumped": Jon Pareles, "Wham Facing Up to New Popularity," *The New York Times*, February, 13, 1985.

p. 47 "I don't know where I lost the plot": Steve Pond, "George Michael, Seriously," *Rolling Stone*, January 28, 1988, p. 32.

p. 47–48 "People like Madonna": Pond, "George Michael, Seriously," *Rolling Stone*, January 28, 1988, p. 49.

p. 48 "He even knows what he'll do": Ibid.

p. 48 "Walter was a clever, sophisticated man" and "just bluff": Simon Napier-Bell, "Does a happy artist equal profit?" *Applause*, undated clip.

p. 48 "All of us agreed": This and subsequent Michael Lippman quotes from July 1997 author interview.

p. 49 "Trying to get the best" and "be preferable to see a bit more": Paul Russell witness statement in *Between: Panayiotou and Sony Music Entertainment*.

p. 49 "Take it or leave it time": George Michael witness statement in *Between: Panayiotou and Sony Music Entertainment*.

p. 49 "I had little alternative": Ibid.

p. 50 "For the first time in my career" and "whether or not my record company would support me": Ibid.

p. 51 "That I considered that I could have a very long-term career": Ibid.

p. 51 "Just kind of accepted it": George Michael cross-examination in *Between: Panayiotou and Sony Music Entertainment.*

p. 51 "A high degree of mutual antipathy": Justice Parker in *Between: Panayiotou and Sony Music Entertainment.*

p. 52 "A deliberate policy decision": George Michael quoted in *Between: Panayiotou and Sony Music Entertainment.*

p. 52 "The competition an edge": Andy Stephens letter to George Michael, November 1, 1990.

p. 52 "He was totally depressed" and "the straw that broke": Tony Russell witness statement in *Between: Panayiotou and Sony Music Entertainment.*

p. 52 "Rescuable": George Michael cross-examination.

p. 53 "I am the last one to look": Mark Schwartz memo quoted in *Between: Panayiotou and Sony Music Entertainment.*

p. 54 Several of them contacted Michael's camp: Author interview with Dick Leahy, November 1992. Lack of record companies' cooperation confirmed in a July 1997 author interview with Sony solicitor David Davis.

p. 54–55 "Basically a counterpart": Author interviews with Don Engel, May 1997 and November 1992.

p. 55 "David Geffen told us": Author interview with Don Engel, July 1997.

p. 55 In March 1993, Henley filed a countersuit: Calif. Labor Code Sec. 2855. In the 1980s, the Recording Industry Association of America successfully lobbied the California legislature to permit record companies to seek money damages for product an artist in a seven-year statute suit had yet to deliver under a recording contract.

p. 55–56 "David Geffen's company is no longer the one": Chuck Philips, "EMI Offer Intensifies Henley Feud With Geffen," *Los Angeles Times*, April 29, 1993.

p. 56 "I'm about as concerned about this": Chuck Philips, "Henley Ups the Ante in Geffen Fight," *Los Angeles Times*, September 1, 1993.

p. 56 "Don Engel argued before the judge": Stan Soocher, "Bit Parts" column, *Entertainment Law & Finance*, June 1994, p. 8.

p. 56 "A vehicle for settling the case": Ibid.

p. 56–57 "Geffen was under pressure": Author interview with Don Engel, July 1997.

p. 57 In 1974, songwriter Tony Macaulay: *A. Schroeder Music Publishing Co. v. Macaulay*, (1974) 3 All ER 616 (HL).

p. 57 In 1988, the High Court ruled: *Zang Tumb Tuum Records Ltd. v. Johnson*, High Court of Justice, Chancery Division, 1987 Z No. 4889.

p. 57 Then in 1991, the High Court found: *Silvertone Records Ltd. v. Mountfield*, High Court of Justice, Queen's Bench Division, 1990 S No. 6909. The last major U.K. artist to challenge a major label contract on restraint of trade grounds was Rod Stewart, after he hit big in the early 1970s. But the issue wasn't reached because it was determined that Stewart's label, Mercury Records, improperly assigned his contract. Representing Stewart was solicitor David Davis, who represented Sony in the George Michael case.

p. 57 "But there was such huge interest": This and subsequent Cyril Glasser quote from July 1997 author interview.

p. 59 "Corrupt and dishonest way": Justice Parker in *Between: Panayiotou and Sony Music Entertainment*.

p. 60 "Inaccurate interpretation": Jeffrey Jolson-Colburn, "Superstar pacts revealed in Yetnikoff statement," *Hollywood Reporter*, November 30, 1993.

p. 61 "Thoroughly unreliable": Justice Parker in *Between: Panayiotou and Sony Music Entertainment*.

p. 62 The 400-page settlement: Details of settlement compiled from several sources, especially Paul Gorman, "George Michael—The bitter battle—and how peace was won," *Music Business International*, August 1995, pp. 11-13.

p. 63 "I think George is worried": Andrew Smith, "Can We Listen Without Prejudice?" London *Sunday Times*, January 7, 1996.

Chapter 4

p. 65 "We brought the Shirelles in": This and subsequent Sam Lipshie quotes from December 1996 author interviews, unless otherwise indicated. Artist Rights Enforcement chief Chuck Rubin noted in a July 1997 author interview, "One of the issues in the case was whether the defendants had been selling the original tracks, or re-recordings that had been done by some of the Shirelles. We prepped the ladies by playing them the re-recordings. They got caught up in it, stood up and started singing bits and pieces of the songs."

p. 65 "Beverly and Doris had been fighting": This and subsequent Chuck Rubin quotes from July 1997 author interviews, unless otherwise indicated.

p. 66 "I don't know anyone who's even seen him": Author interview with J. David Wykoff, December 1996.

p. 66 "He'd tell me": Lytle also raised show dogs and cattle.

p. 66–67 "A white knight of rock": Jon Pareles, "Tracing Lost Royalties: A White Knight of Rock," *The New York Times*, December 2, 1986; "more pit bull" and "a guy who didn't happen": Stephen Fried, "You're Cheatin' Art," *GQ*, January 1990, p. 60.

p. 67 "It was very difficult to track": Deposition of Doris Coley Kenner Jackson, June 7, 1988, in *Thomas v. Gusto Records Inc.*, 3-87-0975, in the U.S. District Court for the Middle District of Tennessee.

p. 68 "There were federal investigations": The government disallowed most such tax shelters. Some master recording tax shelter participants went to jail.

p. 69 "An after-market record company": Author interview with Grant Smith, July 1997.

p. 69 "We were selling it to": Peter Watrous, "Record Label Reissues A Treasured Collection of Rhythm-and-Blues," *The New York Times*, June 7, 1994.

p. 69 Lytle claimed Rubin never provided: Affidavit of Moe Lytle, May 3, 1990, in *G.M.L. Inc. v. Rubin*, 90-6165, transferred from the U.S. District Court for the Middle District of Tennessee to the Southern District of New York.

p. 69 "We just don't pay": Chuck Rubin trial testimony in *Thomas v. Gusto Records Inc.*

p. 70 "We've all known each other": Doris Jackson deposition.

p. 70 "This was the first case": Author interview with Grant Smith, July 1997.

p. 70 District Judge Thomas Higgins oversaw the juryless trial: There was no jury because a suit for an accounting, like one for an injunction, has traditionally been considered one for equitable relief, which is granted by a judge.

p. 76 "We had no idea what monies": Author interview with Fred Wolinsky, September 1997.

p. 78 "Particularly with '50s and '60s artists": Author interview with Tom Bonetti, September 1997.

p. 79 "Highland has no full-time employees": Stephen Hawkins also testified that he used his nine to ten employees in Canada "to save me having to divide my resources, to act as staff for Highland."

p. 79 "I've never seen a witness drink": Author interview with Ira Greenberg, July 1997.

p. 80 "These artists, while perhaps not 'superstars'": *Thomas v. Gusto Records Inc.*, 939 F.2d 395.

p. 80 "The defendants claimed the rights": *Thomas v. Gusto Records Inc.*, 939 F.2d 395 (6th Cir. 1991).

p. 80 "Why don't artists come forward": Author interview with Bob Emmer, September 1997.

p. 81 "I booked mostly country artists": This and subsequent Moe Lytle quotes from August 1997 author interview.

p. 82 The court allowed Gusto to continue: *CBS Inc. v. Gusto Records Inc.*, 403 F.Supp. 447 (M.D.Tenn. 1974).

p. 83 "If I wanted to win": David Willman, "Rights to Rock Treasure Chest at Issue in Trial," *Los Angeles Times*, August 16, 1992.

p. 83 "It was the judgment in the B.J. Thomas case": Author interview with Tom Bonetti, September 1997.

p. 83 But the day Lytle's lawyers were applying: Author interviews with G.M.L.'s lawyer, Robert Besser, October 1997 and April 1998. Author also interviewed Sehorn bankruptcy counsel, Rudy Cerone, in October 1997.

p. 83 Meanwhile, Moe Lytle continued to battle: Lytle was also involved in a suit for non-payment of royalties brought against his G.M.L. by the Kingsmen, who had a hit with "Louie, Louie" in 1963. In April 1998, the 9th U.S. Circuit Court of Appeals upheld a district court ruling that the Kingsmen's master recordings, which Lytle had purchased, should revert to the band. *Peterson v. Gusto Records Inc.*, 1998 U.S. App. Lexis 7149.

Chapter 5

p. 85 Across town that same day: The settlement agreement was signed on November 7, 1989.

p. 86 For dropping the litigation: Author's confidential sources reported in Stan Soocher, "You Never Give Me My Money," *Rolling Stone*, January 25, 1990, pp. 14, 15.

p. 86 "They couldn't find anything to sue": Jeff Giles, "Come Together," *Newsweek*, October 23, 1995, p. 66.

p. 87 "I always felt retrospectively": Timothy White, "Magical Mystery Tour: Harrison Previews 'Anthology Volume 2,'" *Billboard*, March 9, 1996, p. 89.

p. 87–88 The band members themselves got only: Chet Flippo, *Yesterday: The Unauthorized Biography of Paul McCartney* (New York: Doubleday, 1988), p. 199.

p. 88 "We used to ask them" and "the first time I actually saw checks": Chris Salewicz, "Tug of War," *Musician*, October 1986, p. 62.

p. 88 In a gesture of generosity; but when Epstein negotiated: Philip Norman, *Shout!—The Beatles in Their Generation* (New York: MJF Books, 1981), p. 196.

p. 88 "So I put down the first figure": Norman, *Shout!—The Beatles in Their Generation*, p. 209.

p. 89 In 1967, Nizer settled: Norman, *Shout!—The Beatles in Their Generation*, pp. 305-306.

p. 89 "Very keen, able and well-spoken": Author interview with Louis Nizer, November 1989.

p. 89 $50,000 retainer and "the Seltaeb deal was my fault": Peter Brown and Steven Gaines, *The Love You Make: An Insider's Story of the Beatles* (New York: McGraw-Hill, 1983), p. 163.

p. 89 "Your personal finances": Stephen Maltz letter quoted in Norman, *Shout!— The Beatles in Their Generation*, p. 350.

p. 90 "The first real sophistication": This and subsequent Nat Weiss quote from author interview, November 1989.

p. 90 "A cross between": A.E. Hotchner, *Blown Away* (New York: Fireside, 1991), p. 187.

p. 90–91 "And I got a lot of guilt": Salewicz, *Musician*, October 1986, p. 60.

p. 91 "Paul was the same with Brian": Jann Wenner, "One Guy Standing There Shouting 'I'm Leaving,'" *Rolling Stone*, May 14, 1970, p. 6.

p. 91 Lennon penned a series: *Between: McCartney and Lennon*, In the High Court of Justice, Chancery Division, Group B, 1970 M. No. 6315.

p. 91 "A second-rate salesman": Justice Stamp quoted in Hotchner, *Blown Away*, p. 198.

p. 92 "I never did believe": Author interview with Allen Klein, Winter 1985.

p. 92 "This is one of the few cases": Author interview with Joseph Santora, April 1998. Author also interviewed Allen Klein's lawyer, Donald Zakarin, in April 1998. In the end, Harrison owned full rights in "He's So Fine." Klein's ABKCO retained a worldwide percentage interest in "My Sweet Lord," excluding the U.S. and Canada.

p. 93n "Chapman believes without question": Author interview with Jonathan Marks, June 1981.

p. 93 In his deposition, Lennon stated: Reported in Anthony DeCurtis, "Beatles Planned Film Reunion," *Rolling Stone*, July 17-31, 1986, p. 15.

p. 93 "I met with them in their apartment": Author interview with Leon Wildes, November 1989.

p. 93 "It just seemed like a toothache" and "But they kept pullin' me back": Pete Hamill, "Long Night's Journey Into Day," *Rolling Stone*, June 5, 1975, p. 73.

p. 93 "Everybody's sued each other": Transcript of Harrison press conference published in *Beatlefan*, Vol. I, No. 3.

p. 94 John Lennon signed the letter: Author interview with Stephen Tenenbaum, November 1989.

p. 95 "There were several Yoko Ono songs" and "that escalation clause": This and subsequent Joseph Wheelock attribution and quotes from author interviews, August 1996, unless otherwise indicated.

p. 95 Grand Funk settlement figure attribution and subsequent Daniel Murdock quotes from author interview, August 1996.

p. 96 "We don't have a witness": This and subsequent John Eastman quotes—as well Paul McCartney, Linda McCartney and Lee Eastman quotes—from a tape recording of a mid-'80s meeting among these individuals.

p. 100 "That's just sheer nonsense": Anthony DeCurtis, "Illegal Sale of Beatles LP's Alleged," *Rolling Stone*, May 22, 1986, p. 14.

p. 100 "Our plant manager sold": Deposition of Dennis White, March 21, 1986, in *Apple Records Inc. v. Capitol Records Inc.*, 08041/79, in the Supreme Court of the State of New York, County of New York.

p. 100 Walter Lee...admitted: Deposition of Walter Lee, March 20, 1986, in *Apple Records Inc. v. Capitol Records Inc.*

p. 100 "Isolated incident" and "completely successful": "Beatles' Apple Records Lawsuit Vs. Capitol Draws Press Barbs," *Variety*, May 7, 1986, p. 535.

p. 100 "If their claims are proven": Justice Michael Donzin ruling in *Apple Records Inc. v. Capitol Records Inc.*, 08041/79, July 28, 1986.

p. 101 Leonard Marks claimed that Capitol: Affidavit of Leonard M. Marks in Opposition to Motion to Dismiss, December 17, 1986, *Apple Records Inc. v. Capitol Records Inc.*

p. 101 "Pension funds run by the Mafia": J. Kordosh, "Fab! Gear!—The George Harrison Interview," *Creem*, December 1987, p. 46.

p. 101 "Like a scam cooked up by": Author interview with Michael Donzin, October 1996.

p. 101 "Insufficient manufacturing capacity": David Fricke, "Capitol To Release Beatles CD's," *Rolling Stone*, February 26, 1987, p. 25.

p. 102 Jackson compiled a list: Jay Cocks, "Wanna Buy a Revolution," *Time*, May 18, 1987, p. 78.

p. 103 "Definitely": Deposition of Daniel Gittelman, March 11, 1988, in *Apple Records Inc. v. Capitol Records Inc.*

p. 103 "A competitor of mine phoned": Soocher, *Rolling Stone*, January 25, 1990, pp. 14, 15.

p. 103 Settlement talks. . .soon resumed: "Beatles, Ono eye Capitol-EMI settlement," *Variety*, February 7, 1989, p. 123.

p. 103 $300 million: "Beatles on magical money tour," Jeffrey Jolson-Colburn, *The Hollywood Reporter*, December 20, 1995.

p. 104 $2.26 per CD: *Capitol Records Inc. v. Donovan Leisure Newton & Irvine*, 106494/93, in the Supreme Court of the State of New York, County of New York.

p. 105 "I was handling mostly corporate matters": Author interview with Denis O'Brien, September 1996.

p. 105 "That, if Mr. Harrison sued": Reply Declaration of Bertram Fields in Support of Motion for Summary Judgment, November 11, 1995, in *Harrison v. O'Brien*, BC120397, in the Superior Court of the State of California for the County of Los Angeles.

p. 106 "Had I made such a statement": Notice of Filing of Original Declaration of Defendant Denis O'Brien in Opposition To Plaintiff's Motion for Summary Adjudication, October 25, 1995, in *Harrison v. O'Brien.*

p. 106 "George saved himself $30 million": Author interview with Denis O'Brien, September 1996.

p. 107 "He was most unhappy" and "total chaos resulted": O'Brien declaration, October 25, 1995.

p. 107 "For some reason, Harrison has refused": Memorandum of Points & Authorities by Daniel Germain, October 17, 1995, attached to Opposition of Defendant Denis O'Brien To Motion For Order Concerning United States Trademarks in *Harrison v. O'Brien*

p. 108 By the end of the year: In February 1998, the California Court of Appeal affirmed Judge Todd's ruling for Harrison and denied Denis O'Brien's motion to transfer the case to England. *Harrison v. O'Brien*, B100692, in the Court of Appeal of the State of California, Second Appellate District, Division One.

p. 108 "I've hardly ever picked up" and "we've got to follow him": White, *Billboard*, March 9, 1996, p. 91.

Chapter 6

p. 109 "It started to wobble": Bill Bottrell trial testimony in *Cartier v. Jackson*, 92-1115, in the U.S. District Court for the District of Colorado.

p. 109 "I turned the lights on": Brad Sundberg trial testimony in *Cartier v. Jackson.*

p. 110 A copyright infringement suit involving Michael Jackson's "The Girl Is Mine": Details of the Fred Sanford trial proceedings from *Sanford v. CBS Inc.*, 594 F.Supp. 711 (1984); Morry Roth, "Jackson Testifies 'Girl Is Mine' Not Stolen From Suing Tunesmith," *Variety*, December 12, 1985, p. 2; "Jackson didn't steal hit song—court," *New York Post*, December 15, 1984; Christopher Andersen, *Michael Jackson: Unauthorized*, pp. 168, 169; and author interviews with Sanford counsel Jerold Jacover, January 1985, and CBS counsel James Klenk, January 1985.

p. 110 Generally, an infringement plaintiff: Access may be inferred if the songs at issue are "strikingly similar."

p. 111 "My tape was sent out": Fred Sanford quote from his appearance on "Good, Bad & Dangerous: The Trials of Michael Jackson Continue," *Geraldo* TV show, March 2, 1994.

p. 111 "Michael wanted to show": Author interview with John Branca, January 1985.

p. 112 "One of the jurors called me": Author interview with Jerold Jacover, January 1985.

p. 112 According to Robert Altschuler: Author interview with Robert Altschuler, January 1985.

p. 112 At least three and as many as 15 litigation matters: Affidavit of Eve Wagner, July 18, 1994, in *Cartier v. Jackson.*

p. 112 "We had just left the judge's bench": Author interview with Eve Wagner, August 1996.

p. 113 "I believe that Mr. Jackson received": Eve Wagner affidavit.

p. 113 "More than accidentally similar": Deposition of Jim Mason, April 29, 1993, in *Cartier v. Jackson.*

p. 113 But Mason also admitted: Jim Mason deposition.

p. 114 "She alleged, for the first time": Memorandum in Support of Defendants' Motion for Summary Judgment, May 21, 1993, in *Cartier v. Jackson.*

p. 114 "There was a press report": This and subsequent Richard Gabriel quotes from September 1996 author interview.

p. 115 "The tape of my song": Robert Smith quote from his appearance on "Good, Bad & Dangerous: The Trials of Michael Jackson Continue," *Geraldo* TV show. Fred Sanford, Robert Smith, Reynaud Jones and Crystal Cartier all appeared on the same broadcast.

p. 115 "Conservatively estimated at $750 million" and plaintiff's $20 million settlement demand: "Defense Verdicts—A Roundup of Major 1994 Cases," *The National Law Journal*, April 24, 1995, p. A24.

p. 115 Jones claimed that Jackson offered the plaintiffs $100,000: Figure from "Good, Bad & Dangerous: The Trials of Michael Jackson Continue," *Geraldo* TV show.

p. 116 "Was worded in such a manner": Ibid.

p. 116 In June 1996, however, the 9th U.S. Circuit Court of Appeals affirmed: *Smith v. Jackson*, 84 F.3d 1213 (1996).

p. 116 "I don't know if he knew": Michael Roberts, "Dangerous Liaisons," *Westword*, February 2, 1994, p. 10.

p. 117 "Anyone connected with the music business": This and subsequent Crystal Cartier quotes from September 1996 author interview, unless otherwise indicated. As is often the case in copyright infringement suits, the Eberhardts took Cartier's case on a contingency fee basis. Because Cartier timely registered her song in the Copyright Office, the court had the ability to award her attorney fees, if she prevailed over Jackson.

p. 122 "Was not on his schedule": "Jackson to Skip trial in Denver," *The Denver Post*, February 7, 1994.

p. 122 "That's the one day": Author interview with Eve Wagner, August 1996.

p. 122 "When Cartier walked in": Author interview with Ed Pierson, September 1996.

p. 122 Some of his fans obtained seats: Sue Lindsay, "Jackson 'performs' for court," *Rocky Mountain News*, February 15, 1994.

p. 127 "For him this is a tax-deductible expense": Eric Anderson, "Star's fans dazzled; Cartier unfazed," *The Denver Post*, February 15, 1994.

p. 128 But the appeals court ruled against her: *Cartier v. Jackson*, 59 F.3d 1046 (1995).

Chapter 7

p. 129 In 1966, the U.S. Supreme Court upheld: *Davis v. U.S.*, 384 U.S. 953.

p. 130 "Royal was aware": Luther Campbell & John R. Miller, *As Nasty As They Wanna Be: The Uncensored Story of Luther Campbell of the 2 Live Crew* (Fort Lee, N.J.: Barricade Books Inc., 1992), p. 70.

p. 130 "The best evidence": *Paris Adult Theatre I v. Slaton*, 413 U.S. 49 (1973).

p. 131 To be obscene under U.S. Supreme Court guidelines: The Supreme Court's guidelines are laid out in *Miller v. California*, 413 U.S. 15 (1973); the national standard was discussed in *Pope v. Illinois*, 481 U.S. 497 (1987). Obscenity differs from "indecency," which generally applies to government-regulated broadcast media, such as radio and TV. Indecent material refers to sexual or excretory functions that, in context, are patently offensive under community standards. Unlike works that are ruled obscene, indecent material is entitled to First Amendment protection and has been regulated by limiting it to late-night broadcast hours, rather than banning it altogether.

p. 131 "If the jury is aroused": Shawn Ryan, "Ala. Retailer Cleared In Obscenity Case," *Billboard*, March 10, 1990, p. 1.

p. 131 "Conservative Southerners don't like": Author interview with Bobby Segall, April 1990.

p. 131 "We're definitely in the middle": Author interview with Martin Garbus, May 1990.

p. 132 To head off forced labeling: The music industry continued to be troubled by proposed labeling laws and efforts to tighten state harmful-to-minors statutes well into the 1990s. In 1997 and 1998, for example, the music industry battled sound-recording legislation in more than half a dozen states. Mickey Granberg, legislative consultant to the National Association of Recording Merchandisers, noted in a March 1997 author interview that NARM continued to participate in weekly discussions of First Amendment issues with such entertainment industry organizations as the Motion Picture Association of America, the Recording Industry Association of America and the Video Software Dealers Association.

p. 132 "They tore the place apart": Author interview with Suzanne Stefanac, June 1990.

p. 132 "I felt it was a DEA drug raid": Biafra's spoken word album *High Priest of Harmful Matter*, Alternative Tentacles Records, 1989/1992.

p. 133 "What they're really trying to do": Don Bolles, "Punk v. Prosecutor," *The National Law Journal*, September 7, 1987, p. 6.

p. 133 "There was no such thing": John R. Miller, "Give The Devil His Due," *The Miami Herald Tropic* magazine, November 18, 1990, p. 10. Details of Luther Campbell's biography based on the Miller article, Campbell & Miller, *As Nasty As They Wanna Be*, and March 1997 author interview with Luther Campbell.

p. 133 "I didn't learn to read": Miller, *The Miami Herald Tropic* magazine, November 18, 1990, p. 11.

p. 133 "Luther used to shake up": Ibid.

p. 134 On New Year's Day: Details of Jack Thompson's first exposure to the 2 Live Crew's lyrics from February 1997 author interview with Jack Thompson.

p. 134 "A clarion call": James LeMoyne, "Three Men Who Took Aim at Rap Group," *The New York Times*, June 12, 1990.

p. 134 "I was stunned": Miller, *The Miami Herald Tropic* magazine, November 18, 1990, p. 16.

p. 135 "A lot of people don't realize it": Chuck Philips, "The 'Batman' Who Took On Rap," *Los Angeles Times*, June 18, 1990.

p. 135 "A hick area": Campbell & Miller, *As Nasty As They Wanna Be*, p. 73.

p. 136 But, according to Campbell, record stores throughout the state: Author interview with Luther Campbell, March 1997.

p. 136 But "it was Thompson's complaint": James F. McCarty, " 'Persistent' lawyer pressed sheriff to act on band," *The Miami Herald*, June 7, 1990.

p. 137 "It was like Mafia stuff": Author interview with Luther Campbell, March 1997.

p. 137 "I heard my godson singing": Author interview with Willie Logan, April 1990.

p. 138 "The theme that runs through my cases": Dexter Filkins, "Nova prof takes rap into court," *The Miami Herald*, May 28, 1990.

p. 138 "Even if you lose": This and subsequent Bruce Rogow quotes from March 1997 author interview, unless otherwise indicated.

p. 138 "Holding the record hostage": Author interview with Bruce Rogow, April 1990.

p. 138 "We used to serve those orders everyday": This and subsequent Nick Navarro quotes from March 1997 author interview.

p. 139 "Navarro may want the dispute in state court": Stan Soocher, "Bit Parts" column, *Entertainment Law & Finance*, April 1990, p. 8.

p. 139–140 "Anyone can sample 'Voodoo Chile'": Stan Soocher, "Aftermath of Obscenity Decision," *Entertainment Law & Finance*, July 1990, p. 6.

p. 140 The *Teasers* video would be missing: Confirmed by Bruce Rogow in a March 1997 author interview.

p. 141 "She says that she has never": Campbell & Miller, *As Nasty As They Wanna Be*, p. 84. Campbell claimed that he modeled himself after a long line of "blue humor" comedians that included Redd Foxx and Richard Pryor.

p. 142 "It wouldn't affect the type of lyrics": Author interview with Luther Campbell, May 1990.

p. 143 "The plaintiffs' rights to publish": This and subsequent Judge Gonzalez quotes from his ruling in *Skyywalker Records Inc. v. Navarro*, 739 F.Supp. 578 (1990). Given his musical tastes, it's unlikely that Judge Jose Gonzalez would have been sympathetic to the 2 Live Crew's brand of rap. In June 1990, *The Miami Herald* reported that Gonzalez's extensive collection of social protest music included Woody Guthrie, Pete Seeger and Josh White albums. But Bruce Rogow recalled seeing Judge Gonzalez at a local symphony orchestra performance the week of the federal 2 Live Crew trial. In a March 1997 conversation with the author about the violent lifestyles of gangsta rappers, Gonzalez waxed effusive about Barbra Streisand's sentimental recording "Evergreen."

p. 143 "He told me right on camera": Author interview with Jack Thompson, June 1990.

p. 143–144 After midnight Friday: Details of Club Nu show from Marilyn Marks and Jean Marie Lutes, "2 Live Crew laces shows with profanity," *The Miami Herald*, June 10, 1990; James LeMoyne, "Rap Singers Seized on Obscenity Charge," *The New York Times*, June 11, 1990; and author interview with Luther Campbell, March 1997.

p. 144 "So far I have yet to receive": Deborah Wilker, "Backlash Over Crew Leerics Ebbs," *Variety*, June 13, 1990, p. 3.

p. 144 "Navarro took a dive": Author interview with Jack Thompson, June 1990.

p. 144 "Jolly wouldn't return my phone calls": Author interview with Jack Thompson, February 1997.

p. 144 "Hate faxes": Soocher, *Entertainment Law & Finance*, July 1990, p. 6.

p. 144–145 "As long as these hundred-dollar bills": Stephen Smith, "2 Live sales go from boom to a bust," *The Miami Herald*, June 9, 1990.

p. 145 On Saturday night: Details of Club Futura shows and subsequent arrests from Marks and Lutes, *The Miami Herald*, June 10, 1990; "Two Of Crew Arrested In Fla.," *Daily Variety*, June 11, 1990; and author interviews with Luther Campbell and Nick Navarro, March 1997.

p. 145 "We were going to settle": Author interview with Allen Jacobi, November 1996.

p. 145 Law enforcement officials acted swiftly: Just how far-reaching the obscenity crackdown was is a matter of perspective. In his "Essay: Too Live a Crew," *Nova Law Review*, Vol. 15, No. 1, Winter 1991, p. 242, Bruce Rogow wrote that "out of tens of thousands of prosecutors, police and public officials, only a handful warred with *As Nasty As They Wanna Be*" and that "the few prosecutor-players were those with a track record of over-zealousness."

p. 146 "Record retailing has become": Author interview with Robyn Blumner, April 1990.

p. 146 "The shame of it": Author interview with Bryan Turner, June 1990.

p. 147 The National Association of Recording Merchandisers: NARM President Pam Horovitz—executive vice president in 1990—said in a March 1997 author interview that, as a result of these First Amendment concerns, her organization doubled its budget in 1990.

p. 147 "Bruce and Luther can go to hell": Chuck Philips, "Boss Apparently OKs Crew's Use of 'U.S.A.'," *Los Angeles Times*, June 26, 1990. Springsteen charged Campbell the minimal compulsory license fee provided for by copyright law, but no additional fee for using "Born in the U.S.A." with new lyrics.

p. 147 "In the end, it may not matter": Jon Pareles, "In Rap Music, the Beat and the Lawsuits Go On," *The New York Times*, October 23, 1990.

p. 148 But on October 3, the jurors voted to convict: Despite the Freeman conviction, there was good news for free speech advocates on at least one front in the obscenity war. On October 5, a jury in Cincinnati—long a hotbed of obscenity crackdowns—voted to acquit the Contemporary Arts Center and its director, Dennis Barrie, of the illegal use of minors and pandering obscenity. The charges had been based on several homoerotic photos by Robert Mapplethorpe that had been included in a museum exhibit. Never before had a legitimate arts museum been tried for obscenity. Pedro Dijols said in a November 1996 author interview that during the Freeman case the Broward prosecutors called the Cincinnati prosecutors to find out how they planned to prove their charges.

p. 148 "This verdict sends": "Reaction to Rap Verdict," *The Miami Herald*, October 4, 1990. Thompson's words would prove prophetic. After the initial assault on independent labels, watchdog groups led by the likes of former Education Secretary William Bennett and C. Dolores Tucker, chairperson of the National Political Congress of Black Women, began applying pressure over violence and sex in rap lyrics to such major companies as Time Warner and MCA.

p. 148 "What the fuck is this shit": March 1997 author interviews with Bruce Rogow and Luther Campbell.

p. 150 "That's your verdict" and "I laugh when I convict": Dexter Filkins, "Jury's note to judge is a real laugher," *The Miami Herald*, October 18, 1990.

p. 150 One reason was: In a March 1997 author interview, Luther Campbell said he didn't believe he was arrested as a result of the chant. Instead, "Navarro ordered that we be arrested as soon as I said *one bit* of profanity," Campbell said.

p. 150 "We agreed with": Sara Rimer, "In Rap Obscenity Trial, Cultures Fail to Clash," *The New York Times*, October 22, 1990.

p. 151 "The big mistake": Author interview with Pedro Dijols, November 1996.

p. 151 "No religious fundamentalist": Ibid.

p. 151 "Unethical conduct": Author interview with Jack Thompson, February 1997.

p. 151 "Intentionally throwing" and "we ignored him": Author interview with Pedro Dijols, November 1996.

p. 151 "Phony Christian affiliations": Affidavit of John B. Thompson quoted in Jim Mullin, "Jack Thompson and the Truly Obscene," *New Times*, October 31-November 6, 1990, p. 13.

p. 151 "There was a problem": Ibid.

p. 152 "We reject the argument": *Luke Records Inc. v. Navarro*, 960 F.2d 134 (1992).

p. 152 "One of the security guys": Author interview with Luther Campbell, March 1997. Use of Nick Navarro's security service on yacht confirmed in March 1997 author interviews with Navarro and Bruce Rogow.

Chapter 8

p. 153 "The judge told the attorneys": This and subsequent Kenneth McKenna quotes from October 1996 author interview.

p. 154 "Do what?": This and subsequent Elliot Hoffman quote from October 1996 author interview.

p. 154 "Obtaining semi-automatic or automatic weapons": Defense Motion for Summary Judgment, April 11, 1989, in *Vance v. Judas Priest*, 86-5844, in the Second Judicial District of the State of Nevada in and for the County of Washoe.

p. 155 "Jay recited those lyrics like scripture": Ivan Solotaroff, "Subliminal Criminals—Judas Priest in the Promised Land," *Village Voice*, September 4, 1990, p. 29.

p. 156 "I remember that there was a big, I think, exchange": Deposition of James Vance, September 26, 1988, in *Vance v. Judas Priest*.

p. 156 "Getting amped on the music" and "and I said this guy is saying": Ibid.

p. 156 "I thought the answer" and "hugged each goodbye": Deposition of James Vance, September 12, 1988.

p. 156 "I sure fucked up" and "there was so much blood": Deposition of James Vance, September 26, 1988.

p. 157–158 According to the suit: *Roberson v. Judas Priest*, 86-3939, in the Second Judicial District of the State of Nevada in and for the County of Washoe.

p. 158 "The doctors told me": Chuck Philips, "'My Heart Aches'—Mothers in Judas Priest Trial Tell of Their Five-Year Ordeal," *Los Angeles Times*, July 24, 1990.

p. 159 "It was a frightening experience": This and subsequent Thomas Anderson quotes from October 1996 author interview.

p. 159 "There must have been 50 film crews waiting": This and subsequent Ozzy Osbourne quotes from December 1996 author interview.

p. 159 "It is not just the words" and "it was actually as if": *McCollum v. Osbourne*, C571832, Second Amended Complaint, October 7, 1986, in the Superior Court of the State of California for the County of Los Angeles.

p. 159 "A progression of songs": Ibid.

p. 160 "Musical lyrics and poetry" and "unintelligible": *McCollum v. CBS Inc.*, 249 Cal.Rptr. 187 (Cal. App. 1988), *review denied*, California Supreme Court, October 1988.

p. 160–161 "Very clear that a situation": William Vogeler, "Appeal Court Rules Suicide's Parents Can't Sue Musician," *Los Angeles Daily Journal*, July 15, 1988.

p. 162 "Given their library" and "I might have given CBS": Author interview with Judge Jerry Carr Whitehead, October 1996.

p. 163 "The First Amendment right of an individual": Judge Whitehead's ruling in Order Denying Summary Judgment, August 23, 1989, in *Vance v. Judas Priest*.

p. 163 "He was reluctant to antagonize": Judge Whitehead ran uncontested for reelection to the six-year term.

p. 164 "If the lunatics prevail": Judy Keen, "Nevada judge will decide landmark suit," *USA Today*, July 16, 1990.

p. 164 "It's like chasing phantoms": Chuck Philips, "Subliminal Messages at Heart of Case," *Los Angeles Times*, July 31, 1990.

p. 164 "It's not the subliminal that really concerns me": Keen, *USA Today*, July 16, 1990.

p. 164 "Due to the high level of interest": Author interview with Suellen Fulstone, November 1996.

p. 165 "They said I was the closest thing": Mike Henderson, "Lawyer says 'try suicide' message hidden in music," *Reno Gazette-Journal*, July 17, 1990.

p. 166 The one plaintiffs' witness: Author interview with Judge Whitehead, October 1996.

p. 168 "The plaintiffs have submitted a forceful argument" and "the plaintiffs did not lose this case because": Judge Whitehead's ruling in *Vance v. Judas Priest*, 86-5844, in the Second Judicial District of the State of Nevada in and for the County of Washoe, August 24, 1990.

p. 168 "If artists who use subliminals": Timothy Post editorial, "Mind Intrusion Is the Worst Kind of Invasion of Privacy," *Los Angeles Times*, August 27, 1990.

p. 168 "Almost criminally irresponsible": Craig Rosen, "Judge Rules For Judas Priest, But 'Subliminal' Door Still Ajar," *Billboard*, September 8, 1990, p. 85.

p. 168 "After I heard . . . a thousand times": David Hinckley, "Subliminal message or silly conclusion," New York *Daily News*, September 27, 1990.

p. 169 "Ozzy had the solution": Author interview with Ben Mills, September 1990.

p. 169 "In a world full of traps": This and subsequent Judge Fitzpatrick quotes from his ruling in *Waller v. Osbourne*, 763 F.Supp. 1144 (M.D.Ga. 1991).

p. 169 The 11th U.S. Circuit Court: *Waller v. Osbourne*, 958 F.2d 1084 (1992), *cert. denied*, 506 U.S. 916 (1992).

p. 169 In May 1993, the Nevada Supreme Court affirmed: *Robinson v. Judas Priest*, 109 Nev. 1413 (1993).

Chapter 9

p. 171 "Because of the Anita Hill thing": Author interview with Luther Campbell, March 1997.

p. 171 "There was no eye movement": Ibid.

p. 171 Cases involving rock music: In one case, the Supreme Court denied punitive damages to the promoter of a summer concert series in Newport, Rhode Island, who sued after the city council canceled a concert for fear that Blood, Sweat and Tears (!) would attract a rowdy rock crowd. *Newport v. Fact Concerts Inc.*, 453 U.S. 247 (1981). In another case, the Supreme Court held that the City of New York could control concert volume levels in Central Park so long as the sound engineer the city hired consulted with the concert sponsor about how the vocals and instruments were mixed. *Ward v. Rock Against Racism*, 491 U.S. 781 (1989).

p. 172 "There's an important First Amendment issue": Stan Soocher, "Supreme Justice: Rap's Day In Court," *Rolling Stone*, November 11, 1993, p. 13.

p. 172 The 2 Live Crew's "Pretty Woman" used the opening lyrics: Acuff-Rose's musicologist, Earl V. Speilman, stated in an affidavit for the case that the guitar riff on the 2 Live Crew recording may have been sampled from the Orbison recording. The issue was never resolved in court proceedings; the suit charged infringement of the musical composition, not violation of the sound recording. In a March 1997 author interview, however, Luther Campbell admitted he sampled the riff from the Orbison track.

p. 172 "A typical encounter in the hood": Soocher, *Rolling Stone*, November 11, 1993, p. 13.

p. 172 Under the federal Copyright Act's compulsory licensing provision: 17 U.S.C. Sec. 115.

p. 172 "Roy was playing guitar": Author interview with Bill Dees, May 1997. Orbison composing the guitar lick confirmed by Jerry Kennedy, a lead guitarist on the "Oh, Pretty Woman" recording session, in comment to author in May 1997. If the guitar riff had been part of the sound recording, rather than the underlying musical composition, it may not have been entitled to federal copyright protection, which doesn't apply to recordings registered before February 15, 1972.

p. 172–173 "At first, I think Roy": Author interview with Bill Dees, August 1993.

p. 173 "I said, 'Don't put it on *As Nasty*": This and subsequent Allen Jacobi quotes from November 1996 author interview.

p. 173 Weird Al Yankovic: In a fall 1993 author interview, Weird Al's manager, Jay Levey, confirmed that Weird Al's parodies were pre-licensed and that permission had been refused on only one or two occasions. In court documents in the "Oh, Pretty Woman" case, nationally syndicated radio host Dr. Demento noted, however, that Weird Al began his career by doing unlicensed parodies.

p. 173 "Acuff-Rose wrote back": Gerry Teifer, director of licensing for Acuff-Rose claimed he hadn't listened to the 2 Live Crew track before denying the license request. He later stated, "I use that word parody to describe any derivative work; i.e., any work in which the melody of an existing work is coupled with new lyrics. Based on my experience in the music industry, I consider this a common custom and usage surrounding the term." Declaration of Gerald E. Teifer, August 28, 1990, in *Acuff-Rose Music Inc. v. Campbell*, in the U.S. District Court for the Middle District of Tennessee, 3-90-0524.

p. 173 "The timing of the suit": This and subsequent Eddie Wayland quote from May 1997 author interview.

p. 174 The Act provides a four-part test: 17 U.S.C. Sec. 107.

p. 174 "It wasn't meant as an admission": Author interview with Alan Mark Turk, April 1997.

p. 174 "If I offered you money": Author interview with Bill Dees, August 1993.

p. 175 "A song is difficult to parody": *Acuff-Rose Music Inc. v. Campbell*, 754 F. Supp. 1150 (M.D.Tenn. 1991).

p. 175 "It's that Judge Wiseman": This and subsequent F. Casey Del Casino quote from May 1997 author interview.

p. 175 Begrudgingly assuming: The appeals court noted in a footnote to its decision, "The mere fact that both songs have a woman as their central theme is too tenuous a connection to be viewed as critical comment on the original."

p. 175 "The factors involving the commercial nature": *Acuff-Rose Music Inc. v. Campbell*, 972 F.2d 1429 (6th Cir. 1992).

p. 176 "Mr. Mathis's rather singular vocal range" and "parodists will seldom get permission": *Fisher v. Dees*, 794 F.2d 434 (9th Cir. 1986).

p. 176 "Roy had pretty much hit the bottom": This and subsequent John Mason quotes from May 1997 author interview.

p. 177 "I am shocked and hurt": "Orbison Sues Rose, Alleging Fraud, Mishandling of Career," *Variety*, September 15, 1982, p. 77.

p. 177 "I'll end up with": Ellis Amburn, *Dark Star—The Roy Orbison Story* (New York: Lyle Stuart, 1990), p. 185.

p. 178 "We didn't ask": Martin Ashton, "Blue Angel—The Last Testament of Roy Orbison," *BAM*, February 24, 1989, p. 17.

p. 178 "I wrote ten songs with Roy": Author interview with Bill Dees, May 1997.

p. 178 "Barbara immediately called": Ibid.

p. 179 "Hip Hop Comes to the Hallowed Halls": Frank Jackman, "2 Live Crew's high copy-wrong rap," New York *Daily News*, March 30, 1993.

p. 179 But the only parody case the Supreme Court had: *Loew's Inc. v. Columbia Broadcasting System*, 131 F. Supp. 165 (S.D. Cal. 1955), *aff'd sub nom, Benny v. Loew's Inc.*, 239 F.2d 532 (9th Cir. 1956); *aff'd by an equally divided court*, 356 U.S. 43 (1958). Benny described his skit, "Autolight," as "one of my all-time favorites." See Jack and Joan Benny, *Sunday Nights At Seven—The Jack Benny Story* (New York: Warner Books, 1990), p. 242. There are several theories why Justice Douglas declined to vote. Mercedes Eichholz, who was married to Douglas in the 1950s, said in a May 1997 conversation with the author that it was most likely Douglas saw a conflict of interest based on his friendship with Benny. Charles Rickerhauser, Douglas's law clerk during the 1957-58 term, noted in a May 1997 conversation with the author that, based on Douglas' voting record on free speech issues, the justice would likely have voted in favor of Benny. In fact, Douglas, who was assigned to write the court's majority decision, did vote for Benny and CBS. But Douglas withdrew from the case after he learned that CBS was negotiating with his literary agent for the possible purchase of the TV rights to Douglas's book *An Almanac of Liberty*. See Douglas's March 11, 1958 memo to Chief Justice Earl Warren.

p. 179 In 1984: *Sony Corp. of America v. Universal City Studios Inc.*, 464 U.S. 417 (1984).

p. 179 In 1985: *Harper & Row Publishers Inc. v. Nation Enterprises*, 471 U.S. 539 (1985).

p. 179 Would stand to lose": Tony Mauro, "Is it rap—or a rip-off?" *USA Today*, November 8, 1993.

p. 179–180 "Would Irving Berlin": Ibid. Thirty years earlier, Irving Berlin lost a case before the 2d U.S. Circuit Court of Appeals in which he sued *Mad* magazine over a written parody of "A Pretty Girl Is Like a Melody." *Berlin v. E.C. Publications Inc.*, 329 F.2d 541 (2d Cir.), *cert. denied*, 379 U.S. 822 (1964). In the "Oh, Pretty Woman" case, parodist Weird Al Yankovic filed an *amicus* brief *in favor* of Acuff-Rose, perhaps, speculated 2 Live Crew counsel Alan Mark Turk, because Weird Al had an ongoing licensing relationship with Michael Jackson. "The song that changed my life the most was probably 'Eat It' [Weird Al's parody of Jackson's 'Beat It']," Yankovic said in a May 27, 1997 appearance on the TV show *Politically Incorrect*. "After that song came out, I was able to buy a house."

p. 180 Conservative Justice Clarence Thomas: Despite Justice Thomas's conservative leanings, he may not have found the 2 Live Crew's raw female depictions completely unpalatable. For years, Thomas reportedly had been a fan of pornographic magazines and videos. See Jane Mayer and Jill Abramson, *Strange Justice: The Selling of Clarence Thomas* (Boston, New York: Houghton Mifflin Co., 1994), pp. 55-58, 106-108.

p. 180 "I imagine most of the justices": Author interview with Alan Mark Turk, July 1993.

p. 180 "I think the Supreme Court justices'll be looking": Author interview with Luther Campbell, September 1993.

p. 180 "I'd never even read the copyright statute": Author interview with Bruce Rogow, March 1997.

p. 181 Rogow defined parody: A parody has been defined in fair use cases as at least commenting on the original work itself, while a satire, which is aimed strictly at society at large, is considered possible without using the underlying work.

p. 184 Only Justices Harry Blackmun: Justice Blackmun was the Supreme Court's most liberal sitting justice when the "Oh, Pretty Woman" case was heard, but he also had a history of voting against findings of fair use.

p. 184 "It is not a bull session" and "The truth is": William H. Rehnquist, *The Supreme Court—How It Was, How It Is* (New York: William Morrow and Co. Inc., 1987), pp. 291, 290.

p. 184 "If I had to guess": Author interview with Alan Mark Turk, April 1997. Ginsburg's daughter, Jane, teaches copyright at Columbia University School of Law and is the co-author of a casebook on copyright law.

p. 184 "Lived alone in a dilapidated farmhouse": Charles Moritz, editor, *Current Biography Yearbook 1991* (New York: The H.W. Wilson Co., 1991), p. 546.

p. 185 "Has that British satirical sense": Quoted in Moritz, *Current Biography Yearbook 1991*, p. 544.

p. 185 In what turned out to be a 9-0 vote: Unanimous Supreme Court rulings aren't as rare as publicly thought. One week after the 2 Live Crew ruling, for example, Chief Justice Rehnquist authored a 9-0 opinion that rocker John Fogerty, the prevailing defendant in a song copyright infringement suit brought by Fantasy Inc. (Fantasy claimed Fogerty had infringed on songs he wrote that Fantasy now owned), could be reimbursed attorney fees without establishing that Fantasy's suit was frivolous or in bad faith. *Fogerty v. Fantasy Inc.*, 510 U.S. 517 (1994). In any event, the Supreme Court's unanimous parody ruling may not have been all that surprising in light of the fact that, when Congress rewrote the Copyright Act in 1976, it recognized a parody might pass as a fair use. H.R. Rep. No. 1476, 94th Cong., 2d Sess., 65 (1976).

p. 185 "The more transformative the new work": This and subsequent Justice Souter quotes from his opinion in *Campbell v. Acuff-Rose Music Inc.*, 114 S. Ct. 1164 (1994).

p. 185 "Free speech to an absurd level": Chuck Philips, "Ruling on Parodies Stuns Music Execs," *Los Angeles Times*, March 9, 1994.

p. 185 "Made absolutely clear": Author interview with Sidney Rosdeitcher, April 1997.

p. 186 Whether the 2 Live Crew had hurt Acuff-Rose's ability to license non-parody rap versions: In his essay, "The Piracy of Parody," *Entertainment and Sports Lawyer*, Vol. 12, No. 3, Winter 1994, p. 19, entertainment attorney Alvin Deutsch noted that he asked three musicians to create a nonparodic rap version of Roy Orbison's "Oh, Pretty Woman." Deutsch wanted to see whether that version could be deemed a compulsory use—because the basic melody and character of the song remained true to the original—for which a statutory license under the Copyright Act would automatically be granted without a need for Acuff-Rose's permission. Musicologist Thomas Z. Shepard concluded the musicians achieved such a result, leading Deutsch to cite this as a flaw in Souter's opinion.

p. 186 "Neither has enough money": Arnold Markowitz, "2 Live Crew members suing Miami rapper Campbell," *The Miami Herald*, December 11, 1991.

p. 186 "They go and spend their money stupidly": Ibid.

p. 187 "I was the producer": John Lannert, "2 Live Crew members file trademark suit vs. Luther Campbell," Ft. Lauderdale *Sun-Sentinel*, January 14, 1992.

p. 187 Campbell admitted that Hobbs founded: Leonard Pitts, "Some thoughts about 'Luke,'" *The Miami Herald*, February 26, 1992.

p. 187 "Luther agreed to give us": This and subsequent Richard Wolfe quotes from March 1997 author interview, unless otherwise indicated.

p. 187 "Luther's created a lot of bad blood": Author interview with James Leshaw, April 1996.

p. 187 According to court documents: Summary of Schedules in *In re: Luke Records Inc.*, 95-11447, in the U.S. Bankruptcy Court for the Southern District of Florida.

p. 188 "Tremendous talent" and subsequent James Feltman quotes: Examiner's Report and Recommendations, July 13, 1995, in *In Re: Luke Records Inc.*

p. 188 "To review the Atlantic paperwork": Author interview with Stuart Silfen, May 1997.

p. 188 "Jacobi was probably only the second lawyer": This and subsequent Luther Campbell quotes from March 1997 author interview.

p. 188 Miami litigator Nick Manzini: Author discussed Campbell/Jacobi dispute with Nick Manzini in May 1997 interview.

p. 189 "When gangsta rap became more popular": This and subsequent Joe Weinberger quote from March 1997 author interview.

p. 189 "The seating was alphabetical": Author interview with Richard Wolfe, May 1997.

p. 190 Under the agreement, Acuff-Rose gave the 2 Live Crew: In addition, Acuff-Rose agreed to waive copyright fees accumulated by the 2 Live Crew prior to August 1995, and the rap group waived its right to $10,628 in court costs it had been awarded by the Supreme Court.

p. 190 "There was a delay": Author interview with Bruce Rogow, March 1997.

p. 190 "First, Mr. Rogow advised us": Letter of Sarah Nordlund, counsel for Acuff-Rose, to District Judge Thomas Wiseman, August 4, 1995, in *Acuff-Rose Music Inc. v. Campbell.*

p. 190 Richard Wolfe, Campbell's nemesis: The lawyers involved in Campbell's legal problems continued to fight after Campbell's bankruptcy was settled. For example, as Campbell's bankruptcy trustee, Richard Wolfe sued Campbell litigator Nick Manzini alleging malpractice in the Peter Jones litigation—a case in which Wolfe had then been on the other side. Joe Weinberger sued Manzini, claiming that Manzini refused to give up Campbell master recordings after Weinberger bought the tapes in the bankruptcy proceeding. Weinberger hired Wolfe to file the suit. Manzini in turn sued Weinberger for malicious prosecution.

p. 191 "Two plastic bags" and "less than $350": Complaint to Revoke Confirmation of Joint Plan and Discharge of Luther Campbell, in *In re: Luke Records Inc.*

Index

About the Author

Stan Soocher has served as editor-in-chief of the Manhattan-based *Entertainment Law & Finance* since its start in 1985. He is also an entertainment attorney, and has received ASCAP Deems Taylor Awards for excellence in music journalism for his music law articles in *Rolling Stone*, *The National Law Journal*, and *Musician* magazine.